高等院校“十三五”应用型规划教材 ·

国际结算与单证

主 编 冯明好

快速导航，学习要点
拓展知识，轻松提高
下载课件资源

南京大学出版社

图书在版编目(CIP)数据

国际结算与单证 / 冯明好主编. —南京:南京大学出版社，2018.6

高等院校“十三五”应用型规划教材. 国际贸易专业

ISBN 978-7-305-20326-8

Ⅰ. ①国… Ⅱ. ①冯… Ⅲ. ①国际结算—高等学校—教材 ②国际贸易—业务核算—原始凭证—高等学校—教材 Ⅳ. ①F830.73

中国版本图书馆CIP数据核字(2018)第117904号

出版发行 南京大学出版社
社　　址 南京市汉口路22号　　邮编 210093
出 版 人 金鑫荣

书　　名 国际结算与单证
主　　编 冯明好
责任编辑 尤　佳　　编辑热线 025-83592123

照　　排 南京理工大学资产经营有限公司
印　　刷 南京京新印刷有限公司
开　　本 787×1092 1/16 印张 12.25 字数 283千
版　　次 2018年6月第1版 2018年6月第1次印刷
ISBN 978-7-305-20326-8
定　　价 32.00元

网　　址:http://www.njupco.com
官方微博:http://weibo.com/njupco
微信服务号:njuyuexue
销售咨询热线:(025)83594756

前　言

近年来随着中国国际贸易的发展，对外贸易在国家经济中的地位愈来愈重要，这对于从事国际贸易业务的人员也提出了越来越高的要求。国际贸易业务操作的成功与否，除了成功的谈判之外，能否顺利收回货款也是重要体现。而由于国际货物贸易中货款的结算主要体现在单据的买卖，所以卖方能否准确、及时的提供出买方需要的单据，直接关系到货款能否顺利收回。所以，学习国际贸易相关专业的学生，除了要掌握国际贸易理论与实务的相关知识外，还须掌握国际贸易相关单证制作这一技能。

编写《国际结算与单证》这一教材的主要目的就是让学生学会国际贸易相关单证的制作。本教材在编写过程中，参考了数家外贸公司在进出口业务操作过程中所使用的单证，总结了数名外贸制单人员的单证制作技巧，广泛收集了外贸公司单证制作的实例，让学生的学习过程如同工作中的实际操作。

本书以国际货物出口贸易操作流程为主线，按照操作流程中的各环节所需要的单证展开讲述，使学生充分认识到单证在国际货物贸易操作流程中的重要性。

本书参照了中小外贸企业的实际操作流程，一改以往教材中签订合同即开始备货的流程，要求学生在实际操作中面对小金额合同要先催收定金或催证、审证、改证，然后再开始备货，以避免货物备好而定金或信用证未到的被动局面。

本书共分为十四章，重点讲述货物进出口贸易中买卖双方办理清关手续必须的商业发票、装箱单、提单、产地证四个基本单证，并分章节说明在不同的结算方式中，四个单证的制作依据及注意事项。本教材把信用证结算方式下单证的制作作为重中之重来讲述，结合编者的单证制作经验，详细讲解了信用证的阅读、分析以及根据信用证制作单据的技巧和要求。

本书主编冯明好现系烟台南山学院讲师、国际商务师。曾在烟台某大型外贸公司从事货物进出口工作多年。本书总结了编者数年的外贸工作经验以及国际商务专业的教学经验，内容详实，更切近于实际工作需要。

本书在编写的过程中参考了许多专家、学者的名作，在此表示万分感激。由于编者水平有限，书中不足之处在所难免，敬请广大读者提出宝贵意见。

作　者

2018 年 5 月

目　录

第一章　国际结算与单证概述

学习目标

了解国际结算的形式、单证在国际结算中的重要性，把握制作外贸单证的原则。

第一节　国际结算

一、国际结算的定义

国际结算(International Settlements)是指国际间由于政治、经济、文化、外交、军事等方面的交往或联系而发生的，以货币表示债权债务的清偿行为或资金转移行为，分为有形贸易类和无形贸易类。有形贸易引起的国际结算为国际贸易结算，无形贸易引起的国际结算为非贸易结算。本书主要讲述国际贸易结算。

二、国际结算的基本工具

国际结算中使用的支付工具主要是金融票据，金融票据是出票人签发的，无条件约定自己或要求其他人支付一定金额，经背书可以转让的书面支付凭证。金融票据一般包括汇票、本票、支票。

结算使用的单据，分为基本单据和附属单据。

(1) 基本单据指出口方向进口方提供的单据，有商业发票、运输单据、保险单据等。

(2) 附属单据是出口方为符合进口方政府法规或其他要求而提供的特殊单据，如熏蒸证明、UL证书等。

三、国际结算的基本方式

(一) 国际汇付(Remittance)

国际汇付是一种通行的结算方式，是付款方通过银行将款项转交给收款方。共涉及四个当事人：汇款人、收款人、汇出行、汇入行。

(二) 托收(Collection)

托收是出口方委托当地银行向国外进口方收取款项的一种国际贸易结算方式。

托收有跟单托收和光票托收。跟单托收是出口商在货物装船后，将提单等货运单据和汇票交给托收银行，托收行寄单给代收行，代收行在进口商付款或承兑后，将货运单据交进口方。光票托收是委托人交给托收银行一张或数张汇票委托收款，没有附带单据。跟单托收又分为付款交单(D/P)和承兑交单(D/A)两种。

(三) 信用证(L/C)

信用证是进口国银行应进口商要求，向出口商开出的，在一定条件下保证付款的一种书面文件，即有条件的银行付款保证书。

在信用证付款方式下，出口商发货后要根据信用证提出的单据要求备齐单据，且所有单据要表面符合信用证所列条款，然后在信用证规定的交单日期内送至指定的议付行交单议付，议付行审单无误后，先行垫付货款给出口商或直接将单据寄至信用证指定付款行，付款行最终审核单据合格后付款给议付行，再由议付行拨交给出口商。

通过对国际结算相关知识的了解可以得知，在国际贸易结算中，单证是结算的工具和凭据。因此可以说，国际结算和单证制作是分不开的，若想保证国际结算顺利进行，必须学会正确制作国际贸易中的相关单证。

第二节 国际贸易单证

一、国际贸易单证的含义及作用

(一) 国际贸易单证的含义

国际贸易单证是指在国际贸易业务中所使用的各种单据(documents)和证书(certificates)，主要有下面几种：

1. 国际货款支付工具

汇票(Bill of Exchange)、支票(Cheque)、本票(Promissory Note)。

2. 议付用单据

商业发票(Commercial Invoice)、装箱单(Packing List)、提单(Bill of Lading，B/L)、产地证(Certificate of Origin)等。

3. 报检、报关单据

进出境货物报检单、进出境货物报关单、出口收汇核销单等。

4. 信用证中需要受益人提交的证明

装船通知(Shipping Advice)、受益人证明(Beneficiary's Certificate)、船公司证明(Shipping Company's Certificate)等。

(二) 国际贸易单证的作用

1. 国际贸易单证是结算的基本工具

国际贸易与国内贸易不同，国内贸易中买卖双方经常是看货交易，付款方式主要通过汇付或现金，而国际贸易由于买卖双方地处不同的国家，卖方主要通过向买方提供相关单证来证明自己的货物质量、数量以及装船日期，买方往往是见到单证符合自己的要求后才能向卖方支付货款，所以在国际贸易中体现的是单据的买卖。可以这样说，在国际贸易中，单据制作的是否准确在一定程度上可以决定卖方能否及时收回货款。

2. 国际贸易单证是履行合同的必要环节

在国际贸易中，进出口合同的条款一般会包含卖方应该向买方提供的单据，所以卖方能否按合同要求提供单证，是履行合同条款必不可少的环节。除此之外，合同履行中卖方需要做出口报检、报关工作，买方需要做进口报检、报关工作，期间需要向商检、海关部门提供必需的单证。由此可见，外贸单证的制作是履行合同的重要环节。

3. 国际贸易单证是出口企业经营管理的重要环节

单证工作贯穿于合同履行的全过程，合同的内容、信用证的条款、报检报关、交单议付等直接关系到企业的经济效益。单证工作能反映出一个企业的外贸业务管理水平的高低，如果在某个环节上不能正确、及时的缮制或流转相关单证，就会影响整个合同履行的过程。一个企业如果制单工作做好了，就会减少差错，保证外汇及时收回，这样就加速了企业资金流转速度，保证企业正常运行。如果单证做的不及时、有错误，轻则给企业带来不必要的麻烦，重则使企业的外汇不能收回，并影响企业的声誉。

4. 国际贸易单证工作的涉外性强

国际贸易单证是涉外性商业文件，它不但具有经济意义，还具有政治意义，体现出一个国家的对外贸易方针，因此单证的制作必须严格按照有关国家的各项法规和制度办理。例如普惠制产地证是进口国执行普遍优惠制和海关减免税的依据。

二、国际贸易单证工作的基本要求

国际贸易单证主要由出口商制作，主要工作包括审证、制单、审单、交单和归档五个环节。总的要求是“一致”：“证同一致、单证一致、单单一致、单货一致”。证同一致主要指信用证和合同保持一致，信用证开立的主要依据是合同，如果卖方收到信用证后发现其与合同的内容不一致，可以要求买方修改信用证；单证一致是指信用证付款方式下单据的制作要符合信用证的要求；单单一致是指同一批货物下的单据内容必须一致；单货一致是指单据中描述的货物名称、数量、包装等必须和实际货物一致。在做到上述几个一致的基础上，单证工作还必须做到“正确、完整、及时、简明、整洁”。

（一）正确

正确是单证工作的前提和核心。所谓正确，首先是指所有单据在内容上必须真实地反映该批装运的货物，如果是根据信用证制作单据，内容还必须符合信用证的要求。其次在形式上必须正确，各种单据作用不同，其基本的格式要求必须正确。单据在内容和形式上都正确，既能体现出一个外贸公司的水平，又能确保货款的顺利回收。

（二）完整

所谓完整，主要体现在如下两个方面：

1. 单据种类要符合买方或信用证的要求

在国际商务谈判中，买方对单据的要求有时候会列入合同的条款中，不同国家的买方对单据种类的要求是不一样的。买方要求卖方提供的单据一般包括商业发票、装箱单、提单、产地证四种，但有些国家例如澳大利亚，对所有进口的木制或草制品还要求提供熏蒸证明。这就要求卖方签订合同以前必须弄明白买方需要哪些种类的单据，以免造成遗漏影响结汇，耽误买方办理进口手续。如果付款方式是信用证，买方往往在信用证中罗列出自己需要的单据，这时候卖方在准备单据时不仅要参考信用证对单据提出的内容要求，还要满足信用证对单据的种类及数量要求。

2. 每一种单据本身的内容完整

每一种单据都有其不同的作用，这些不同的作用是通过单据的内容体现出来的，例如装箱单，必须体现出来货物的包装数量。如果单据的内容不完整，就体现不出来它的作用。信用证付款方式下，信用证对有些单据要求必须有签章，如果没有，就不符合要求。如果信用证要求对汇票、提单、保险单进行背书，卖方也不能漏掉。

(三) 及时

1. 每一种单证的出单日期要及时、有序、合理

制作单据的时间顺序，一般是合同在先，然后依次是商业发票、装箱单、产地证、提单，如果买方还要求提供其他单据，其日期一般应在产地证和提单之间。在信用证付款方式下，所有单据的时间要符合信用证的要求。

2. 交单议付时间要及时

货物装运后，卖方要及时备齐买方需要的单据，按照付款方式及时向买方收取货款。如果付款方式是信用证，则交单议付时间必须符合信用证的要求。

(四) 简明

所谓简明，是指单据的内容应该按照信用证规定和国际贸易惯例填制，力求简明，这样既可以节省时间，又便于买方或相关当事人审核单据。

(五) 整洁

所谓整洁，是指单据的布局要美观大方，其格式的设计和缮制力求标准化和规范化。单据的外观在一定程度上反映了一个国家的科技水平和一个企业的业务水平。单据是否整洁，不但反映出制单人制单的熟练程度和工作态度，还会直接影响出单的效果。

总而言之，单证的制作作为国际贸易流程中必不可少的一个环节，外贸业务人员必须予以高度重视。一般中型以上的外贸公司都有专门的单证制作部门，单证制作员经过培训后方能上岗。通过学习本书后面各类单证的制作，学生即可初步掌握外贸业务中基本单据的制作，为以后的实际工作打下基础。

本章小结

作为课本的开篇，本章主要介绍国际结算相关知识以及国际结算与单证的关系，要求学生通过本章学习，意识到单证在国际贸易中的重要性，并且要知晓制作国际贸易相关单证的要求和原则。

复习思考题

1. 国际结算的工具和方式有哪些？
2. 外贸单证主要有哪些种类？
3. 外贸单证工作有哪些要求？
4. 结合外贸实例说明单证在进出口业务中的作用。

第二章　国际贸易合同的制定和履行

通过本章学习，要求学生掌握国际货物销售合同的主要条款，学会编写合同；把握进出口贸易的基本流程，了解流程中各环节所需要的单证以及制作单证的依据。

第一节　国际贸易合同

一、国际贸易合同的形式

合同的形式是指当事人订立合同达成协议的表现形式。订立合同的形式一般有三种：书面形式、口头形式和其他形式。《联合国国际货物销售公约》规定："销售合同无须以书面订立或者书面证明，在形式方面也不受任何其他条件的限制。"我国的新合同法对合同的形式也采取了非常宽容的态度，不再要求涉外合同必须采用书面形式。尽管如此，由于国际货物买卖往往由于交易金额大，履行期限长，容易产生纠纷，建议尽量建立书面合同。

二、书面合同的意义

（一）买卖双方谈判的主要依据

在国际贸易谈判中，买卖双方需要谈哪些方面？尤其是初次参加谈判的参与者，往往因为没有谈判经验而无所适从，或者是谈判结束后才发现有些方面没有和客户谈及。如果谈判者在谈判之前先准备好一份完整的合同，在谈判的过程中按照合同所列的条款逐一与客户商谈，就可以解决这一问题。

（二）买卖双方履行合同的主要依据

合同签订后，卖方要依据合同的要求备货、发货，买方要依据合同要求按时付款、接货，这就要求买卖双方签订的合同中必须全面、清楚、具体地明确双方的权利和义务，否则就可能给双方带来不便甚至发生纠纷。

三、书面合同的种类

（一）合同(Contract)

合同的条款相对完善，除商品名称、规格、包装、数量、单价、装运港、目的港、装运期、付款方式、唛头外，还包括商品的品质、争议的处理、不可抗力等。如果买卖双方交易的金额较大，建议采用条款完善的合同，以利于明确双方的责任和权利，也利于纠纷的解决。

合同主要分为进口合同(Importing Contract)和出口合同(Exporting Contract)，出口合同又称为销售合同(Sales Contract，S/C)。

（二）确认书(Confirmation)

它是一份简式合同，其中的条款较少，主要包括商品名称、规格、包装、数量、单价、装运港、目的港、装运期、付款方式、唛头等条款，当买卖双方交易的金额较小时，为了节省谈判时间，可以采用确认书的形式。确认书包括售货确认书(Sales Confirmation)和购货确认书(Purchase Confirmation)。

合同和确认书的区别只是内容的繁简，其法律效力是一样的。

四、书面合同的内容

销售合同

SALES CONTRACT

卖方(Seller)：______________　　合同号(Contract No.)：______________

地址(Address)：______________　　合同日期(Date)：______________

签约地点(Place)：______________

买方(Buyer)：______________

地址(Address)：______________

双方同意按下列条款由卖方出售、买方购进下列货物：

The seller agrees to sell and the buyer agrees to buy the following goods according to the terms and conditions stipulated below：

(1) 唛头 Marks	(2) 名称 Name of Commodity	(3) 数量 Quantity	(4) 单价 Unit Price	(5) 金额 Amount
	Total：			

________% more or less allowed.

(6) 货物总值(Total Amount)：

(7) 付款方式(Terms of Payment)：

买方须于____年____月____日前开出本批交易的信用证(或付出定金)，否则，售方有权不经过通知取消本合同，并有权提出索赔。

The buyers shall establish the covering Letter of Credit (or effect the payment of deposit) before ________, falling which the Seller reserves the right to lodge a claim.

(8) 装运期限(Time of Shipment):

(9) 装运港/目的港(Port of Loading & Port of Destination):

(10) 分批及转船(Partial Shipment and Transshipment):

(11) 品质及检验(Quality & Inspection):

(12) 包装(Packing):

(13) 单据要求(Documents Required):

(13) 品质/数量异议:如买方提出索赔,凡属品质异议须于货到目的口岸____日内提出,凡属数量异议须于货到目的口岸____日内提出,对所装货物所提任何异议属于保险公司,船公司等其他有关运输或邮递机构,卖方不负任何责任。

Quality/Quantity Discrepancy: In case of quality discrepancy, claim should be filed by the Buyer within ____ days after the arrival of the goods at port of destination; while for quantity discrepancy, claim should be filed by the Buyer within ____ days after the arrival of the goods at port of destination. It is under stood that the seller shall mot be liable for any discrepancy of the goods shipped due to causes for which the Insurance Company, Shipped Company other transportation organization/ or Post Office are liable.

(14) 本确认书内所述全部或部分商品,如因人力不可抗拒的原因,以致不能履行或延迟交货,卖方概不负责。

The Seller shall not be held liable for failure of delay in delivery of the entire lot or a portion of the goods under this Sales Confirmation in consequence of any Force Major incidents.

(15) 仲裁(Arbitration):本合同在执行过程中若发生争议,双方应通过友好协商方式解决;如果协商不成,则应提交北京中国国际经济贸易仲裁委员会裁决。裁决是终局的,对双方均有约束力。仲裁费用由败诉方承担。

All disputes arising from the execution of the contract shall be settled by friendly negotiation, falling which the case should be submitted to the China International Economic & Trade Arbitration Commission, Beijing. The Decision is final and binding upon both parties. The fee shall be borne by the losing party.

(16) 买方收到本售货确认书后请立即签回一份,如买方对本确认书有异议,应于收到后五天内提出,否则认为买方已同意接受本确认书所规定的各项条款。

The buyer is requested to sign and return one copy of the Sales Confirmation immediately after the receipt of same. Objection, if any, should be raised by the Buyer within five days after the receipt of this Sales Confirmation, in the absence of which it is understood that the Buyer has accepted the terms and condition of the sales confirmation.

The Buyer:(签字盖章) The Seller:(签字盖章)

第二节　出口合同的履行

买卖双方经过交易磋商签订合同之后，当事人必须严格履行自己的义务，执行合同的各项规定。卖方要负责及时备货、交货、提供买方需要的各种单证；买方要负责及时支付定金或开立信用证，如果按照贸易术语由买方租船订舱，买方还要及时订舱并通知卖方己方货代的相关信息。对于卖方来说，一般应遵循如下出口操作流程（交易条件 CIF，如图 2-1）

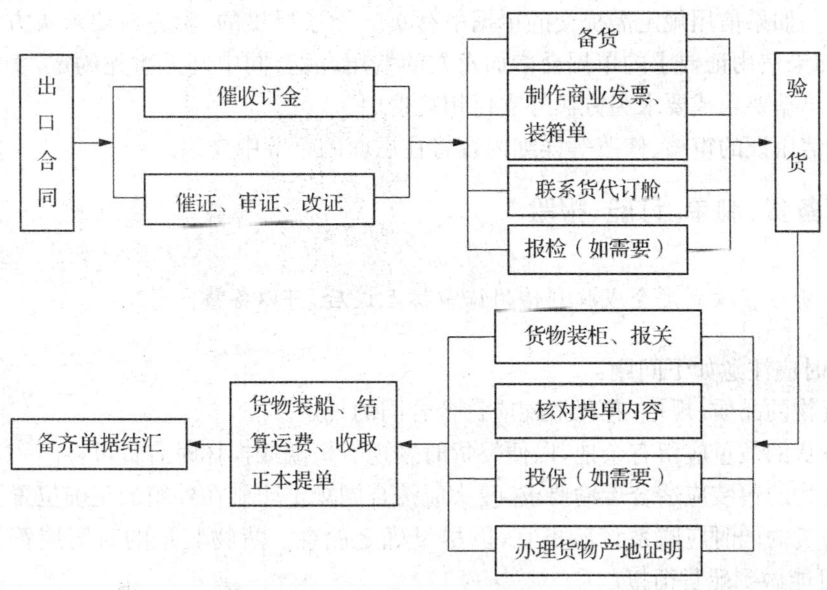

图 2-1　货物出口操作流程

从以上货物出口贸易流程图中可以看到，在流程中的每一个环节，都离不开单证，本书后面的单证也将根据流程的顺序逐一讲述。出口合同在履行的过程中，卖方还应注意如下问题：

一、催收定金或催开信用证

合同签订之后，如果合同金额较小，卖方不应急于备货，而是应该按照合同中规定的付款方式，催买方付定金或开信用证。因为小额合同的法律意义不大，即使买方违约了，卖方也不值得去提起仲裁或诉讼。一般是等收到了买方的定金再开始备货，以免使自己陷入货物备好而定金未到的被动局面。

如果合同规定付款方式是信用证，卖方在收到信用证后应该认真审核，主要审核如下几点：

（一）信用证的真伪和开证行的信誉

信用证应由开证行按照卖方提供的 SWIFT 账号开到卖方指定的银行，然后经银行通知后，由卖方去领取。如果是买方直接寄给卖方信用证或卖方从其他渠道收到信用证，该信用证可能是假的。此外，卖方也可以向信用证的通知行咨询，以求证信用证的真伪。至于开证行的信誉问题，卖方也可以向通知行咨询，如果开证行的信誉不好，卖方可以要求买方开立由信誉较好的银行保兑的信用证或直接拒绝接受该证。

（二）信用证的条款是否符合合同的规定

信用证是根据合同开立的，如果信用证中的条款（例如装船日期、信用证金额等）不符合合同的规定且对卖方不利，卖方可以要求买方修改不利条款。

（三）信用证要求卖方提交的单据

卖方对这一条款主要是审核信用证要求的单据己方能否提供，如果能够提供，是否会增加费用。如果信用规定需提交的单据中有卖方无法提供的，卖方应要求买方删除该单据要求；如果信用证要求的单据会增加卖方的费用，而合同中又无事先约定，卖方可以要求删除该单据要求或要求买方额外支付相关费用。

关于信用证的审核、修改等详细内容将在后面的章节中介绍。

二、备货、制单、订舱、报验

（一）卖方在收到定金或收到信用证审核无误后，可以备货

备货时应注意如下问题：

1. 货物的品质、规格、花色搭配应符合合同的规定。

2. 备货的数量应留有余地，以便发货时发现有短缺或损坏时有货可补。

3. 货物的包装应适合运输要求，唛头应按合同规定印刷在外箱的正确位置。

4. 备货的同时应联系订舱事宜，以尽早确定船期。货物装运的时间应符合合同规定，并尽可能做到船货衔接。

（二）货物在生产的过程中，卖方应及时制作商业发票和装箱单，以便为接下来的订舱、报检提供数据

1. 商业发票的制作主要依据是合同以及买方的相关要求，具体细节要求将在以后章节讲述。

2. 装箱单的制作主要是依据商业发票以及货物的具体包装情况，其中的净重、毛重、尺码必须是经过实际测量得出来的数据，详细内容将在以后章节讲述。

（三）订舱

如果合同是以 FOB 条件成交的，卖方要及时联系买方指定的货代，给货代发运输委托书，货代订舱后，会发给卖方入货通知书，入货通知书中详细说明了该次运输的船名、航次、预计开航日期、截港日期和结关日期，卖方收到入货通知书后，要及时给买方发装船通知，及时联系生产工厂做好船货衔接准备工作。

如果合同是以 CIF 或 CFR 成交的，卖方要及时联系货代，洽谈运费，同信誉好、规模较大的货代签订运输合同。

（四）报检

凡是国家规定需要经过出入境检验检疫局检验后方能出口的货物，或合同规定需要

官方机构出具相关检验证明的货物，都要报检。报检的时间一般是在货物发运前 7 天，报检时需要卖方填写出口货物检验申请单并提供合同副本、厂检单、包装性能检验结果单等单据，出入境检验检疫局接受报检后，卖方应至少在验货前 3 天和检验检疫局相关人员约定验货时间，验货时应积极配合检验人员，货物检验合格后，检验人员给卖方出具通关单或其他申请的单证，卖方凭以报关或结汇。

三、验货

验货是国际货物出口贸易中的一个重要环节，在货物装运或离开生产工厂之前，卖方一定要再三确认货物是否需要检验。

1. 如果货物是按国家规定必须经检验检疫方能出口的，要及时联系商检局相关人员验货。

2. 如果货物不是法检产品，要确认合同中检验条款有无买方指定相关部门验货，如果有，要及时联系相关验货人员。

3. 核对在合同执行过程中买方在往来函电中有无验货的附加要求。

四、货物装柜、报关、投保、审核提单、办理产地证书

1. 卖方在确认货物检验合格后，就可以按照入货通知书提供的集装箱场站地址，联系卡车拖柜到工厂装货了。货物装柜时要注意清点数量，货物在柜内要摆放平整、紧凑，避免出现货柜晃动时货物在柜内相互碰撞的情况。装完货柜后要用货代提供的铅封锁柜，并记录下货柜编号和铅封号留待核对提单内容时用。重柜（装满货后的集装箱）返回场站的时间要严格遵守入货通知书上截港时间之规定，以免被甩箱。

2. 货物装完后应按实际数量更改商业发票及装箱单，然后按实际发货数量报关。报关可以委托货代代为申报，也可以自行报关，报关的时间要按入货通知书上结关时间的规定，如遇海关抽检货物，卖方应及时派人到现场配合海关查验。

3. 投保。如果按合同成交方式由卖方投保，卖方应在货物装船前按合同规定险别、保额投保。如果付款方式是信用证，保险单的内容一定要符合信用证的要求；如果按合同成交方式规定由买方投保，卖方在货物装船前要及时给买方发转船通知，提醒买方投保。

4. 核对提单内容。重柜返回场站后，货代会将一份提单的电子版发给卖方，确认其中的内容是否需要更改。卖方应当按照商业发票、装箱单内容认真审核，做到单单一致。如果付款方式是信用证，还应使提单符合信用证的要求。凡是需要更改的地方，应一次向货代提出，避免多次更改产生费用。

5. 如果买方需要卖方提供普惠制产地证书或一般产地证书，卖方应在货物装船前到商检局或贸促会办理。如果付款方式是信用证，产地证书的内容一定要符合信用证的要求。

五、货物装船、结算运费、收取正本提单

重柜按入货通知书的要求返回场站，货物按时通关后，由货代负责安排货柜装船事宜。货物装船后，货代会将本次代办发货的费用清单发给卖方确认，费用清单中若有卖方

不明白的费用,应及时问清楚。费用结清后,货代应及时把全套提单寄给卖方。卖方收到提单后,应按提单所载的正本提单的份数清点提单。

六、备齐单据结算

如上一章所讲,国际贸易体现的是单据的买卖,所以卖方发完货后同买方结算货款时,必须提供买方需要的单证。一般来说,买卖双方在签订合同时,就应将买方所需的单据列明,以免发货后引起纠纷。在汇付和托收付款方式下,卖方一般提供给买方的单据包括商业发票、装箱单、提单、产地证、保险单(CIF 或 CIP 成交),如果买方还需要其他单证,应该在贸易谈判时声明并列在合同上。卖方在备齐单据后,应先通过电子邮件发送单据副本供买方确认。买方确认后,如果付款方式是汇付,卖方应在收到全额货款后通过正规的国际快递公司把全套正本单证寄给买方;如果付款方式是托收,卖方则根据合同规定的托收方式送单至当地银行委托收款。

第三节 进口合同的履行

在进口合同的履行过程中,买方工作的重中之重是选择可靠的供货商。合同签订后,买方一般按下列程序执行合同:

一、开立信用证或向买方支付定金

合同签订后,进口商应及时根据合同的规定开立信用证或支付定金。作为进口商,如果能在谈判的过程中为自己争取有利的付款方式(如 D/P 或 D/A),则可以免除开证或支付定金的麻烦以及由此产生的费用。

二、租船订舱

按照 FOB 贸易术语成交的合同,买方需要租船订舱。买方应在合同签订后及时落实船期,联系货代,并同货代签订运输委托合同,然后及早让货代联系卖方商定发货事宜。

三、投保

以 FOB 或 CFR 成交的合同,买方要负责办理货物海上运输保险事宜。买方应及时联系卖方,让卖方在货物装船前发装船通知,以便及时投保。

四、审单付汇

卖方通过电子邮件或银行发来的单证,买方务必认真审核,确认单据符合自己的进口清关要求后,买方应及时付款赎取正本单据。

五、报关、验收、拨交货物

货物运抵目的地后,由进口企业或其代理人向海关办理申报手续,并配合海关查验货物;需要经商检局检验方能进口的货物,要及时报检。验货时若发现货物数量短缺或质量与合同不符，应保留检验证据以供将来索赔时用。货物清关后，进口商可与实际用货单位结算货款并办理拨交手续。

六、进口索赔

进口商发现货物数量短缺或质量与合同不符合时，应按合同索赔期限的规定，及时向卖方提出索赔。如果是由于保险范围内自然灾害或意外事故造成的货物损失，应及时凭相关单证向保险公司提出索赔。

本章小结

本章主要介绍了国际货物销售合同的形式、内容及操作流程。通过本章的学习，要求学生能够掌握国际货物销售合同的基本内容，并在领会国际贸易实务相关内容的基础上学会填制合同；通过进出口操作流程的学习，要求学生能够掌握流程中的注意事项，以避免在工作中出现错误和遗漏。

复习思考题

1. 签订书面合同的意义是什么？
2. 备货时应注意哪些问题？
3. 根据下列资料草拟一份合同：

卖方：YANTAI BRIGHT FURNITURE CO.，LTD.
　　260 JIEFANG RAOD，YANTAI，CHINA.
买方：GENERAL TRADING COMPANY
　　NO. 32 FLOWER ST.，NEW YORK，USA
商品名称：木制课桌（WOODEN DESKS）
数量：A002　1000 张（1000PCS），
　　B013　1000 张（1000PCS）
包装：纸箱装，每××张一箱
单价：A002　USD20.00
　　B013　USD25.00　CIF NEW YORK
装运期：2015 年 10 月 30 日前，可分批装运，可转船
付款方式：即期不可撤销信用证
品质要求：同样品一致

第三章　信用证的审核与修改

学习目标

了解信用证的概念、性质、特点，学会审核信用证的条款，对于审核中发现的问题，要及时修改。

第一节　认识信用证

一、信用证的基本概念

信用证(Letter of Credit，简称 L/C)是银行开立的有条件的承诺付款的书面文件。即开证行根据进口商的申请和指示向出口商开立的一定金额的、并在一定期限内凭规定的单据承诺付款的书面文件。

二、信用证的性质与特点

（一）单据买卖

信用证业务处理的是单据，不是单据项下的货物。例如我国青岛某公司向韩国出口海产品，由于青岛离韩国很近，进口商未拿到单据时货物早已到达，进口商发现货物并没有达到规定的质量标准，于是向开证行要求拒付款。但开证行审核单据并在单单相符、单证相符的前提下，立即付了款；只是因为信用证处理的是单据，不是货物，只要单证相符，就必须付款，货物的实际情况与信用证无关。至于货物的问题如何处理，应由买卖双方自行洽商。

（二）独立文件

信用证的开立是以合同的条款为依据的，但信用证经开证行开出后，如果卖方接受，便实际形成了开证行与卖方之间的契约关系，脱离合同而成为一份独立的文件。卖方只有提供符合信用证要求的单据，银行才能付款。如我国某公司出口一批木质椅子，合同中规定的最晚装船日期是 2015 年 12 月 30 日，而信用证规定的最晚装船日期是 2015 年 12 月 25 日，卖方收到信用证后并未提出异议。2015 年 12 月 28 日卖方在货物装船后取得提单，并备齐其他单据到银行交单议付，虽然卖方的交货期并没有违反合同的规定，但却遭到银行拒付。这一案例给我们的警示就是必须要理解信用证作为独立文件的含义，银行的付款与否就是看卖方提供的单据是否符合信用证的要求，与合同无关。

（三）银行信用

根据信用证的定义可知，信用证是银行开出的有条件的付款承诺书，只要卖方满足信用证中所载明的条件，银行就要履行付款承诺，故它是一种银行信用。

三、信用证的主要内容及类型

（一）信用证的开立形式

信用证的开立形式可分为信开信用证和电开信用证，信开信用证是开证行开出信用证后通过邮寄方式送到卖方，电开信用证是通过电讯方式先开至卖方所在地的银行，然后由银行通知卖方领取。

（二）信用证的主要内容

1. 信用证本身固有的内容

开证行的名称、地址、信用证的类型、名称、信用证的号码、开证日期、金额、受益人、开证申请人、通知行、有效期、开证文句及兑付方式等。

2. 汇票的条款

汇票的出票人、付款人、汇票期限、金额等。

3. 单据

商业发票、运输单据、保险单据等。

4. 货物条款

货物描述、包装等。

5. 装运条款

起运港和目的港，分批装运和转运、装运期等。

6. 开证行担保条款

7. 其他条款

8. 根据 UCP600 条款的开证文句

信用证示例(3－1)

BASIC HEADER　　F　01 BKCHCNBJA940 0542 763485

APPLICANTION HEADER　Q 700 1043 011214 SCBKHKHHBXXX 3414 633333 1048 N

* SHANGHAI COMMERCIAL BANK LIMITED

* HONG KONG

USER HEADER

SERVICE CODE　103：

BANK. PRIORITY　113：

MESG USER REF.　108：

BBIBMEY036P40000

INFO. FROM CI　115：

SEQUENCE OF TOTAL 27：1/1
FORM OF DOC. CREDIT 40 A：IRREVOCABLE
DOC. CREDIT NUMBER 20：LCBB61561
DATE OF ISSUE 31 C：041214
EXPIRY 31 D：DATE 050129 PLACE AT OUR COUNTER IN HONGKONG
APPLICANT 50：ABLENDID DEVELOPMENT LTD
UNIT 10—6，15/F MENAL ASIA GRANITE
34 WAI YIP STREET，KOWLOON HONG KONG
BENEFICIARY 59：SOHO TEXTILE AND LIGHT INDUSTRY CO. LTD.
120 TAIPING ROAD.
NANJING，CHINA
AMOUNT 32 B：CURRENCY USD AMOUNT 108,750.00
POS. / NEG. TOL. (%) 39 A：10/10
AVAILABLE WITH/BY 41 D：ANY BANK
BY NEGOTIATION
DRAFTS AT … 42 C：AT SIGHT
DRAWEE 42 D：SHANGHAI COMMERCIAL BANK LTD. HONGKONG FOR FULL INVOICE VALUE
PARTIAL SHIPMENTS 43 P：ALLOWED
TRANSSHIPMENT 43 T：ALLOWED
LOADING IN CHARGE 44 A：ANY PORT IN CHINA
FOR TRANSPORT TO … 44 B：AARHUS，DENMARK
DESCRIPTION OF GOODS 45 A：
FABRIC CRUSHED VELOUR，150CM，AT USD7.5/M
AS PER S/C NO. 2K11121，JSL ORDER NO. 4500207220
ART. 5360004/10，1,000M VANILLA
ART. 5360025/30，2,000M BURGUNDY
ART. 5360029/40，10,700M HUNTER GREEN
ALL CIF AARHUS，DENMARK
DOCUMENTS REQUIRED 46 A：

1. FULL SET OF CLEAN 'ON BOARD OCEAN VESSEL' BILL OF LADING ISSUED TO ORDER AND BLANK ENDORSED NOTIFYING JYSK CO. LTD.，AND MARKED 'FREIGHT PREPAID' SHOWING NAME AND ADDRESS OF SHIPPING COMPANY'S AGENT AT DESTINATION.
2. SIGNED COMMERCIAL INVOICES IN TRIPLICATE SHOWING

CIF VALUE OF THE MENTIONED GOODS AND STATING 'WE HEREBY CERTIFY THAT THE GOODS HEREIN INVOICED CONFORM WITH P/O NO., JSL ORDER NO. AND ART. NO.'

3. PACKING LISTS IN TRIPLICATE SHOWING NUMBER OF CARTONS, GROSS WEIGHT, NET WEIGHT AND SPECIFIED PER CONTAINER,
4. GSP CERTIFICATE FORM A IN DUPLICATE ISSUED BY COMPETENT AUTHORITY OF P. R. CHINA
5. INSURANCE POLICY OR CERTIFICATE IN ASSIGNABLE FORM AND ENDORSED IN BLANK FOR 110 PCT OF INVOICE VALUE WITH CLAIMS PAYABLE AT DESTINATION IN CURRENCY OF DRAFT COVERING ICC (A), INSTITUTE WAR CLAUSES (CARGO), INSTITUTE STRIKES CLAUSES (CARGO), WAREHOUSE TO WARHOUSE CLAUSES AND SHOWING NO. OF ORIGINALS ISSUED.
6. CERTIFICATE OF INSPECTION ISSUED BY KETHEREN.

ADDITIONAL COND. 47 A:

1. CHARGES INCURRED IN RESPECT OF ANY TELEGRAPHIC TRANSFER/CHARTS PAYMENT/PAYMENT ADVICE BY SWIFT/TELEX ARE FOR ACCOUNT OF BENEFICIARY.
2. A HANDLING COMMISSION OF USD50.00 OR EQUIVALENT, PLUS TELEX CHARGES, IF ANY, WILL BE DEDUCTED FROM THE PROCEEDS FOR EACH SET OF DOCUMENTS WITH DISCREPANCIES PRESENTED UNDER THIS LETTER OF CREDIT.
3. ALL DOCUMENTS MUST BE PRESENTED THROUGH BENEFICIARY'S BANKER AND EXTRA COPY OF INVOICE AND TRANSPORT DOCUMENT FOR L/C ISSUING BANK'S FILE REQUIRED.

WE HEREBY ENGAGE WITH THE DRAWERS, ENDORSERS AND BONA FIDE HOLDERS THAT DRAFTS DRAWN AND NEGOTIATED IN COMPLIANCE WITH THE TERMS AND CONDITIONS OF THIS CREDIT WILL BE DULY HONOURED ON PRESENTATION.

THIS DOCUMENTARY CREDIT IS SUBJECT TO THE UNIFORM CUSTOMS AND PRACTICE FOR DOCUMENTARY CREDITS (1993) REVISION, INTERNATIONAL CHAMBER OF

COMMERCE, PUBLICATION NO. 500.

DETAILS OF CHARGES 71 B: ALL BANKING CHARGES OUTSIDE HONG KONG
ARE FOR ACCOUNT OF BENEFICIARY.

PRESENTATION PERIOD 48: ALL DOCUMENTS MUST BE PRESENTED TO AND REACH OUR COUNTER IN HONG KONG
WITHIN 7 DAYS AFTER B/L DATE.

CONFIRMATION 49: WITHOUT

INSTRUCTIONS 78:

1. PLS FORWARD THE WHOLE SET OF DOCUMENTS IN ONE LOT TO OUR BILLS PROCESSING CENTRE (KOWLOON) AT 2/F., 666 NATHAN ROAD, KOWLOON, HONG KONG VIA COURIER SERVICE AT BENEFICIARY'S EXPENSES.
2. IN REIMBURSEMENT, WE SHALL REMIT PROCEEDS IN ACCORDANCE

WITH YOUR INSTRUCTIONS UPON RECEIPT OF THE DOCUMENTS

ADVISE THROUGH 57 D: YOUR JIANGSU BRANCH,
148 ZHONGSHAN SOUTH ROAD, NANJING, CHINA

（三）信用证的类型

1. 可撤销信用证和不可撤销信用证

若信用证条款中有 irrevocable,则该信用证是不可撤销信用证;若信用证载明 revocable,则该信用证是可撤销信用证。若信用证中既没有 irrevocable,也没有 revocable,则该信用证是不可撤销信用证。

2. 即期信用证和远期信用证

若信用证 42C 内容之后是 at sight,则表明该信用证是即期信用证。若 42C 后面的内容是 at xx days after sight,则表明该信用证是远期信用证。

3. 跟单信用证和光票信用证

如果信用证名称为 documentary letter of credit,或者信用证内容中有 DOCUMENTS REQUIRED,则表明该信用证是跟单信用证,受益人议付时除了要出具汇票外还要按信用证要求提供单据。若信用证中没有单据的要求,受益人议付时只需要出具汇票就可以,这样的信用证就是光票信用证。

4. 可转让信用证和不可转让信用证

若信用证中条款中明确规定 transferable 或者 the third party documents acceptable,则表明该信用证是可转让的信用证。若没有类似的规定,则该信用证是不可转让信用证。

5. 保兑信用证和不保兑信用证

信用证 confirmation 后面内容如果是 without,该信用证是不保兑信用证。若后面的内容是由某某银行保兑,该信用证是保兑信用证。保兑信用证中的保兑行和开证行一样承担第一付款人的责任。

四、信用证项下的单证流转程序

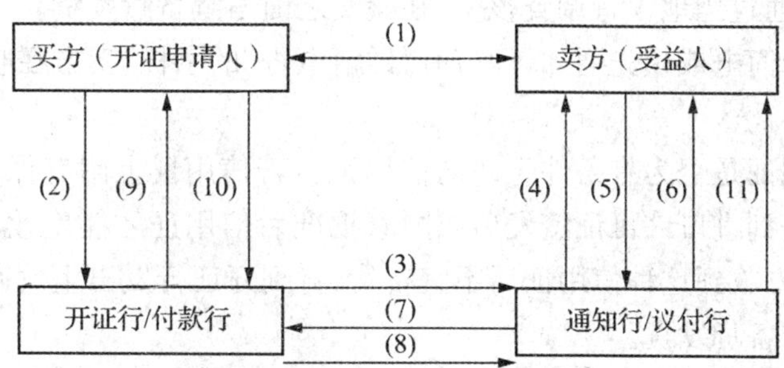

(1) 买卖双方签订贸易合同，在合同中规定使用信用证作为付款方式。

(2) 买方向当地银行提出申请，开立信用证。

(3) 开证行接受买方的申请后向卖方当地银行开出信用证。

(4) 卖方当地银行收到信用证后，核对密押或印签，通知卖方领取信用证。

(5) 卖方收到信用审核无误后，备货发货，然后根据信用证的要求备齐单据，开出汇票，按信用证的要求送至议付行交单议付。

(6) 议付行收到单据审核无误后，按汇票金额扣除利息，把货款垫付给卖方。

(7) 议付行将单据和汇票寄至信用证中规定的付款行索偿。

(8) 付款行审单无误后付款给议付行。

(9) 开证行取得单据后向买方提示单据，要求买方付款赎单。

(10) 买方到开证行付款赎单。

(11) 议付行收到付款行的货款后，为企业结汇入账，并收回垫款。

第二节　信用证的审核与修改

一、审核信用证

信用证的付款原则是“单单相符、单证一致”，如果受益人提交的单据不符合信用证的要求，就会遭到拒付，所以，在卖方拿到信用证后，必须就信用证的条款进行严格审核，如果信用证的条款中有与合同不符或卖方提供不出来的单据，就要及时要求买方修改。审核信用证时一般从下面几个方面进行：

(一) 审核信用证的真实性、安全可靠性

信用证一般是通过卖方所在地通知行转交给卖方的，这种方式的信用证通知比较安全。根据 UCP600 的有关规定，通知行应对所通知的信用证的真实性负责，所以，卖方从通知行拿到信用证后，首先要认真查看“信用证通知面涵”上或信用证上是否有“密押核符”(电开证)或“印签核符”(信开证)的表示或批注。如果有，则说明通知行已证实信用证的真实性；如果看到是“密押、印签待核，仅供参考”，就说明通知行不能确认信用证的真实

性。对密押、印签不符的信用证,在收到通知行证实信用证“密押相符”的书面通知之前,不应按信用证的要求发货。

如果信用证是由买方直接寄送的,或是从本地某个地址寄来的,卖方要警惕该信用证可能是假的,可以通过当地银行调查核实,在核实之前不宜备货发货。

如果信用证为简电或预先通知,即带有“详情电告”的字样,卖方在收到正式的信用证之前不宜备货。

要查看该信用证是否为有条件生效的信用证。若信用证上附有保留或限制性条款,如信用证规定要等到进口许可证签发后或国家批准后信用证才能生效等类似条款,属于未生效信用证,卖方收到这种信用证后不宜备货,直到开证行发出生效通知后卖方才能开始按照信用证要求备货发货。

要查看信用证是否为不可撤销信用证,如果信用证 40A 条款中标明的是 revocable,则该信用证是可撤销信用证,卖方不能接受;只有标明的是 irrevocable,说明该信用证是不可撤销信用证(信用证未标明是否可撤销时,该信用证视为不可撤销),卖方才能接受。

要查看保兑的信用证是否按要求由有关银行进行了保兑。

要查看信用证开证行的资信。开证行资信的好坏,直接关系到信用证使用的安全性。按照 UCP600 的规定,开证行开出信用证后,就承担了第一付款人的责任。资信差的开证行开出的信用证其他银行难以接受,受益人融资困难。因此,对于资信较差的开证行,卖方可以要求其在开证时由信誉较好的银行加以保兑。

(二) 审核信用证与合同条款是否一致,信用证条款是否合理,有无前后矛盾的现象

要审核信用证有效期是否晚于最迟装船日期,以便有足够的时间准备交单议付;如果信用证的装船日期和到期日是同一天,即通常所称的“双到期”,卖方在实际业务操作中,就要把装船日期提前 10 天左右,以留出足够的时间备单议付。

信用证中规定了分批装运的时间和数量应该注意能否办到,否则,当有一批货物未按期出运时,该期信用证即告失效。如信用证中规定了每一批货物出运的确切时间,则必须按此照办,如不能办到,必须修改。除非信用证另有规定,货物是允许分批装运和转运的。

检查信用证的金额、币种与合同规定是否一致,如信用证的金额是否正确,信用证中的单价与总值是否准确,大小写是否一致等。

如合同允许数量上可以有一定幅度的伸缩,那么信用证是否也规定了在支付金额时允许有一定伸缩幅度。如果在信用证的金额、数量或单价前使用了“大约”一词,其意思是允许金额、数量或单价有 10%的增减幅度。除非信用证规定数量不得有增减,那么,在付款金额不超过信用证金额的情况下,即使不准分批装运,货物数量也允许有 5%的增减。这种货物数量可以有 5%增减的规定一般适用于大宗货物,对于以包装单位或个体为计算单位的货物不适用。如:1000PCS 100% Cotton Shirts 由于数量单位是件,实际交货时只能是 1 000 件,而不能有 5%的增减。

(三) 审核信用证是否包括软条款

软条款信用证削弱了信用证付款保证的完整性和可靠性,以致被不法分子利用作为行骗的工具或赖账的手段,所以受益人必须对此提高警惕。信用证的软条款有两类。

一类是在单据上做文章，如信用证规定：

1. 受益人必须提交买方或其代理人签发的货物收据，其签字必须与开证行或通知行持有的签字样本相符。

2. 受益人必须提交买方或其指派人员出具的货物检验证明，其签字必须与开证行或通知行持有的签字样本相符。

3. 受益人必须提交买方出具的证明书，证明货物与形式发票相符，或证明货物已通关，其签字必须与开证行或通知行持有的签字样本相符。

4. 商检证或其他单据须由买方或其指派人员的会签，其签字必须与开证行或通知行持有的签字样本相符。

以上各种条款，买方及其代理人是否会签发这些单据，其签字是否与开证行或通知行的持有的签字样本相符，都不是受益人能够主动控制的。一般来说，对于信用证要求提交的单据，如果卖方不能确定能否办理，应要求买方删除此单据要求。对于信誉好、规模大的进口商开来的信用证，如果有些单据(例如验货证明)要求是其惯常做法，可以考虑接受。

5. 信用证规定 2/3 套正本提单交单议付，1/3 正本提单直接寄送开证申请人。对于这样的条款也要根据客户所在地距离的远近和客户的信誉如何认真加以分析，以判断其合理性，分析其真实的用意所在。

另一类软条款是在付款条款上做文章，如信用证规定：

1. 只有在货物再出口得到货款后才付款。

2. 只有在货物清关或由主管当局批准进口后才付款。

3. 本信用证为背对背信用证，只有在原信用证项下货款收进后才付款。

4. 本信用证货款用某国政府的贷款(或援助款)支付，我行在得到该贷款(或援助款)以后才能付款。

以上各种条款能否实现，均非受益人能主动控制。如果接受上述条款，受益人在正常处理信用证业务的主动权很大程度上掌握在对方手里，影响安全收汇。

二、信用证修改的要求

通过对信用证的全面审核，如果发现问题，应及时处理。对于影响收汇、难以接受或难以做到的信用证条款，必须要求国外客户进行修改。关于信用证的修改应明确下列问题：

1. 凡是需要修改的内容，应做到一次性向对方客户提出，避免多次修改产生费用。

2. 对于不可撤销信用证中任何条款的修改，都必须取得当事人的同意方能生效。

3. 只有买方(开证申请人)有权接受是否修改信用证的要求；只有卖方(信用证受益人)有权决定是否接受信用证的修改。

4. 受益人收到修改的信用证后，应及时检查改证是否符合要求，并做出接受或拒绝的表示。

5. 对于修改的内容应全部接受或拒绝，部分接受或拒绝无效。

6. 修改的信用证必须通过原证通知行的通知后方能生效，直接由买方送达的改证无效。

7. 信用证修改产生的费用应明确由谁承担，一般按照改证的责任归属来确定。

本章小结

本章主要讲述的信用证的相关知识。通过本章学习，要求学生了解信用证的定义、特点和种类，以便在贸易谈判中知晓采用何种信用证作为付款方式。通过本章学习，学生还要学会审核信用证，尤其是学会审核信用证的内容，这直接关系到卖方能否顺利议付结汇。能否理解信用证的内容，也是能否按照信用证要求正确制单的关键所在。

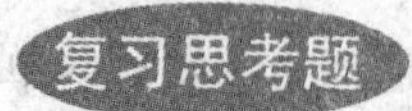

1. 简述信用证的定义、性质。
2. 简述信用证的议付流程。
3. 审核信用证时应注意那些问题？
4. 分析上述第一节(3-1)信用证，回答下列问题：

(1) 信用证的有效期和装运期有何规定？

(2) 卖方应在何时交单？

(3) 信用证要求卖方议付时提交哪些单证？哪些单据是卖方能够制作的？哪些单据不是卖方能够制作的？

第四章　托运单证

学习目标

通过本章学习，学生应学会制作商业发票、装箱单、运输委托单，掌握订舱的基本流程。

根据货物出口业务流程，卖方在收到定金或收到信用证审核无误后，就可以开始着手备货了。在货物生产的过程中，卖方可以制作商业发票、装箱单，取得货物的详细数据，为之后的订舱、报检提供货物信息。此时制作商业发票、装箱单，主要依据是合同以及货物的实际数量、净重、毛重、尺码，这是货物的第一手信息，卖方在采集相关货物信息时一定要亲自动手称重、量包装尺码，切不可凭空估计。

第一节　商业发票

一、商业发票的概念及作用

商业发票(Commercial Invoice)是出口商对进口商开立的发货价目清单，它全面反映合同内容，是装运货物的总说明。商业发票主要供进口商凭以收货、支付货款，是进出口双方记账、报关、纳税的依据，是各种单据的核心。其主要作用体现在如下几个方面：

1. 商业发票对于卖方而言，它是卖方向买方出售货物的总说明和凭证，是卖方制作货运单据的依据。

2. 商业发票对于买方而言，它是买方向卖方付款的凭据。

3. 商业发票是买卖双方进出口报关、报检、纳税计算的重要单据之一。

二、商业发票的内容及缮制注意事项

(一) 出口商的公司名称和地址

一般印在发票的正上方作为标头，如果付款方式是信用证，出口商的公司名称应该和信用证受益人一致，除非信用证另有规定。

(二) 发票名称

印在出口商公司名称正下方，一般印为 Commercial Invoice 字样。

(三) 发票编号(Invoice No.)

由出口商根据本公司的实际情况编写。

(四) 出票的日期(Date)

发票制作的实际日期,日期应在合同签订日期之后和装船日期之前。

(五) 买方的公司名称和地址

此处是发票抬头,一般印在发票的"TO"之后。

(六) 运输方式和路线

此处根据实际运输方式和路线填写,如"Shipment from Qingdao port, China to New York, USA by sea"。

(七) 唛头及编号(Marks & Nos)

此栏根据合同填写唛头,如果发票中所载的货物名称较多,本栏可以填写上货物的序列号。如果没有唛头,记为"N/M"。

(八) 商品名称(Name of Commodity)

此栏填写货物的名称、货号,与合同一致。

(九) 单价(Unit Price)

根据合同填写商品的单价及对应的贸易术语,填制要规范,如 10 美元应制为"USD10.00"。

(十) 数量(Quantity)

此处填写实际发货的数量,数量应符合合同的要求。

(十一) 金额(Amount)

对应填写单价和数量的乘积,要注意计算准确、填制规范。

(十二) 金额大写

如总金额是 10 000 美元应记为"SAY U. S. DOLLARS TEN THOUSAND ONLY",划线单词为金额大写的固定格式。

(十三) 声明文句

根据买方的要求,卖方有时需要在发票上添加诸如制造商公司名址、非木质包装声明等字句,卖方把这些文句填写在发票的下端即可。

(十四) 受益人签章

发票的右下角要盖有出口商法人代表签字的公章。

在实际业务操作中,缮制发票的时候可以不写中文,只用其中的英文部分。除此之外,货物出口到不同国家,买方可能要求在发票上添加其他内容。例如出口到美国的货物,买方一般要求在商业发票上添加非木制包装声明。还有些买方要求在商业发票上注明货物的实际生产厂商公司名称、地址或者货物零部件的价值等等。卖方把这些内容添加在发票下部的空白处即可。为了避免遗漏此类添加语句,卖方在同买方进行商务洽谈时可以就单据内容咨询买方。

商业发票填制示例见表 4-1。

三、其他种类的发票

（一）海关发票(Custom Invoice)

海关发票是进口商向进口国海关报关的证件之一。是根据某些国家海关的规定，由进口商提供电子或纸质版本，出口商填制的，供进口商凭以报关用的特定格式的发票，其内容较一般商业发票复杂。海关发票的作用是供进口国海关核定货物的原产地国，以采取不同的国别政策；供进口商向海关办理进口报关、纳税等手续；供进口国海关掌握进口商品在出口国市场的价格情况，以确定是否低价倾销，以便征收反倾销税；供进口国海关作为统计的依据。采用海关发票的有加拿大、澳大利亚、新西兰等国家。

（二）领事发票(Consular Invoice)

领事发票是由进口国驻出口国的领事出具的一种特别印制的发票，是出口商根据进口国驻在出口地领事所提供的特定格式填制，并经领事签证的发票。这种发票证明出口货物的详细情况，为进口国用于防止外国商品的低价倾销，同时可用作进口税计算的依据，有助于货物顺利通过进口国海关。对于领事发票各国有不同的规定，如允许出口商在商业发票上由进口国驻出口地的领事签证(Consular Visa)，即“领事签证发票”。出具领事发票时，领事馆一般要根据进口货物价值收取一定费用。这种发票主要为中东、拉美国家所采用。

（三）厂商发票(Manufacturer Invoice)

厂商发票是出口货物的制造厂商所出具的，以本国货币计算，用来证明出口国国内市场出厂价格的发票。要求提供厂商发票的目的是检查出口国出口商品是否有销价倾销行为，供进口国海关估价，核税以及征收反倾销税之用。

（四）形式发票(Proforma Invoice)

形式发票(P/I)是国际贸易中常用的一种非正式发票，买方常常需要形式发票，以作为申请进口和批准外汇之用。形式发票中除了商业发票的基本内容之外，还应加上付款方式、交货期、卖方的银行资料等。形式发票示例见表 4 - 2。

第二节　装箱单

一、装箱单的概念及作用

装箱单是指记载或描述商品包装情况的单据。不同的商品往往需要不同的装箱单。装箱单是商业发票的补充单据，是对商业发票上商品包装情况的描述，便于国外买方在货物到达目的港时，供海关检查和核对货物，也便于买方了解包装件号的具体内容，以方便销售。

二、装箱单的内容及缮制时注意事项

（一）出口商的公司名称和地址

一般印在装箱单的正上方作为标头，如果付款方式是信用证，出口商的公司名称应该

和信用证受益人一致,除非信用证另有规定。

(二) 标题

印在出口商公司名称正下方,一般印为 Packing List 字样。

(三) 发票编号(Invoice No.)和日期(Date)

装箱单是商业发票的补充,所以应该填上相应的发票编号和日期。

(四) 运输方式和路线

此处根据实际运输方式和路线填写,如"Shipment from Qingdao port, China to New York, USA by sea"。

(五) 唛头及编号(Marks & Nos)

此栏根据商业发票填写唛头,如果装箱单所载的货物名称较多,本栏可以填写上货物的序列号。如果没有唛头,记为"N/M"。

(六) 商品名称(Name of Commodity)

此栏填写货物的名称、货号,与商业发票一致。

(七) 数量(Quantity)

装箱单的数量包括两项内容,一项是货物的数量,数量及数量单位应和商业发票一致;另一项内容是货物的包装数量,应根据货物的实际包装数量及包装种类填写。

(八) 净重(Net Weight)

此处应对应填写该款货物总的净重,取整数填写即可。

(九) 毛重(Gross Weight)

此处应对应填写该款货物总的毛重,取整数填写即可。

(十) 尺码(Measurement)

此处应对应填写该款货物总的立方数,此栏数据关系到订舱的货柜规格和数量,为精确起见,应保留到小数点后两位数字。

(十一) 合计(Total)

此栏把对应列的数量、净重、毛重、尺码合计。

(十二) 包装数量大写

此处应将装箱单总的包装数量的英文大写。

(十三) 声明文句

根据买方的要求,卖方有时需要在装箱单添加诸如制造商公司名址、非木质包装声明等字句,卖方把这些文句填写在装箱单的下端即可。

(十四) 受益人签章

装箱单的右下角要盖有出口商法人代表签字的公章。

装箱单填制示例见表 4-3。

三、其他种类的包装单据

（一）重量单(Weight List)

以重量单位计价成交的货物(例如化肥、矿石等)，买方或者信用证可能要求卖方提供重量单。卖方在制作重量单时，除了把标题改为 Weight List 之外，其他内容和装箱单是一致的。为了明确货物的单位包装重量，在重量单中卖方一般要说明每一包装的净重、毛重、尺码，以供买方安排运输存储时参考。

（二）尺码单(Measurement List)

单位尺码计价成交的货物(例如布匹、绳索等)，买方或者信用证可能要求卖方提供尺码单。卖方在制作尺码单时，除了把标题改为 Measurement List 外，还应重点加注每件、每种规格的尺码和总尺码，如果包装内不是统一尺码则应逐一加以说明。

第三节　托运单

无论以什么条件成交的货物，卖方都要和货代洽谈运输事宜，以确定船期、货物入仓时间、通关时间等等，以保证货物顺利装船发运。货代一般会要求卖方填写订舱委托书，以便据此订舱。

一、卖方订舱发运货物的一般流程

（一）卖方联系货代。如果合同是按 FOB 成交，卖方最好是在洽谈合同时就让买方直接告知其货代的联系方式，以便及早联系，落实船期。如果合同时按 CIF 或 CFR 成交，卖方需要自行落实货代，洽谈海运费，签订运输委托合同。卖方在落实货代时，要做到货比三家，选定规模大、信誉好、报价低的货代作为自己运输代理。

（二）卖方制作货运委托书发给货代。卖方同货代取得联系后，货代一般会要求卖方填写货运委托书，据此订舱。卖方在填写货运委托时，要根据商业发票和装箱单的相关货物信息，如实填写。货运委托书示例见(图表 4 - 4)。

（三）收到卖方的货运委托书后，货代订舱。订舱后货代会给卖方发一份入货通知书，入货通知书里列明了船名、航次、预计开航日期、集装箱场站地址及联系电话、截港日期、结关日期。卖方收到入货通知书后要仔细阅读，按照船期同供货商落实好船货衔接问题。

（四）收到入货通知书后，卖方应及时给买方发送装船通知，按 FOB 或 CFR 术语成交的，卖方还要提示买方及时办理货物运输保险。

（五）拖柜装货、报关。备货完毕后，货物需要检验后方能出口的，一定要在拖柜装货前做好货物检验工作。验货合格后，卖方应按入货通知书中集装箱场站地址，联系卡车拖柜装货，并告知卡车司机重柜返场时间，以免过了截港日期被甩柜。自行报关的，要在重柜返场前报关；让货代代理报关的，要及早把报关材料寄给货代。如遇海关抽检，卖方应及时派员到现场配合海关人员验货，以免错过入货通知书规定的结关时间。

（六）审核提单，同货代结算费用。重柜返场后，货代一般会把提单的电子版发给卖方审核内容，卖方要认真按照商业发票、装箱单、信用证等单证要求认真审核，做到“单单一致、单证相符”。审核无误后查看货代的费用清单，清单中有不明白的费用一定要问清楚，结算费用后及时向货代收取正本提单。让货代代理报关的，还应让货代及时退还报关单及出口收汇核销单的海关应退还联。

二、订舱委托书的填制

（一）货运委托书的编号和时间

可以按发票号填写，日期就是填制委托书当天的日期。

（二）托运人（出口商）的公司名称和地址

按商业发票填写，应补充上汉语公司名称、地址及联系电话，以方便货代联系。

（三）收货人（进口商）的公司名称和地址

按商业发票填写，也可以要求货代在缮制正本提单时在此栏直接填写 TO ORDER.

（四）通知人

即货到目的港后通知谁来提货。如果买方或信用证告知了提货人的公司名址，直接按买方或信用证给出的提货人名址填写即可，如果没有告知，可以直接填写收货人的公司名址。

（五）货物存放地点

如果需要货代拖柜装货，此处应填写货物的存放地点的详细地址；如果出口商自行拖柜装货，此处可以免填。

（六）预订船期

出口商应根据合同、信用证及备货时间综合考虑预订船期，以便货代据此订舱。

（七）发货港

按商业发票填写。

（八）目的港

按商业发票填写。

（九）目的地

根据成交方式不同，D 组贸易术语成交的，应填写目的地，其他贸易术语成交的可以不填。

（十）正本提单的份数

如果付款方式是信用证，正本提单的份数应该根据信用证要求填写。例如有些信用证规定提交的提单应是“3/3 clean on board ocean bill of lading”，就需要提交 3 份正本提单。

（十一）唛头及编号

此栏根据商业发票填写唛头，如果装箱单所载的货物名称较多，本栏可以填写上货物的序列号。如果没有唛头，记为“N/M”。

（十二）商品名称、包装数量及预订集装箱的型号和数量

此栏货物的名称、货物包装数量按装箱单的货物名称、总的包装数量填写。如果是整箱装运的货物，应按装箱单货物总的体积计算出所需订集装箱的型号及数量。一般来说，常用的集装箱型号有3种，20′、40′、40′H，分别能装30立方米、60立方米、70立方米的货物，最大载重量为18吨、24吨、24吨，所以体积小、重量大的货物应选择20′型号的集装箱。如(图表4－3)装箱单所示货物体积114.01立方米，毛重未超过集装箱载重量，故可以选择2个40′型号的集装箱，在托运单上记为“2X40′FCL”即可，意即订2个40′型号集装箱，整箱装货。

（十三）毛重

此处应按装箱单填写货物总的毛重。

（十四）尺码

此处应按装箱单填写货物总的立方数，此栏数据关系到订舱的货柜规格和数量，为精确起见，应保留到小数点后两位数字。

（十五）运费

如果是以CIF或CFR成交的货物，卖方在和货代谈妥海运费后，可以将海运费标注在此处；如果是以FOB成交的货物，此处标注FREIGHT COLLECT(运费到付)即可。

（十六）声明文句

如果出口商想让货代提供船公司提单，可以在托运单上特别说明；如果货物运往美国，出口商可以特别要求货代提供提单时要在提单上特别注明该次运输适用中国法律。(原因将在后面关于提单的章节中详细介绍)

（十七）货代签章

出口商把货运委托书发给货代后，可以让货代签字盖章后回传一份留底，以备遇到纠纷时作为处理凭证。

货运委托书示例见表4－4。

本章小结

本章主要是按照出口合同的操作流程介绍了商业发票、装箱单的制作以及订舱的一般流程。商业发票、装箱单是以后章节要讲述的单据的填制依据，所以这两个单据一定要制作准确、完整。下一章要讲述的报检、报关流程中，商业发票、装箱单是必须向相关部门提交的单据之一。

根据下列资料缮制商业发票和装箱单。

SALES CONFIRMATION

NO.：03CAN－1108

DATE：NOV. 08，2004

THE SELLER：JIANGSU INTERNATIONAL IMP. & EXP. CORP. LTD.
80 ZHONGSHAN ROAD，NANJING，CHINA

THE BUYER：SHEMSY NEGOCE ID CORP.
75 ROUTE 96570 DARDILLY，FRANCE

THIS SALES CONFIRMATION IS HEREBY MUTUALLY CONFIRMED，TERMS AND CONDITIONS ARE AS FOLLOWS：

NAME OF GOODS AND SPECIFICATIONS	QTY	UNIT PRICE	AMOUNT
LEATHER BAGS		FOB SHANGHAI	
ITEM NO. SL100	1000PCS	USD2. 00/PC	USD2000. 00
ITEM NO. SG120	2000PCS	USD1. 50/PC	USD3000. 00
ITEM NO. SF200	3000PCS	USD3. 00/PC	USD9000. 00
TOTAL	6000PCS		USD14000. 00
SAY US DALLARS FOURTEEN THOUSAND ONLY			

SHIPPING MARKS：

SNIC
03CAN－1108
C/N0. 1－UP

SHIPMENT：TO BE MADE（45 DAYS BY SEA AFTER RECEIVED 30％ T/T PAYMENT）FROM SHANGHAI PORT，CHINA TO MARSEILLE，FRANCE，PARTIAL SHIPMENTS AND TRANSHIPMENT TO BE ALLOWED.

PAYMENT：30％ T/T IN DEPOSIT，70％ D/P AT SIGHT

PACKING：PACKED IN PLASTIC BAGS PER PIECE，THEN IN CARTON，10PCS/CTN

其他货物信息：

ITEM NO. SL100　净重：1 千克/个

ITEM NO. SG120　净重：1. 2 千克/个

ITEM NO. SF200　净重：1. 5 千克/个

包装箱重量：3 千克/个，尺码：60 cm×40 cm×30 cm

表 4-1　商业发票

<table>
<tr><td colspan="3">SELLER(卖方):
GUANGZHOU IMP. & EXP. CO.,LTD
ADD.:160 ZHONGSHAN ROAD,
GUANGZHOU,CHINA</td><td colspan="2" rowspan="2">COMMERCIAL INVOICE

商 业 发 票</td></tr>
<tr><td colspan="3">BUYER(买方):
GENERAL TRADING COMPANY
ZP2280,SUNFLOWER ROAD,NEWYORK,
U.S.A.</td></tr>
<tr><td colspan="3">S/C NO.(合同号): GG5019
L/C NO.(信用证号:LL80993278</td><td colspan="2">INVOICE NO(发票号): GB160
DATE(发票日期): OCT.20,2016</td></tr>
<tr><td colspan="5">运输路线和方式:
SHIPMENT FROM GUANGZHOU PORT,CHINA TO NEW YORK,USA BY SEA</td></tr>
<tr><td>唛头
MARK</td><td>货物名称
DESCRIPTION OF GOODS</td><td>数量
QUANTITY</td><td>单价
UNIT PRICE</td><td>金额
AMOUNT</td></tr>
<tr><td>N.Y.
USA</td><td>WOODEN DESKS
A012
B018</td><td>200PCS
500PCS</td><td>FOB
GUANGZHOU
USD30.00
USD20.00</td><td>USD6000.00
USD10000.00</td></tr>
<tr><td></td><td>TOTAL:</td><td>700PCS</td><td></td><td>USD16000.00</td></tr>
<tr><td colspan="5">TOTAL AMOUNT(金额大写):SAY U.S. DOLLARS SIXTEEN THOUSAND ONLY.</td></tr>
</table>

GUANGZHOU IMP. & EXP. CO.,LTD

(法人代表签字章)

表 4-2 形式发票

MINGR TRADING CO. ,LTD.

Room 2901, HuaRong Mansion, Guanjiaqiao 85#, Shanghai, China.

PROFORMA INVOICE

TO: ______________________ INVOICE NO. : ____________

______________________ DATE: ____________

SHIPMENT FROM ________ **TO** ____________ **BY SEA**

MARKS	NAME OF GOODS	UNIT PRICE	QUANTITY	AMOUNT
	TOTAL:			

1. TERMS OF PAYMENT:
2. TIME OF DELIVERY:
3. INSURANCE:
4. SELLER'S BANK INFORMATION:

MINGR TRADING CO. ,LTD
(法人代表签字章)

表 4-3　装箱单示例

GUANGZHOU IMP. & EXP. CO. ,LTD

ADD. :160 ZHONGSHAN ROAD,GUANGZHOU,CHINA

PACKING LIST

INVOICE NO. : GB160　　　　DATE: OCT. 20,2016

SHIPMENT FROM GUANGZHOU PORT,CHINA TO NEW YORK,USA BY SEA

MARKS	NAME OF GOODS	QUANTITY		N. W.	G. W.	MEAS.
N. Y. USA	WOODEN DESKS A012 B018	200PCS 500PCS	200CTNS 500CTNS	2000KGS 5000KGS	3000KGS 7500KGS	35. 78CBM 78. 23CBM
	TOTAL:	700PCS	700CTNS	7000KGS	10500KGS	114. 01CBM

SAY SEVEN HUNDRED CARTONS ONLY.

GUANGZHOU IMP. & EXP. CO. ,LTD
（法人代表签字章）

表 4－4　订舱委托书

<table>
<tr><td colspan="2">Shipper(发货人)
广州进出口有限公司
地址:广州市中山路 160 号
联系电话:020－8516682
GUANGZHOU IMP. & EXP. CO.,LTD
ADD.:160 ZHONGSHAN ROAD,
GUANGZHOU,CHINA</td><td colspan="2" rowspan="3">**订舱委托书**
NO.:GB1603
DATE:2016.10.25</td></tr>
<tr><td colspan="2">Consignee(收货人)
TO ORDER</td></tr>
<tr><td colspan="2">Notify Party(通知)
GENERAL TRADING COMPANY
ZP2280,SUNFLOWER ROAD,NEWYORK,
U.S.A.</td></tr>
<tr><td>货物存放地点:
×××仓库</td><td>Port of Loading(发货港)
GUANGZHOU PORT,CHINA 广州港</td><td colspan="2">Port of Discharge(目的港)
NEWYORK,U.S.A.</td></tr>
<tr><td>预订船期:
2016.11.20</td><td>Place of Delivery 目的地</td><td colspan="2">正本提单的份数:3</td></tr>
<tr><td>Marks and/Numbers
(唛头)</td><td>No. of Container / Packages / Description of Goods
(集装箱数量 / 包装数量 / 货物名称)</td><td>Gross Weight
(Kgs)(毛重)</td><td>Measurement
(cu-metres)(立方米)</td></tr>
<tr><td>N.Y.
USA</td><td>2×40′集装箱
700CARTONS 箱
WOODEN DESKS 木制课桌

注意:该次运输适用中国法律.
请提供船公司提单</td><td>**10500**</td><td>**114.01**</td></tr>
<tr><td colspan="3">FREIGHT & CHARGES(运费):FREIGHT COLLECT</td><td>(货代确认盖章)</td></tr>
</table>

第五章　出口报检、报关单证

学习目标

通过本章学习，掌握出口报检、报关的业务流程，学会填制货物出口报检单、报关单及其他报检、报关所需单证。

第一节　出口货物报检

按照货物出口操作的业务流程，在订舱程序完成后，如果货物需经商检局检验合格后才能出口，出口商就可以备齐单据、准备报检了。

一、出口货物报检概述

（一）出口货报检的范围

1. 根据《中华人民共和国进出口商品检验法》及其实施条例、《中华人民共和国进出境动植物检疫法》及其实施条例、《中华人民共和国国境卫生检疫法》及其实施细则、《中华人民共和国食品卫生法》等有关法律、行政法规的规定，须经商检部门检验检疫合格后方能出口的货物；

2. 进口国家或地区规定必须凭货物出口国商检局出具的相关证书方准入境的货物；

3. 有关国际条约规定必须要检验检疫的货物；

4. 申请签发普惠制产地证或一般原产地证的货物；

5. 对外贸易关系人申请的鉴定业务和委托检验；

6. 对外贸易合同、信用证规定出口商需提供由官方机构出具证书的货物。

（二）报检的时间和地点

1. 出口货物最迟应于装船前 7 天报检，对于检验检疫周期长的货物，应留有相应的检验检疫时间。隔离检疫出境的动物应在出境前 60 天预报，隔离前 7 天报检。

2. 货物检验的地点。除活的动物需由口岸检验检疫机构检验检疫外，其他货物应在产地检验。如果货物的生产地和出境地距离甚远，出口商可以委托生产商在当地报检，由当地商检机构验货合格后，出具《出境货物换证凭单》或凭条，出口商再凭《出境货物换证凭单》或凭条在出口地商检机构报检换取《出境货物通关单》即可。

二、报检的操作流程及相关单证

(1) 出口商网上填写货物信息。初次报检的出口商应先持相关证书到当地商检局注册,注册成功后按照商检局的要求安装报检系统软件,然后按照报检系统的要求填写货物出境的相关信息,具体信息参照出境货物报检申请单内容。填完信息后保存发送。

(2) 商检局网上初步审核。商检局在收到出口商发送的货物报检信息后,一般在 24 小时内初步审核并发送反馈信息。

(3) 出口商现场交单。出口商在网上申报完报检信息后,可在当日或次日查看商检局反馈的信息。如果反馈的信息中显示有不合格的地方,出口商可以修改后再次发送;如果反馈的信息显示为合格,出口商应备齐所需单据,到商检局现场交单。主要单据包括《出境货物检验申请单》《销售合同》复印件、货物出厂检验合格单(由货物生产厂家提供)、《出境货物运输包装性能检验结果单》(由包装材料生产厂家提供),如果货物已经在异地检验了,还应提供《出境货物换证凭单》或凭条。根据国家规定需要经相关部门许可才能出口的货物,出口商还应提供相关的法律批文。对于按样品成交的货物,出口商报检时还应提供买卖双方确认的样品。

(4) 商检局核对出口商提交的相关单证及要求出具的证书,审核无误后按规定收取费用。

(5) 出口商报检成功后应同商检局相关验货人员预约验货时间,并按时配合相关人员验货。

(6) 验货合格后,验货人员将验货信息录入系统,出口商到签证放行处领取《出境货物通关单》或其他已申请单证。

三、出口货物报检的填制

(1) 报检单位:此处加盖出口商报检专用章即可。

(2) 报检单位登记号:报检单位在商检局的注册号。

(3) 联系人:报检人员姓名。

(4) 联系电话:报检人员的联系电话。

(5) 报检日期:当天报检的日期。

(6) 发货人名称:出口公司的中英文名称。

(7) 收货人(英文):按合同买方填写。

(8) 货物名称(中英文):按合同的货物名称填写。

(9) H. S. 编码:从海关核发的商品编码表查询货物编码,填写前 8 位数字。

(10) 产地:按实际填写。

(11) 报验数/重量:按实际应检验商品数量填写。

(12) 货物总值:按合同金额填写。

(13) 包装种类及数量:按装箱单包装种类及总的包装数量填写,散装货则填"IN BULK"。

(14) 运输工具名称:报检时如尚未订舱,可不填。

(15) 贸易方式：如果是一般货物进出口，填写“一般贸易”，其他贸易方式则根据实际情况填写“来料加工”“进料加工”等。

(16) 存货地点：报验时若需对检验商品取样，则应到其存货地点。

(17) 合同号：按随附的合同号码填写。

(18) 信用证号：如果付款方式是信用证，填上信用证号即可，如果是其他付款方式，如实填写，如“T/T”“D/P”。

(19) 用途：指本货物的进口商用途，可填写民用、种用、食用、药用等。

(20) 输往国别与地区：按合同填写。

(21) 许可证/审批单号：须经国家行政主管部门批准方能出口的，要提供相关批文号。

(22) 启运地：合同的发货港。

(23) 到达口岸：合同的目的港。

(24) 生产单位注册号：货物的生产商在商检的注册号。

(25) 集装箱规格、数量及号码：填写装运报检货物所需要的集装箱型号及数量，如果需要一个40′集装箱，填写1x40′，集装箱的号码如报检时不知道可不填。

(26) 合同、信用证特殊要求的检验检疫条款或特殊要求，如果有，则需附上信用证复印件；如果没有，填写“无”。

(27) 标记及号码：按合同唛头填写。

(28) 随附单据：在相应方框内打√，需要卫生证时，要有卫生注册证及厂检合格单。需换证凭单(出口货物不在出运口岸而在发运地商检)时，要有预验结果单。

(29) 需要证单名称：在相应的证单上打√。

(30) 检验检疫费：由商检局填写。

(31) 报检人郑重声明：由报检人员亲自签名。

(32) 领取单证：报检人员在领取所需单证后签名。

注意：一批商品需要一份申请，不能涂改；所填的项目必须和所附单据内容一致；如果要修改报检内容或添加所需单证，则应填写报检修改通知书，办理更改手续，需要缴费的，则要缴纳相关费用。

四、商检机构可出具的单证的种类及作用

(一) 种类

1. 品质检验证书(Inspection Certificate of Quality)。

2. 重量检验证书(Inspection Certificate of Weight)。

3. 数量检验证书(Inspection Certificate of Quantity)。

4. 兽医检验证书(Veterinary Inspection Certificate)。

5. 卫生(健康)检验证书(Sanitary Inspection Certificate)(Inspection Certificate of Health)。

6. 消毒检验证书(Disinfection Inspection Certificate)。

7. 产地检验证书(Inspection Certificate of Origin)。

8. 价值检验证书(Inspection Certificate of Value)。

9. 验残检验证书(Inspection Certificate on Damaged Cargo)。

10. 验舱检验证书(Inspection Certificate on Tank/Hold)。

11. 货载衡量检验证书(Inspection Certificate on Cargo Weight & Measurement)。

12. 温度检验证书(Inspection Certificate of Temperature)。

(二) 作用

1. 如果买方在合同或信用证中要求卖方提供由官方出具的上述单据,那么它就是卖方交单结汇或银行凭以付款的重要依据。如果卖方不能提供合同或信用证要求的单据或提供的单据与要求不符,将遭买方或银行拒付。

2. 这些单据是卖方交货的品质、数量、质量的有效证明。

3. 如果买卖双方因货物的品质、数量问题引发纠纷,这些单据将是法院或仲裁庭判决的重要依据。

根据货物出口贸易的操作流程,在完成货物的报检后,卖方应按与商检局验货人员约定的验货时间,跟踪备货情况,力争如期备货完毕,按约定时间验货。商检人员验货的过程中,卖方应派业务负责人员及货物生产工厂技术人员积极配合,对于商检人员在验货中提出的问题,要虚心接受并及时整改,直至货物检验合格。除了商检人员验货外,卖方还要仔细核实该批货物买方是否要委派其他人员前来验货。验货合格并取得相应的单证后,卖方就可以根据入货通知书的要求安排拖柜装货了。货物装柜后,卖方应及时备好相关单据报关,以便在入货通知书规定的结关日期之前使货物通关。

出境货物报检单如表 5-1 所示。

表 5-1　出境货物报检单

中华人民共和国出入境检验检疫

出境货物报检单

报检单位(加盖公章):　　　　　　　　＊编号＿＿＿＿＿

报检单位登记号:　　联系人:　　电话:　　报检日期:　　年　　月　　日

<table>
<tr><td rowspan="2">发货人</td><td colspan="5">(中文)</td></tr>
<tr><td colspan="5">(外文)</td></tr>
<tr><td rowspan="2">收货人</td><td colspan="5">(中文)</td></tr>
<tr><td colspan="5">(外文)</td></tr>
<tr><td>货物名称(中/外文)</td><td>H.S.编码</td><td>产地</td><td>数/重量</td><td>货物总值</td><td>包装种类及件数</td></tr>
<tr><td></td><td></td><td></td><td></td><td></td><td></td></tr>
<tr><td>运输工具名称号码</td><td></td><td>贸易方式</td><td></td><td>货物存放地点</td><td></td></tr>
<tr><td>合同号</td><td></td><td>信用证号</td><td></td><td>用途</td><td></td></tr>
<tr><td>发货日期</td><td></td><td>输往国家(地区)</td><td></td><td>许可证/审批号</td><td></td></tr>
<tr><td>启运地</td><td></td><td>到达口岸</td><td></td><td>生产单位注册号</td><td></td></tr>
</table>

（续表）

<table>
<tr><td colspan="2">集装箱规格、数量及号码</td><td colspan="3"></td></tr>
<tr><td colspan="2">合同、信用证订立的检验
检疫条款或特殊要求</td><td>标记及号码</td><td colspan="2">随附单据(划"√"或补填)</td></tr>
<tr><td colspan="2"></td><td></td><td>□合同
□信用证
□发票
□换证凭单
□装箱单</td><td>□厂检单
□包装性能结果单
□许可/审批文件
□
□</td></tr>
<tr><td colspan="4">需要证单名称(划"√"或补填)</td><td>＊检验检疫费</td></tr>
<tr><td rowspan="3">□品质证书
□重量证书
□数量证书
□兽医卫生证书
□健康证书
□卫生证书</td><td colspan="3" rowspan="3">□动物卫生证书
□植物检疫证书
□熏蒸/消毒证书
□出境货物换证凭单
□通关单</td><td>总金额
(人民币元)</td></tr>
<tr><td>计费人</td></tr>
<tr><td>收费人</td></tr>
<tr><td colspan="4" rowspan="3">报检人郑重声明：
1. 本人被授权报验。
2. 上列填写内容正确属实，货物无伪造或冒用他人的厂名、标志、认证标志，并承担货物质量责任。

签名：________</td><td>领取证单</td></tr>
<tr><td>日期</td></tr>
<tr><td>签名</td></tr>
</table>

第二节　一般贸易货物出口报关

一、报关概述

报关是办理货物出口手续的必要环节之一。报关是指进出口货物的收发货人、进出境运输工具的负责人、进出境物品的所有人或者他们的代理人，向海关办理货物、物品或运输工具进出境手续及相关海关事务的过程，包括向海关申报、交验单据证件，并接受海关的监管和检查等。

根据报关对象不同，可分为进出境的运输工具报关和货物报关、物品报关三类。由于性质不同，其报关程序各异。运输工具如船舶、飞机等通常应由船长、机长签署到达、离境报关单，交验载货清单、空运、海运单等单证向海关申报，作为海关对装卸货物和上下旅客实施监管的依据。而货物和物品则应由其收发货人或其代理人，按照货物的贸易性质或物品的类别，填写报关单，并随附有关的法定单证及商业和运输单证报关。如属于保税货物，应按"保税货物"方式进行申报，其应办事项及监管办法与其他贸易方式的货物有所区别。本节主要讲述一般货物出口报关，贸易方式为"一般贸易"。

二、货物出口报关的操作流程

1. 报关前做好准备工作。

(1) 初次报关的,应到海关办理注册登记手续。注册完毕后,按照海关的要求购买并安装《电子口岸系统》软件。

(2) 备齐报关所需单证。基本单证主要有商业发票、装箱单、合同复印件等,法检货物需要提供商检局签发的通关单。除此之外,需要相关机构批准方能出口的货物还需要提供出口许可证或其他官方证明文件。货物出口报关之前,出口商还应登录电子口岸系统申领出口收汇核销单,然后到外汇管理局领取纸质版,领回后再次登录电子口岸系统备案。纸质版的出口收汇核销单是报关的必备单证之一。

2. 自理报关的出口商,在货物运抵海关监管区后,装船的 24 小时以前,登录电子口岸系统录入货物报关信息。委托报关行或货代代理报关的,要将报关委托单以及其他报关所需单证寄给代理人。

3. 现场交单缴费。网上申报货物信息通过后,出口商或代理人应备齐所需单据到海关交纸质报关单及其他所需单据,海关审单后收取手续费。

4. 海关查验。海关一般对出口报关货物抽检,如果被抽到,出口商应及时到场站配合海关人员查验货物,按照海关人员的要求搬移、开拆被查验的货物。

5. 缴纳税费。对于出口需要缴纳关税的货物,出口商或其代理人在收到海关发出的税费缴纳通知后,应及时缴纳税费。

6. 通关放行。海关在查验货物完毕并收取了相关税费后,即办理通关放行手续,出口申报的货物显示“已通关”。货代即可安排货物装船。

7. 货物通过放行后 14 天左右,到海关领回海关签注后应退还的报关单出口退税证明联、出口收汇证明联、企业留存联以及出口收汇核销单。

三、出口货物报关单的填制

出口货物报关单的填制,有特别的要求,它必须要符合海关的规定,并全部用中文填制而成,其中预录入编号、海关编号由出口地海关填制,其余各项的填制要求如下:

(一) 出口口岸

货物出境时我国港口和国境口岸的名称。

(二) 备案号

一般贸易项下,本栏不填,加工贸易项下填《登记手册》编号。

(三) 出口日期、申报日期

用 6 位阿拉伯数字表示,出口日期应比申报日晚。

(四) 经营单位

对外签订并执行合同的中国境内企业或单位及其 10 位数编码。

(五) 运输方式

江海、铁路、汽车、航空、邮政、其他(包括人扛、驮畜、管道、输电网)等。

（六）运输工具名称

江海运输——船名/航次；

汽车、铁路——车牌号(车次)/进出境日期(8 位阿拉伯数字)；

航空——航班号、8 位进出境日期/总运单号；

邮政——包裹单号/8 位进出境日期；

其他——填具体的运输方式名称。

（七）提运单号(只能有一个)

江海、铁路运输，填提、运单号，航空运输填分运单号，无分运单的填总运单号，其他运输方式下不填。

（八）发货单位

出口货物在境内的生产或销售单位，可以与经营单位不同。

（九）贸易方式

一般贸易、来料加工(B)、进料对口或非对口(C)、不作价、加工贸易设备(D)、合资、合作、外资设备(Z)、补偿贸易、无偿援助、捐赠物资。

（十）征免性质

海关对进出口货物实施征、减、免税管理的性质类别。根据海关核发的《征免税证明》中批注的征免性质填报。

（十一）结汇方式

M/T、T/T、D/D、D/P、D/A、L/C 等。

（十二）许可证号

只有在申领进出口许可证的货物才填报。

（十三）运抵国

出口货物直接运抵的国家。在发生中转运输的情况下，若中转地发生了商业性交易，则为中转地，若未发生商业交易，则以运抵地为准，无实际进出境的，填中国。

（十四）指运港

运往境外的最终目的港。

（十五）境内货源地

出口货物在国内的产地或原始发货地，要填报具体的最小行政区域即区(县)。

（十六）批准文号

出口收汇核销单编号。

（十七）成交方式

具体的贸易术语。

（十八）运费、保费、杂费

货币代码/费用数字/费用代号。其中 1—表示费率，2—表示单价，3—表示总价；常见货币代码—美元(502),港币(110),欧元(300)。例:24 美元运费单价:502/24/2。

(十九) 合同协议号

进出口合同号码。

(二十) 件数

有外包装的货物的实际件数,只能是数字。

(二十一) 包装种类

货物的实际外包装种类,如木箱(WOODEN CASE),纸箱(CTN)、铁桶(IRON DRUM)、裸装(IN NUDE),散装(IN BULK)等。

(二十二) 毛、净重(公斤)

不足 1 公斤,填 1。

(二十三) 集装箱号

集装箱号码×集装箱个数(折合为 20 尺的标准箱个数)。本栏只填一个集装箱号,其余号码写在备注栏。一般 20 尺的集装箱称为一个标准箱,一个 40 尺的箱子可折合为 2 个标准箱。

(二十四) 随附单据

随报关单一起向海关递交的单据,但本栏只填海关监管的证件或批文的代码,不能填合同、发票、箱单、许可证等必备单证。

(二十五) 生产厂家

货物的境内生产企业。

(二十六) 标记唛码及备注

上部:1. 唛头;2. 受三资企业委托为其进口物品的外贸企业名称,如:委托××公司进口;3. 加工贸易结转货物及凭《征免税证明》转内销货物,其对应备案号应填报在本栏目。

下部:1. 24 栏的随附单据编号,如 5:GF1002;2. 23 栏其余的集装箱号码。

(二十七) 项号

分两行,第一行,商品的顺序号,如 01、02 等;第二行,该项货物在《登记手册》中的项号。

(二十八) 商品编码

商品的 8 位 HS 编码。

(二十九) 品名规格型号

分两行,第一行,品名的中文名称;第二行,规格型号,过长可换行,也可填报原文。

(三十) 数量及单位

分三行,海关法定第一、第二计量单位及合同成交单位分别在第一、二、三行填写,若无,则该行空白。

(三十一) 最终目的国

已知的出口货物最后交付的国家,也即最终实际消费、使用或做进一步加工制造的国家。

（三十二）单价

在统一项号下出口货物实际成交的单价，保留到小数点后 4 位数字。例如出口木制课桌单价 30 美元，应计为“30.0000”。

（三十三）总价

在统一项号下出口货物实际成交的总价，保留到小数点后 4 位数字。例如出口木制课桌总价 3000 美元，应计为“3000.0000”。

（三十四）币制

出口货物成交采用的币种，填写实际币种或代码。如美元记为“USD”

（三十五）征免

照章（一般贸易）、全免（备案号首位为 B、C、D、Z 的）、特案、随征免性质、折半征税等。

（三十六）税费征收情况

海关批注出口货物税费征收及减免情况。

（三十七）录入员

货物申报信息预录入人员的姓名。

（三十八）录入单位

电子数据报关单的录入单位名称。

（三十九）申报单位

自理报关的，填写出口商的公司单位名称及海关代码；代理报关的，填写代理人的公司名称及海关代码。

（四十）填制日期

报关员填制报关单的日期，电子数据报关单由计算机自动打印。

（四十一）海关审单批注

海关内部作业时签注，由海关人员手写。其中“放行”栏填写海关对接受申报的出口货物做出放行决定的日期。

报关单内容见出口货物报关单示例表 5-2。

表 5-2　出口货物报关单

中华人民共和国海关出口货物报关单

预录入编号　　　　　　　　　　　　　　海关编号

出口口岸	备案号		出口日期	申报日期
经营单位	运输方式	运输工具名称		提运单号
发货单位	贸易方式	征免性质		结汇方式
许可证号	运抵（国地区）	指运港		境内货源地
批准文号	成交方式	运费	保费	杂费
合同协议号	件数	包装种类	毛重（公斤）	净重（公斤）

（续表）

<table>
<tr><td>集装箱号</td><td>随附单据</td><td colspan="2">生产厂家</td></tr>
<tr><td colspan="4">标记唛码及备注</td></tr>
<tr><td colspan="4">项号　商品编号　商品名称规格型号　数量及单位　最终目的地国（地区）　单价　总价　币制　征免</td></tr>
<tr><td colspan="4"></td></tr>
<tr><td colspan="4"></td></tr>
<tr><td colspan="4"></td></tr>
<tr><td colspan="4"></td></tr>
<tr><td colspan="4">税费征收情况</td></tr>
<tr><td>录入单位</td><td colspan="2">兹声明以上申报无讹并承担法律责任</td><td>海关单批注及放行日期（签章）
审单审价
征税　统计</td></tr>
<tr><td>报关员
单位地址
邮编　电话</td><td colspan="2">申报单位（签章）
填制日期</td><td>查验　放行</td></tr>
</table>

第三节　货物出口许可证

一、出口许可证的定义和范围

（一）出口许可证概述

出口许可证（Export Licence），是指商务部授权发证机关依法对实行数量限制或其他限制的出口货物签发的准予出口的许可证件。

根据国家规定，凡是国家宣布实行出口许可证管理的商品，不管任何单位或个人，也不分任何贸易方式（对外加工装配方式，按有关规定办理），出口前均须申领出口许可证；非外贸经营单位或个人运往国外的货物，不论该商品是否实行出口许可证管理，价值在人民币 1 000 元以上的，一律须申领出口许可证；属于个人随身携带出境或邮寄出境的商品，除符合海关规定自用、合理数量范围外，也都应申领出口许可证。

目前，我国执行审批并签发出口许可证的机关为商务部及其派驻在主要口岸的特派员办事处；各省、自治区、直辖市以及经国务院批准的计划单列市的对外经贸行政管理部门，实行按商品、按地区分级发证办法。

（二）实行出口许可证管理的货物的范围

国家规定有数量限制的出口货物，实行配额管理和出口配额招标管理，其他限制出口货物，实行许可证管理。

1. 实行出口配额许可证管理的货物是：玉米、大米、小麦、玉米粉、大米粉、小麦粉、棉花、锯材、活牛（对港澳）、活猪（对港澳）、活鸡（对港澳）、煤炭、焦炭、原油、成品油、稀土、锑及锑制品、钨及钨制品、锌矿砂、锡及锡制品、白银、铟及铟制品、钼、磷矿石。

2. 实行出口配额招标的货物是：蔺草及蔺草制品、碳化硅、滑石块（粉）、轻（重）烧镁、矾土、甘草及甘草制品。

3. 实行出口许可证管理的货物是：活牛（对港澳以外市场）、活猪（对港澳以外市场）、活鸡（对港澳以外市场）、冰鲜牛肉、冻牛肉、冰鲜猪肉、冻猪肉、冰鲜鸡肉、冻鸡肉、消耗臭氧层物质、石蜡、锌及锌基合金、部分金属及制品、铂金（以加工贸易方式出口）、汽车（包括成套散件）及其底盘、摩托车（含全地形车）及其发动机和车架、天然砂（含标准砂）、钼制品、柠檬酸、维生素C、青霉素工业盐、硫酸二钠。

4. 边境小额贸易出口许可证管理的货物包括：玉米、玉米粉、大米、大米粉、小麦、小麦粉、锌矿砂、锡及锡制品、锑及锑制品、煤炭、原油、成品油、钨及钨制品、锯材、白银（含白银粗加工制品）、锌及锌基合金、部分稀有金属（包括锆、钽、铌、锗、钒、铋、钨、钛、镓、铼、铌、钴、铍、镍、锰、铬、铂、钯、铑、钌、铱、锇、硅铁）、稀土、焦炭、钼、钼制品、铟及铟制品、天然砂、柠檬酸、青霉素工业盐、维生素C、硫酸二钠、磷矿石、蔺草及蔺草制品、碳化硅、滑石块（粉）、氟石块（粉）、轻（重）烧镁、矾土、甘草及甘草锚品、消耗臭氧层物质、摩托车（含全地形车）及其发动机、车架、汽车（包括成套散件）及其底盘。

5. 加工贸易出口列入《禁止出口货物目录》（第一批）未锻造或粉末状铂、板（片）状铂，海关验核出口许可证。

6. 凡列入出口配额许可证、出口许可证管理货物目录的商品，因添加、混合其他成分，或仅简单加工导致商品编号改变的，须按照原海关商品编号的管理方式进行管理。凡申报出口的商品成分中含有（添加或混合）出口配额许可证、出口许可证管理的商品（贵金属超过2%，其他超过10%）的，须按含有出口配额许可证、出口许可证管理商品的管理方式进行管理。如已有管理规定对此问题进行明确的，仍按相关管理规定执行。

“简单加工”指申报出口商品加工工艺或外观达不到其商品描述的要求。一般适用于同类（指同种材料制成的商品，下同）初级产品有管理但深加工产品没有管理的商品。国家、行业有标准的，以国家标准、行业标准作为判定标准；暂无上述标准的，由商务主管部门会同海关协商后认定。

“凡是申报出口的商品中含有出口配额许可证、出口许可证管理的商品”是指申报出口的商品中含有现已公布的出口许可证管理货物目录所列商品编号的商品。

“含有（添加或混合）”是指含有的方式仅限于添加、混合这两种方式。

“添加、混合”是指禁限管理商品与其他商品（无论是否为禁限商品）经过物理混合，并可通过筛分等物理方式还原的。对于经过高温烧结、化学反应混合的，且再分离不可逆（分离困难）或分离成本远高于原管理商品价值的商品，不适用上述管理规定。

“贵金属超过2%、其他超过10%”是指申报出口的商品中含有出口配额许可证、出口许可证管理货物目录中所列商品编号商品的含量标准。对于同类商品中未列入出口配额许可证、出口许可证管理货物目录的，不适用上述管理规定。

出口许可证管理商品中的青霉素工业盐、维生素C暂不适用上述管理规定。

二、出口许可证的申领程序及所需文件

（一）申领程序

1. 查询当年货物出口许可证管理目录，明确出口货物是否属于出口许可证管理范围及应向哪个发证机构申请。

2. 到出证机构领取并填写《出口许可证申请表》，加盖公章，并随附出证机构需要的其他单据。通过网上申领的，应当如实填写电子申请表并传送给出证机构。

3. 出证机构收到申请材料后进行审核。审核通过后，发证机构一般在3个工作日内签发《中华人民共和国出口许可证》，一式四联，将第一、二、三联交给领证人，并收取相关费用。领到许可证后，出口商可凭以报检、报关。

（二）申领时应提交的文件

1. 经批准享有出口经营权的外贸企业，第一次向发证机关申领出口许可证时应提交主管部门批准成立公司（企业）的批文、公司（企业）章程、营业执照以及出口商品经营目录等复印件一套。

2. 经批准成立的外商投资企业，第一次向发证机关申领出口许可证时，应提交有关部门关于项目合同的批件、营业执照以及经国家商务部认可的年度出口计划等复印件一套。

3. 外贸公司凭合同正本（或复印件）；非外贸单位凭主管部门（厅、局级）的批准件。文物，凭文物主管部门的批准料件；书刊，凭出版主管部门的批准件；名人字画（只限近代、现代），凭文化部的批准件；黄金白银（不含饰品），凭中国人民银行的批准件；专利、诀窍、传统技艺，凭国家专利局或主管部门的批准件；居民或村民，凭街道办事处或村民委员会出具的说明情况的证明函和购货发票办理有关手续方可出境。

三、出口许可证填制

（一）出口商

配额管理出口商品，应填写出口配额指标单位的进出口企业全称；一般许可证管理出口商品，应填写有出口经营权的各类进出口企业的全称；还贷、补偿贸易项目出口，应填写有出口经营权的代理公司全称；非外贸单位经批准出运货物，此栏填写该单位名称；企业编码，应按商务部授权的发证机关编定的代码填写（下同）

（二）发货人

配额招标商品（包括有偿和无偿招标）的发货人与出口商必须一致；其他出口配额管理商品的发货人原则上应与出口商一致，但与出口商有隶属关系的可以不一致。还贷出口、补偿贸易出口和外商投资企业委托代理出口时，发货人与出口商可以不一致。

（三）出口许可证号

由发证机关编排。

（四）出口许可证有效截止日期

实行"一批一证"制的商品，其许可证有效期自发证之日起最长为三个月。供港澳（不包括转口）鲜活冷冻商品的许可证有效期为一个月。不实行"一批一证"制的商品、外商投资企业和补偿贸易项下的出口商品，其许可证有效期自发证之日起最长为六个月。许可证证面有效期如需跨年度时，可在当年将许可证日期填到次年，最迟至二月底。

（五）贸易方式

此栏内容有：一般贸易、易货贸易、补偿贸易、进料加工、来料加工、外商投资企业出口、边境贸易、出料加工、转口贸易、期货贸易、承包工程、归还贷款出口、国际展销、协定贸易、其他贸易。进料加工复出口，此栏填写进料加工。外商投资企业进料加工复出口时，贸易方式填写外商投资企业出口。非外贸单位出运展卖品和样品每批价值在 5 000 元以上的，此栏填写"国际展览"。各类进出口企业出运展卖品，此栏填写"国际展览"，出运样品填写一般贸易。

（六）合同号

指申领许可证、报关及结汇时所用出口合同的编码。原油、成品油及非贸易项下出口，可不填写合同号。展品出运时，此栏应填写商务部批准办展的文件号。

（七）报关口岸

指出运口岸，此栏允许填写三个口岸，但仅能在一个口岸报关。

（八）进口国（地区）

指最终目的地，即合同目的地，不允许使用地域名（如欧洲等）。

（九）支付方式

此栏的内容有：信用证、托收、汇付、本票、现金、记账和免费等。

（十）运输方式

可填写海上运输、铁路运输、公路运输、航空运输、邮政运输、固定运输。

（十一）商品名称和编码

按商务部发布的出口许可证管理商品目录的标准名称填写。

（十二）规格等级

规格等级栏，用于对所出口商品做具体说明，包括具体品种、规格（如：水泥 标号、钢材品种等）、等级（如兔毛等级）。同一编码商品规格型号超过四种时，应另行填写出口许可证申请表。"劳务出口物资 "也应按此填写。出运货物必须与此栏说明的品种、规格或等级相一致。

（十三）单位

指计量单位。非贸易项下的出口商品，此栏以"批"为计量单位，具体单位在备注栏中说明。

（十四）数量、单价及总值

数量表示该证允许出口商品的多少。此数值允许保留一位小数，凡位数超出的，一律以四舍五入进位。计量单位为“批”的，此栏填写 1。

（十五）备注

填写以上各栏未尽事宜。

出口许可证示例见表 5-3。

表 5-3　出口许可证

中华人民共和国出口许可证

EXPORT LICENCE OF THE PEOPLE'S REPUBLIC OF CHINA

1. 出口商　　编码 Exporter			2. 出口许可证编号 License No.		
3. 发货人 Consignor			4. 出口许可证许有效期截止日期 Export license expiry date		
5. 贸易方式 Terms of trade			8. 进口国家(地区) Country /Region of purchase		
6. 合同号 Contract No.			9. 支付方式 Payment		
7. 报关口岸： Place of clearance			10. 运输方式 Means of transport		
11. 商品名称 Description of commodity			12. 商品编码 H. S code		
13. 商品规格、型号 Specification	单位 Unit	14. 数量 Quantity	15. 单价(　) Unit Price	16. 总值(　) Amount	17. 总值折美元 Amount in USD
18. 总计 Total					
19. 备注 Supplementary details			20. 发证机关盖章 Issuing authority's stamp 发证日期 Signature Date		

商务部监制　　　　本证不得涂改，不得转让

四、出口许可证的管理

（一）出口许可证申领后，必须在有效期内使用。出口许可证的有效期不得超过六个月。出口许可证跨年度使用时，不得超过次年二月底。

（二）出口许可证管理货物出口报关时，出口许可证号填报在报关单"许可证号"栏，一份报关单只允许填报一个许可证。即出口许可证实行"一证一关"制，即一个出口许可证只能在一个海关报关。

（三）出口许可证使用时实行"一批一证"和"非一批一证"制。

1. "一批一证"指出口许可证在有效期内只能出口报关使用一次。

2. "非一批一证"指出口许可证在有效期内可以多次报关使用，但最多不超过12次。

(1) 下列情形实行"非一批一证"制，发证机构在签发出口许可证时应在备注栏内注明"非一批一证"字样：外商投资企业出口货物、加工贸易方式出口货物、补偿贸易项下出口货物。出口商品为：大米、玉米、小麦、活牛、活猪、活鸡、牛肉、猪肉、鸡肉、原油、成品油、煤炭、汽车（包括成套散件）及其底盘。

(2) "非一批一证"出口许可证每次报关数，是指同一航次运输工具运载的同批货物，海关在许可证上做一次批注，如此类推12次后，该证如有余量不可再使用。海关在第12次批注后，进行总量核注，并将纸面许可证海关留存联正本随附报关单归档。

（四）出口大宗、散装货物溢装数量不得超过出口许可证出口数量的5%。"非一批一证"的大宗、散装货物，每批货物出口时，按其实际出口数量进行核扣，最后一批出口货物出口时，其溢装数量按该许可证实际剩余数量并在规定的溢装上限5%内计算。其中原油、成品油、钢材三种大宗散装货物的溢装货物的溢装数量不得超过出口许可证所列出口数量的3%。

第四节　出口收汇核销单

一、出口收汇核销单定义

出口收汇核销单，是国家为了加强外汇管理，确保国家外汇收入，防止外汇流失，由国家外汇管理局制发、出口单位凭以向海关出口报关、向外汇指定银行办理出口收汇、向国家外汇管理局办理出口收汇核销、向税务机关办理出口退税申报的有统一编号及使用期限的凭证。

它通过建立对企业出口、报关、收汇整个过程实行跟踪的监测系统，以出口收汇核销单为主线，对每一笔出口货物凭出口货物报关单进行跟踪监督。

二、出口收汇核销流程

出口收汇核销工作是一项政策性、规范性很强的工作，出口企业应严格按照国家外汇管理局颁布的《出口收汇核销管理办法》《出口收汇核销管理办法实施细则》以及《出口收汇核销管理操作流程》等规定通过电子口岸出口收汇系统进行。

1. 出口单位取得商务部或其授权单位批准的进出口经营权。

2. 出口单位到海关办理“中国电子口岸”入网手续，并到有关部门办理“中国电子口岸”企业法人 IC 卡和操作员 IC 卡认证手续。

3. 出口单位持有关材料到当地外汇管理机构办理注册登记手续，国家外汇管理局审核无误后，为出口单位办理登记手续，建立出口单位单子档案信息。

4. 出口单位在货物出口报关前登录电子口岸系统进行网上申领出口收汇核销单。每次可按当月出口货物票数申领数张。

5. 出口单位在网上申领 3 个工作日后可凭操作员 IC 卡、核销员证到注册地国家外汇管理局领取纸质出口收汇核销单。纸质核销单正式使用时应加盖单位名称及组织机构代码章，在骑缝处加盖公章。

6. 出口单位在使用核销单报关前，登录电子口岸系统向报关地海关进行核销单的口岸备案。

7. 出口单位出口报关。海关在审核出口单位提交的核销单和其他报关材料，并核对核销单底账无误后，在核销单“海关核放情况”栏加盖“验讫章”，并对核销单电子底账数据进行“已用”核注，结关后应出口单位申请向出口单位签发注有核销单编号的报关单，同时将核销单电子底账的核注情况和报关单电子底账等数据通过电子口岸数据中心传送至国家外汇管理局。

8. 出口单位在报关出口后通过电子口岸出口收汇系统将已用于出口报关的核销单向国家外汇管理机构交单。

9. 出口单位在银行办理出口收汇后，持出口收汇核销单报告表、出口收汇核销单、报关单出口收汇证明联、出口收汇核销专用联及其他规定的核销凭证集中或逐笔向国家外汇管理局办理出口收汇核销手续。

三、出口收汇核销单的填制

出口收汇核销单分为存根、正联、退税联三部分，各部分填写方法是：

（一）存根

1. 编号

应于出口报关单核销联编号一致，该栏由发放空白核销单的当地国家外汇管理局分支机构预先编号。

2. 出口单位

加盖出口单位名称条形印章即可，也可手填。

3. 单位代码

加盖单位组织机构代码章即可，也可手填。

4. 出口币种总价

按商业发票填写出口成交货物总价及使用的币种，应于报关单一致。

5. 收汇方式

合同付款方式，如信用证、汇付、托收，并注明即期或远期。

6. 预计收款日期

应根据预计交单结算日期推算货款到账日期。但需要注意，即期收汇应在货物出口报关 180 天内收汇，远期收汇应在备案期内收汇。对预计收汇日期超过报关日期 180 天以上的，出口单位应在货物报关后 60 天内向国家外汇管理局办理远期收汇备案。出口单位报关后，应在预计收汇日期起 30 天内，持规定的核销凭证集中或逐笔向国家外汇管理局进行出口收汇核销报告。

7. 报关日期

按实际报关日期填写，应与报关单一致。

8. 备注

该栏由出口单位根据实际情况在必要时填写。

9. 有效期

无须填写。

（二）正联

1. 出口单位

同存根。

2. 单位代码

同存根。

3. 银行审签

由收汇银行填写。

4. 海关签注栏

海关审核报关单与出口收汇核销单核对无误后，在此栏内加盖“验讫”章放行。

5. 外汇管理局签注栏

该栏由当地国家外汇管理局分支机构根据核销实际情况填写，并有核销人员签字，加盖“已核销”章。

（三）退税联

1. 编号

同存根。

2. 出口单位

同存根。

3. 单位代码

同存根。

4. 货物名称

同报关单。

5. 货物数量

同报关单。

6. 币种总价

同存根。

7. 报关单编号

按报关单填写。

8. 外汇管理局签注栏

同正联。

四、出口收汇核销期限

2008 年 5 月 21 日，国家税务总局发出《关于出口企业提供出口收汇核销单期限有关问题的通知》(国税发[2008]47 号)称，自 2008 年 6 月 1 日起国家将出口企业在申报出口货物退(免)税时，向主管退税部门提供出口收汇核销单(远期收汇除外)的期限由 180 天内调整为自货物报关出口之日(以出口货物报关单〈出口退税专用〉上注明的出口日期为准)起 210 天内。

出口收汇核销单见表 5－4。

表 5－4　出口收汇核销单

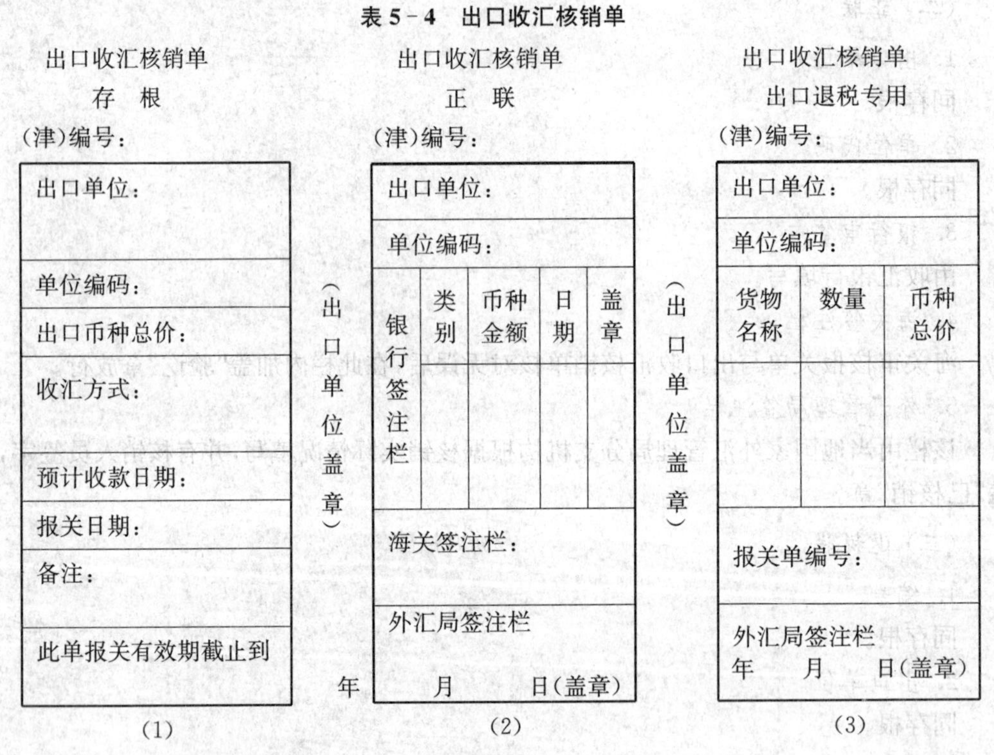

出口收汇核销单
存　根
(津)编号：

出口单位：
单位编码：
出口币种总价：
收汇方式：
预计收款日期：
报关日期：
备注：
此单报关有效期截止到

(1)

(出口单位盖章)

出口收汇核销单
正　联
(津)编号：

出口单位：				
单位编码：				
银行签注栏	类别	币种金额	日期	盖章
海关签注栏：				
外汇局签注栏				

年　　月　　日(盖章)

(2)

(出口单位盖章)

出口收汇核销单
出口退税专用
(津)编号：

出口单位：		
单位编码：		
货物名称	数量	币种总价
报关单编号：		
外汇局签注栏 年　　月　　日(盖章)		

(3)

本章小结

本章主要讲述了卖方在报检、报关时需要的单证操作流程。通过本章的学习，要求学生能够领悟报检、报关的操作流程，学会填制报检单、报关单；掌握出口许可证、出口收汇核销单的申领流程并学会填制相关的内容。其中报关单内容的填制较为复杂，还需要学生在以后的实际工作中逐步掌握。

复习思考题

根据下列材料填制报检单、报关单

卖方：深圳 XX 进出口有限公司

买方：ABULT TRADE GMBH

合同号：SSAB01－0032

产品明细：

MARK	NAME OF GOODS	QTY	UNIT PRICE	AMOUNT
ABULT C/NO. 1－UP	CAR SPEAKER		CIF HAMBURG	
	SQ2013	6000 PAIRS	USD3.50	USD21000.00
	SQ3013	2000 PAIRS	USD5.50	USD11000.00
	TOTAL:	8000 PAIRS		USD32000.00

2016 年 11 月 28 日，深圳 XX 进出口有限公司收到了一份 STATE BANK OF GERMANY，HAMBURG，GERMANY 于 2016 年 11 月 22 日开来的信用证，购买汽车喇叭，信用证号码为 LC201612878，金额为 32000.00，该公司立即与深圳市汽车配件厂联系，并签了生产合同。

货备好后，深圳 XX 进出口有限公司于 2016 年 12 月 9 日向深圳蛇口海关申报出口。

详细信息如下：

SQ2013　净重：2 千克/对　包装：20 对/箱　外箱尺寸：50x40x30CM

SQ3013　净重：4 千克/对　包装：10 对/箱　外箱尺寸：60x50x30CM

外包装箱单个净重：

SQ2013　2.5 千克

SQ3013　3 千克

出口货物通关单编号：98379234

船名/航次：SHENZHEN SEA/S661

租用货柜：2X40’FCL　箱号/封号：SZWY7891012/7891013

SZWY5891017/8310197

提单号码：COSC030189

核销单编号：36548321

运费总价：USD3000.00

保费率：1%

商品编码：8518.2100。

第六章　原产地证明书

学习目标

了解原产地证书的定义和作用，掌握不同种类原产地证书的申办流程和内容填制。

根据一般货物出口操作流程，在完成货物装柜和报关的流程后，就可以着手办理货物的原产地证明书了。根据成交方式需要卖方办理海上货物运输保险的，也需要此时办理。因为根据相关规定，这两项工作要求在货物装船前完成。本章先讲述原产地证书的相关知识及办理流程。

第一节　原产地证明书概述

一、原产地证明书定义

原产地证明书(Certificate of Origin)是出口商应进口商要求而提供的、由公证机构、政府或出口商出具的，证明货物原产地或制造地的一种证明文件。原产地证书是贸易关系人交接货物、结算货款、索赔理赔、进口国通关验收、征收关税的有效凭证，它还是出口国享受配额待遇、进口国对不同出口国实行不同贸易政策的凭证。

二、原产地证书的种类和作用

1. 根据签发者不同，原产地证书一般可分为以下三类：

(1) 商检机构出具的原产地证书，如：中华人民共和国检验检疫局(CIQ)出具的普惠制产地证格式 A(GSP FORM A)；一般原产地证书(CERTIFICATE OF ORIGIN)。

(2) 商会出具的产地证书，如：中国国际贸易促进委员会(CCPIT)出具的一般原产地证书，简称贸促会产地证书(CCPIT CEERTIFICATE OF ORIGIN)。

(3) 制造商或出口商出具的产地证书。

2. 根据产地证书用途不同，又可以分为以下四类：

(1) 普惠制产地证书。主要用于享受关税优惠减免待遇，货物出口到欧盟等 39 国时适用。

(2) 一般原产地证书。主要用来证明货物的产地，为进口国政府征收关税、贸易统计、保障措施、反倾销反补贴、政府采购等提供依据。

(3) 区域性经济集团互惠原产地证书。它是指订有区域性贸易协定的经济集团内的国家官方机构签发，享受互相减免关税的凭证，区域性优惠原产地证上所列的产品应是优惠贸易协定项下的产品，并符合区域性优惠贸易原产地规则。在出口贸易中，我方提供相关的优惠制原产地证，进口商在进口报关时可以少交关税，降低了商品的进口成本，我方出口时报价就可以相应高一些。在进口贸易中，我方要求对方提供相关的优惠制原产地证，我方企业进口报关时就可以享受关税优惠，从而降低了进口成本。目前这类证书主要有《曼谷协定》优惠原产地证书（适用与韩国、斯里兰卡、印度、孟加拉国、老挝相关产品贸易）、中国-东盟自由贸易区优惠原产地证书（Form E）、《中国与巴基斯坦优惠贸易安排》优惠原产地书等。

(4) 专用原产地证书。专用原产地证书是国际组织或国家根据政策和贸易措施的具体特殊需要，针对某一特殊行业的特定产品规定的原产地证书。主要有输往欧盟的蘑菇罐头原产地证书、烟草真实性证书等。

本章主要讲述普惠制原产地证书和一般原产地证书。

第二节　普惠制原产地证书

一、普惠制原产地证书定义及适用国家

（一）普惠制原产地证书定义

普惠制原产地证书（Generalized System of Preferences Certificate of Origin）是指发达国家给予发展中国家或地区在经济、贸易方面的一种非互利的特别优惠待遇。即发展中国家向发达国家出口制成品或半制成品时，发达国家对发展中国家予以免征或减征关税。普惠制于1970年由联合国贸易开发会议第四届优惠特别委员会推行实施。这一制度的实施，对于发展中国家而言，可以扩大出口，多创外汇，加速经济基础发展、促进产业工业化。在我国，该证明由国家质量监督检验检疫总局设在各地的出入境检验检疫分支机构签发。

（二）适用国家

目前给予我国普惠制待遇的有澳大利亚、新西兰、日本、加拿大、挪威、瑞士、土耳其、白罗斯、乌克兰、哈萨克斯坦、列支敦士登等国家。凡是向给惠国出口受惠商品，均须提供普惠制产地证，才能享受关税减免的优惠，所以不管对方是否要求提供这种产地证，我国出口商均应主动提交。普惠制产地证的书面格式名称为格式A（Form A）。但对新西兰还须提供格式59A（Form 59A），对澳大利亚不用任何格式，只需在商业发票上加注有关声明文句。

二、普惠制原产地证书签署条件

1. 货物进口国是给惠国。
2. 该商品是给惠国所列的受惠产品。
3. 该商品完全原产或虽含有进口成分，但符合给惠国规定。
4. 申请单位必须在出入境检验检疫主管部门注册登记。

三、普惠制原产地证书签发程序及所需材料

出口企业应在货物出运前5天到当地进出口检验检疫主管部门办理并购买相关的单证,办理程序及所需资料如下:

1. 根据当地进出口检验检疫主管部门规定先行网上申报。

2. 进出口检验检疫主管部门网上初审并在24小时内反馈审核结果。

3. 网上审核合格后,出口企业应持如下单据到商检局现场交单:

填制准确的《普惠制产地证申请书》、缮制正确、手签并加盖公章的《普惠制产地证明书(Form A)》(一正二副)、商业发票、装箱单、出口货物成本明细表。

4. 进出口检验检疫主管部门审核单据无误后计费,出口企业及时缴费。

5. 进出口检验检疫主管部门审单人员签字并加盖公章,将《普惠制产地证明书(Form A)》(一正一副)交予出口企业,其余单据存档。

四、普惠制产地证明书(Form A)的内容及填制要求

证书号:普惠制原产地证书标题栏(右上角),填上检验检疫机构编定的证书号。

第1栏:出口商名称、地址、国家。此栏出口商公司名称应与注册时相同,必须打上国名、地址。

例: SHENZHEN JIELIIYUAN IMP&EXP CO. ,LTD SHENZHEN,CHINA

第2栏:收货人的名称、地址、国家,除欧盟28国、挪威外,此栏须填上给惠国最终收货人名称。

第3栏:运输方式及路线(就所知道而言)一般应填上装货、到货地点(始启运港、目的港)及运输方式(如海运、陆运、空运)。

例:FROM DONGGUAN TO SHENZHEN BY TRUCK,THEN TRANSHIPPED TO HAMBURG BY SEA. 转运商品应加上转运港,对输往内陆给惠国的商品,如瑞士、奥地利,由于这些国家没有海岸,因此如系海运,都须经第三国,再转运至该国,填证时应注明。例: BY VESSEL FROM SHENZHEN TO HAMBURG, IN TRANSIT TO SWITZERLAND.

第4栏:供官方使用

此栏由签证当局填写,正常情况下此栏空白。特殊情况下,签证当局在此栏加注,例:(1) 货物已出口,签证日期迟于出货日期,签发"后发"证书时,此栏盖上"ISSUED RETROSPECTIVELY"红色印章。(2) 证书遗失、被盗或者损毁,签发"复本"证书时盖上"DUPLICATE"红色印章,并在此栏注明原证书的编号和签证日期,并声明原发证书作废,其文字是"THIS CERTIFICATE IS IN REPLACEMENT OF CERTIFICATE OF ORIGIN NO. …DATED…WHICH IS CANCELLED"。

注意:在录入后发证书时,请在申请书备注栏注明"申请后发",否则计算机退回。

第5栏:商品顺序号

如同批出口货物有不同品种,则按不同品种分列"1""2""3"……,以此类推。单项商品,此栏填"1"。

第6栏：唛头及包装号

填具的唛头应与货物外包装上的唛头及发票的唛头一致；唛头不得出现中国以外的地区和国家制造的字样，也不能出现香港、澳门、台湾原产地字样(例如：MADE IN TAIWAN，HONG KONG PRODUCTS等)；如货物无唛头应填“N/M”。如唛头过多，此栏不够填则打上(SEE THE ATTACHMENT)，用附页填打所有唛头(附页的纸张要与原证书一样大小)，在右上角打上证书号，并由申请单位和签证当局授权签字人分别在附页末页的右下角和左下角手签、盖印。附页手签的笔迹、地点、日期均与证书第11、12栏相一致的。

注意：有附页时，请在申请书备注栏注明“唛头见附页”，否则计算机退回。

第7栏：包件数量及种类，商品的名称包件数量必须有英语和阿拉伯数字同时表示，例如：ONE HUNDRED AND FIFYE (150)CARTONS OF WORKING GLOVES；

注意：

a. 如果包件数量上了千以上，则千与百单位之间不能有“AND”连词，否则计算机退回。应填：TWO THOUSAND ONE HUNDRED AND FIFEYE (2150)CARTONS OF WORKING GLOVES

b. 数量、品名要求在一页内打完，如果内容过长，则可以合并包装箱数和品名。例：ONE HUNDRED AND FIFYE (150)CARTONS OF GLOVE，SCARF，TIE，CAP.

c. 包装必须打具体的包装种类(例：POLYWOVEN BAG，DRUM，PALLET，WOODEN CASE 等)，不能只填写“PACKAGE”。如果没有包装，应填写“NUDE CARGO”(裸装货)，“IN BULK”(散装货)，“HANGING GARMENTS”(挂装)。

d. 商品名称必须具体填明(具体到能找到相对应的4位HS编码)，不能笼统填“MACHINE”(机器)、“GARMENT”(服装)等。对一些商品，例如玩具电扇，应注明为“TOYS：ELECTRIC FANS”，不能只列“ELECTRIC FANS”(电扇)。

e. 商品的商标、牌名(BRAND)及货号(ARTICLE NUMBER)一般可以不填。商品名称等项列完后，应在下一行加上表示结束的符号，以防止加填伪造内容。国外信用证有时要求填写合同、信用证号码等，可加填在此栏空白处。

第8栏：原产地标准

a. 完全原产品，不含任何非原产成分，出口到所有给惠国，填写“P”。

b. 含有非原产成分的产品，出口到欧盟、挪威、瑞士和日本，填写“W”，其后加上出口产品的HS品目号，例如“W”42.02。条件：(1) 产品列入了上述给惠国的“加工清单”符合其加工条件；(2) 产品未列入“加工清单”，但产品生产过程中使用的非原产原材料和零部件经过充分的加工，产品的HS品目号不同于所用的原材料和零部件的HS品目号。

c. 含有非原产成分的产品，出口到加拿大，填写“F”。条件：非原产成分的价值未超过产品出厂价的40%。

d. 含有非原产成分的产品，出口到俄罗斯、乌克兰、哈萨克斯坦、捷克、斯洛伐克六国，填写“Y”，其后加上非原产成分价值占该产品离岸价格的百分比，例如“Y”38%。条件：非原产成分的价值未超过产品离岸价的50%。

e. 输往澳大利亚、新西兰的货物，此栏可以留空。

第9栏:毛重或其他数量

注:此栏应以商品的正常计量单位填,例如"只""件""双""台""打"等。例如:3200 DOZ. 或 6270 KGS. 以重量计算的则填毛重,只有净重的,则净重亦可,但要标上 N. W. (NET WEIGHT)。

第10栏: 发票号码及日期

注:此栏不得留空。月份一律用英文(可用缩写)表示,例如:PHK50016 Apr. 6,2007 此栏的日期必须按照正式商业发票填具,发票日期不得迟于出货日期。

第11栏:签证当局的证明

此栏填打签证机构的签证地点、日期,例如:SHENZHEN CHINA APR. 6,2007 检验检疫主管部门签证人经审核后在此栏(正本)签名,盖签证印章。

注:此栏日期不得早于发票日期(第10栏)和申报日期(第12栏),而且应早于货物的出运日期(第3栏)。

第12栏:出口商的声明

进口国横线上填最终进口国,进口国必须与第三栏目的港的国别一致。

另外,申请单位应授权专人在此栏手签,标上申报地点、日期,并加盖申请单位中英文印章。手签人笔迹必须在检验检疫主管部门注册登记,并保持相对稳定。此栏日期不得早于发票日期(第10栏)(最早是同日)。盖章时应避免覆盖进口国名称和手签人姓名。本证书一律不得涂改,不得加盖校对章。

第三节　一般原产地证明书

一、一般原产地证明书定义

一般原产地证明书(Certificate of Origin,C/O)是用以证明有关出口货物和制造地的一种证明文件,是货物在国际贸易行为中的"原籍"证书,在特定情况下进口国据此对进口货物给予不同的关税待遇。

一般原产地证明书可以分为两种,一种是由中国国际贸易促进委员会(简称 CCPIT)签发,另外一种是由中国进出口检验检疫中心(简称 CIQ)签发。出口企业应根据进口商的要求到相应单位办理。一般原产地证明书适用于除普惠制或跟我国签有关税优惠协议之外的所有国家。

二、一般原产地证明书的签发程序及所需单证

初次办理产地证明书的出口企业首先要到贸促会或进出口检验检疫部门办理注册登记手续,然后按要求购买一般原产地证申请书及一般原产地证明书正本,在货物出运前5天按如下程序办理:

1. 根据当地主办单位规定先行网上申报。

2. 主办单位网上初审并在24小时内反馈审核结果。

3. 网上审核合格后,出口企业应持如下单据到主办单位现场交单:

填制准确的《一般原产地证申请书》、缮制正确、手签并加盖公章的《一般原产地证明书》(一正三副)、商业发票、装箱单、出口货物成本明细表。

4. 主办单位审核单据无误后计费，出口企业及时缴费。

5. 主办单位审单人员签字并加盖公章，将《一般原产地证明书》(一正二副)交予出口企业，其余单据存档。

三、一般原产地证明书的内容及填制要求

第1栏(Exporter)：出口商品名称、地址、国别。此栏出口商名称必须是经进出口检验检疫部门登记注册，其名称、地址必须与注册档案一致。必须填明在中国境内的出口商详细地址、国名(CHINA)。如果出口单位是其他国家或地区某公司的分公司，申请人要求填境外公司名称时可填写。但必须在中国境内的出口商名称后加上 ON BEHALF OF (O/B)或 CARE OF (C/O)再加上境外公司名称。

第2栏(Consignee)：收货人的名称、地址和国别。一般应填写最终收货人名称，即提单通知人或信用证上特别声明的受货人，如最终收货人不明确或为中间商时可填"TO ORDER"字样。

第3栏(Means of transp ort and route)：运输方式和路线。填明装货港、目的港名称及运输方式(海运、空运或陆运)。经转运的，应注明转运地。格式为"FROM... TO... BY...(VIA...)"。多式联运要分阶段说明。

第4栏：(Country/region of destination)目的地，指货物最终运抵港、或国家、地区，一般应与最终收货人(第二栏)一致。不能填写中间商国家名称。

第5栏(For certifying authority use only)：签证机构专用栏，此栏留空。签证机构在签发后发证书、补发证书或加注其他声明时使用。

第6栏(Marks and numbers)：唛头及包装号。此栏应照实填具出口发票上所列唛头的完整图案、文字标记及包装号。如唛头多本栏填不下，可填在第七、八、九栏的空白处，如还不够，可以附页填写。如图案文字无法缮制，可附复印件，但须加盖签证机构印章。如无唛头，应填 N/M 字样。此样不得出现"香港、台湾或其他国家和地区制造"等的字样。

第7栏(Number and kind of packages；description of goods)：商品名称，包装数量及种类。此栏应填明商品总称和具体名称。在商品名称后须加上大写的英文数字并用括号加上阿拉伯数字及包装种类或度量单位。如同批货物有不同品种则要有总包装箱数。最后应加上截止线(＊＊＊)，以防止填伪造内容。国外信用证有时要求填具合同、信用证号码等，可加在截止线下方空白处。

第8栏(H. S Code)：商品编码。此栏要求填写四位数的 H. S. 税目号，若同一证书含有多种商品，应将相应的税目号全部填写。

第9栏(Quantity)：数量和重量。此栏应填写商品的计量单位。以重量计算的要填注毛重或净重。若同一证书包含有多种商品，则量值的填打必须与7、8栏中商品名称、商品编码相对应，有的还必须填写总数。

第10栏(Number)：发票号与日期。此栏不得留空。必须按照所申请出口货物的商

业发票填写。月份一律用英文缩写。该栏日期应早于或同于 11 和 12 栏的申报和签发日期。

第 11 栏(Declaration by the exp orter):出口商声明。该栏由申领单位已在签证机构注册的人员签字并加盖企业中英文印章,手签人的签字与印章不得重合。同时填定申领地点和日期,该栏日期不得早于发票日期(第十栏)。

第 12 栏(Certification):签证机构注明。申请单位在此栏填写签证日期和地点,然后,由签证机构已授权的签证人签名、盖章。签发日期不得早于发票日期(第 10 栏)和申请日期(第 11 栏)。如有信用证要求填写签证机关名称、地址、电话、传真以及签证人员姓名的,需仔细核对,要求准确无误。

本章小结

本章主要讲述了货物原产地证书的定义、种类、作用及申办流程。通过本章的学习,要求学生知晓普惠制产地证书和一般原产地证书的适用国家和出证机构,掌握普惠制产地证的和一般原产地证书的申办流程,学会填制普惠制产地证的和一般原产地证书的申办过程中所需要的各种单据。

复习思考题

根据下列材料,填制一份普惠制产地证申请书和一份普惠制产地证书。

江苏钟表有限公司

JIANGSU TIMEPIECE CO. , LTD.

NO. 188 ZHONGSHAN ROAD, SUZHONG, CHINA

COMMERCIAL INVOICE

TO: SAMRT IMPORT COMPANY　　INVOICE NO. : 170501

NO. 32 EVERHOME ST. , DENMARK　　DATE: OCT. 21, 2017

S/C NO. : 170930　　L/C NO. : LC18975321

SHIPMENT FROM SHANGHAI PORT TO COPENHAGEN

MARKS & NO. S	NAME OF GOODS	Q'TY	UNIT PRICE	AMOUNT
SIC DENMARK C/NO. 1—UP	WALL CLOCKS		FOB SHANGHAI	
	2058	100PCS	USD39. 00	USD3900. 00
	2016	50PCS	USD58. 00	USD2900. 00
	TOTAL:	150PCS		USD6800. 00

SAY US DOLLARS SIX THOUSAND EIGHT HUNDRED AND ONLY.

其他货物相关信息：
货物包装:纸箱装 共150箱
体积:27立方米
货物 H.S.编码:91052900
货物预装船日期:2017年12月30号

表 6-1 普惠制产地证 A 格式申请书

普惠制产地证书申请书

申请单位:(盖章)　　　　　　　证书号:(填上 FORM A 编号)

注册号:(出口单位注册号)

申请人郑重声明:

本人是正式被授权代表出口单位办理和签署本申请书;本申请书及普惠制产地证格式 A 所列内容正确无误;如发现弄虚作假,冒充格式 A 所列货物,擅改证书,自愿接受签证机关的处罚并负担法律责任。现将有关情况申报如下:

<table>
<tr><td>申请单位</td><td colspan="2">(填写出口商公司名称)</td><td colspan="2">联系人电话</td><td colspan="3">(填写报检员电话)</td></tr>
<tr><td>商品名称
(中英文)</td><td colspan="2">(按商业发票填写)</td><td colspan="2">H. S. 税目号
(以六位数码计)</td><td colspan="3">(查询海关商品编码表,填写货物代码的前 6 位)</td></tr>
<tr><td colspan="3">商品(FOB)总值(以美元计)</td><td colspan="2">(按商业发票填写)</td><td>发票号</td><td colspan="2">(商业发票号)</td></tr>
<tr><td>最终消费国</td><td colspan="2">(填写进口商国家)</td><td colspan="2">证书种类划"√"</td><td>加急证书</td><td colspan="2">普通证书</td></tr>
<tr><td colspan="3">货物拟出运日期</td><td colspan="5">(填写预计开船日期)</td></tr>
<tr><td colspan="8">贸易方式和企业性质(请在适用处划"√")</td></tr>
<tr><td>正常贸易
C</td><td>来料加工
L</td><td>补偿贸易
B</td><td>中外合资
H</td><td>中外合作
Z</td><td>外商独资
D</td><td>零售
Y</td><td>展卖
M</td></tr>
<tr><td></td><td></td><td></td><td></td><td></td><td></td><td></td><td></td></tr>
<tr><td colspan="4">包装数量或毛重或其他数量</td><td colspan="4">(按装箱单填写货物总的包装数量)</td></tr>
<tr><td colspan="8">原产地标准 (参见产地证书栏目选填)
本项产品系中国生产,完全符合该给惠国给惠方案规定,其原产情况符合以下第______条:
1. "P"(完全国产,未使用任何进口材料);
2. "W"其 H. S. 税目号为______________;
3. "F"(对加拿大出口产品,其进口成分不超过产品出厂价值的 40%
本批产品系:1. 直接运输从________到________;
2. 转口运输从________中转国(地区)________到__________</td></tr>
<tr><td colspan="8">申请人说明
申请单位:(盖章)
申请人:(签名)
电话:
日期:　　年　　月　　日</td></tr>
</table>

表 6－2　一般原产地证申请书

一般原产地证明书/加工装配证明书

申　请　书

申请单位注册号:(填写出口单位注册号并盖章)　　证书号:(填上产地证书编号)

申请人郑重声明:

本人是正式被授权代表出口单位办理和签署本申请书。

本申请书及一般原产地证明书/加工装配证明书所列内容正确无误;如发现弄虚作假,冒充证书所列货物,擅改证书,本人愿按中华人民共和国出口货物原产地规则的有关规定接受处罚。现将有关情况申报如下:

<table>
<tr><td>生产企业名称</td><td colspan="2">(填写出口商公司名称)</td><td>发票号</td><td colspan="2">(按商业发票号填写)</td></tr>
<tr><td>商品名称
(中英文)</td><td colspan="2">(按商业发票填写)</td><td>H. S. 税目号
(以六位数码计)</td><td colspan="2">(查询海关商品编码表,填写货物代码的前 6 位)</td></tr>
<tr><td colspan="3">商品(FOB)总值(以美元计)</td><td>(按商业发票填写)</td><td>最终目的国家/地区</td><td>(填写进口商国家)</td></tr>
<tr><td>货物拟出运日期</td><td colspan="2">(填写预计开船日期)</td><td>转口国(地区)</td><td colspan="2">(如果没有,填写“无”)</td></tr>
<tr><td colspan="6">贸易方式和企业性质(请在适用处划“√”)</td></tr>
<tr><td colspan="2">一般贸易</td><td colspan="2">三来一补</td><td colspan="2">其他贸易方式</td></tr>
<tr><td>国有企业</td><td>三资企业</td><td>国有企业</td><td>三资企业</td><td>国有企业</td><td>三资企业</td></tr>
<tr><td></td><td></td><td></td><td></td><td></td><td></td></tr>
<tr><td>数量</td><td colspan="2">(按装箱单总的包装数量填写)</td><td>毛重</td><td colspan="2">(按装箱单总的毛重填写)</td></tr>
<tr><td colspan="2">证书种类划“√”</td><td colspan="2">一般原产地证明书</td><td colspan="2">加工装配证明书</td></tr>
<tr><td colspan="6">现提交中国出口货物商业发票一份,一般原产地证明书/加工装配证明书一正三副,以及其他附件________份,请予以审核签证。

申请单位:(盖章)
申请人:(签名)
电话:
日期:　　年　月　　日</td></tr>
</table>

表 6 - 3　出口货物(产品)成本明细表

生产单位:(盖章)

<table>
<tr><td>生产单位</td><td colspan="2"></td><td>企业注册号</td><td></td></tr>
<tr><td>产品名称</td><td colspan="2"></td><td>H. S. 编码</td><td></td></tr>
<tr><td colspan="5">产品原辅料及部件构成情况</td></tr>
<tr><td rowspan="2">原辅料及部件名称</td><td rowspan="2">H. S. 编码</td><td rowspan="2">来源地</td><td colspan="2">单位用料价值</td></tr>
<tr><td>国产</td><td>进口</td></tr>
<tr><td></td><td></td><td></td><td></td><td></td></tr>
<tr><td></td><td></td><td></td><td></td><td></td></tr>
<tr><td></td><td></td><td></td><td></td><td></td></tr>
<tr><td></td><td></td><td></td><td></td><td></td></tr>
<tr><td>合计</td><td colspan="4"></td></tr>
<tr><td>工厂出厂价</td><td colspan="2"></td><td>进口原料占出厂价百分比</td><td></td></tr>
<tr><td>生产工序</td><td colspan="4"></td></tr>
<tr><td>审核机构意见</td><td colspan="4"></td></tr>
</table>

表 6-4　普惠制产地证 A 格式

<table>
<tr><td colspan="3">1. goods consigned from (Exporter's name, address, country)</td><td colspan="3" rowspan="2">Reference No.
GENERALIZED SYSTEM OF PREFERENCES CERTIFICATE ORIGIN
(combined declaration and certificate)
FORM A
Issued in **THE PEOPLE'S REPUBLIC OF CHINA**
(COUNTRY)</td></tr>
<tr><td colspan="3">2. good consigned to (Consignee's name, address, country)</td></tr>
<tr><td colspan="3">3. Means of transport and route(as far as known)</td><td colspan="3">4. For official use</td></tr>
<tr><td>5. Item number</td><td>6. Marks and numbers</td><td>7. Number and kind of packages; description of goods</td><td>8. Origin criterion</td><td>9. Gross weight or other Quantity</td><td>10. Number and date of invoices</td></tr>
<tr><td colspan="3">11. Certification
It is hereby certified, on the basis of control out, that the declaration by the exporter is correct.

Place and date, signature and stamp of certifying authority</td><td colspan="3">12. **Declaration by the exporter**
The undersigned hereby declares that the above details and statements are correct; that all the goods were produced
in **CHINA** and that they comply with the origin requirements specified for those goods in the generalized system of preferences for goods exported to ______. (importing country) ______
Place and date, signature and stamp of certifying authority</td></tr>
</table>

表 6-5　一般原产地证书

<table>
<tr><td colspan="2">1. Exporter</td><td colspan="3" rowspan="2">Certificate No.

CERTIFICATE OF ORIGIN
OF
THE PEOPLE'S REPUBLIC OF CHINA</td></tr>
<tr><td colspan="2">2. Consignee</td></tr>
<tr><td colspan="2">3. Means of transport and route</td><td colspan="3" rowspan="2">5. For certifying authority use only</td></tr>
<tr><td colspan="2">4. Country/region of destination</td></tr>
<tr><td>6. Marks and numbers</td><td>7. Number and kind of packages; description of goods</td><td>8. H. S code</td><td>9. Quantity</td><td>10. Number and date of invoices</td></tr>
<tr><td colspan="2">11. Declaration by the exporter
The undersigned hereby declares that the above details and statements are correct; that all the goods were produced in china and that they comply with the rules of origin of the people's republic of china.
……………………………………
Place and date, signature and stamp of certifying authority</td><td colspan="3">12. Certification
It is hereby certified that the declaration by the exporter is correct.
……………………………………
Place and date, signature and stamp of certifying authority</td></tr>
</table>

第七章　出口投保单证

学习目标

通过学习，了解海洋货物运输投保的基本险别及其承保范围，学会填制保险单；知晓出口信用保险的相关知识，学会运用出口信用保险。

买卖双方以CIF、CIP或D组贸易术语成交的货物，卖方在货物装运前，需要办理海上货物运输保险。投保海上货物运输保险，为货物在海上遇到自然灾害或意外事故遭受损害时提供保障，使买卖双方免除了由此带来的损失。但是，如果货到目的地后，卖方遇到买方违约而拒绝付款提货怎么办？为此，本章除了讲述海上运输保险投保外，还将讲述出口信用保险，为卖方的货物出口收汇提供保障。

第一节　出口货物海上运输保险概述

出口货物在海上运输的过程中，可能会遭遇到无法预测的来自自然界的风险或预想不到的意外事故，由此使货物遭受损失。为了在货物遭受损失后能得到及时、足额的赔偿，卖方必须知晓如何投保。在投保之前，卖方应该先了解货物在海上可能遭遇到哪些风险以及由此而产生哪些损失，怎样投保才能得到赔偿。本节主要就此问题讲述货物在海上遇到的风险与损失，投保的基本险别及保险范围。

一、出口货物海上风险与损失

（一）海上风险与损失

1. 海上风险

海上风险一般包括自然灾害和意外事故两种。

(1) 自然灾害：自然灾害是仅指恶劣气候、雷电、洪水、流冰、地震、海啸以及其他人力不可抗拒的灾害，而非指一般自然力所造成的灾害。

(2) 海上意外事故：海上意外事故不同于一般的意外事故，它所指的主要是船舶搁浅、触礁、碰撞、爆炸、火灾、沉没和船舶失踪或其他类似事故。

2. 海上损失

海上损失（简称海损）是指被保险货物在海运过程中，由于海上风险所造成的损坏或灭失。就货物损失的程度而言，海损可分为全部损失和部分损失；就货物损失的性质而言，海损又分为共同海损（general average）和单独海损（particular average）。

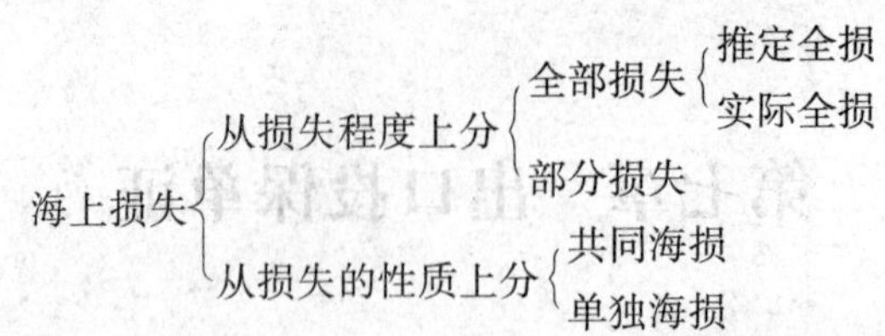

共同海损指在海上航程中，当船舶、货物和其他财产遭遇共同危险时，为了共同安全，有意地、合理地采取措施所直接造成的特殊牺牲、支付的特殊费用，由各受益方按比例分摊的法律制度。只有那些确实属于共同海损的损失才由获益各方分摊，因此共同海损的成立应具备一定的条件，即海上危险必须是共同的、真实的；共同海损的措施必须是有意的、合理的、有效的；共同海损的损失必须是特殊的、异常的，并由救助措施直接造成。

单独海损是指仅涉及船舶或货物所有人单方面利益的损失，它不是人为有意造成的部分损失。

（二）外来风险和损失

1. 一般的外来原因所造成的风险和损失

这类风险损失，通常是指偷窃、短量、破碎、雨淋、受潮、受热、发霉、串味、玷污、渗漏、钩损和锈损等。

2. 特殊的外来原因造成的风险和损失

这类风险损失，主要是指由于军事、政治、国家政策法令和行政措施等原因所致的风险损失，如战争和罢工等。

二、中国保险条款的基本险别

出口商到保险公司投保时，应先选择基本险别之一进行投保，然后再根据货物的类型和实际需要加投附加险别。按照中国保险条款（China Insurance Clause，CIC）的规定，投保时可选择的基本险别包括平安险、水渍险、一切险。

（一）基本险别

1. 平安险（Free from Particular Average，简称 F. P. A.）

平安险这一名称在我国保险行业中沿用甚久，其英文原意是指单独海损不负责赔偿。根据国际保险界对单独海损的解释，它是指部分损失。因此，平安险的原来保障范围只赔全部损失。但在长期实践的过程中对平安险的责任范围进行了补充和修订，当前平安险的责任范围已经超出只赔全损的限制。概括起来，这一险别的责任范围主要包括：

（1）在运输过程中，由于自然灾害和运输工具发生意外事件，被保险货物发生的实际全损或推定全损。

（2）由于运输工具遭搁浅、触礁、沉没、互撞、与流冰或其他物体碰撞以及失火、爆炸等意外事故造成被保险货物的部分损失。

（3）只要运输工具曾经发生搁浅、触礁、沉没、焚毁等意外事故，不论这个事故发生之前或者以后曾在海上遭遇恶劣气候、雷电、海啸等自然灾害所造成的被保险货物的部分损失。

(4) 在装卸转船过程中，被保险货物一件或数件落海所造成的全部损失或部分损失。

(5) 运输工具遭自然灾害或意外事故，在避难港卸货所引起被保险货物的全部损失或部分损失。

(6) 运输工具遭遇自然灾害或意外事故，需要在中途的港口或者在避难港口停靠，因而引起的卸货、装货、存仓以及运送货物所产生的特别费用。

(7) 发生共同海损所引起的牺牲、公摊费和救助费用。

(8) 发生了保险责任范围内的危险，被保险人对货物采取抢救、防止或少损失的各种措施，因而产生合理费用。但是保险公司承担费用的限额不能超过这批被救货物的保险金额。施救费用可以在赔款金额以外的一个保险金额限度内承担。

2. 水渍险(With Particular Average，简称 W. P. A.)

水渍险的责任范围除了包括上列"平安险"的各项责任外，还负责被保险货物由于恶劣气候、雷电、海啸、地震、洪水等自然灾害所造成的部分损失。

3. 一切险(All Risks，简称 A. R.)

一切险的责任范围除包括上列"平安险"和"水渍险"的所有责任外，还包括货物在运输过程中，因一般外来风险所造成保险货物的损失。不论全损或部分损失，除对某些运输途中损耗的货物，经保险公司与被保险人双方约定在保险单上载明的免赔率外，保险公司都给予赔偿。

上述三种险别都是货物运输的基本险别，被保险人可以从中选择一种投保。此外，保险人可以要求扩展保险期，例如，对某些内陆国家出口货物，如在港口卸货转运内陆，无法按保险条款规定的保险期内到达目的地，即可申请扩展。经保险公司出立凭证予以延长，每日加收一定保险费。

不过，在上述三种基本险别中，明确规定了除外责任。所谓除外责任(Exclusion)是指保险公司明确规定不予承保的损失或费用。

(二) 附加险别

一般附加险包括：

1. 偷窃提货不着险(Theft，Pilferage and Non-delivery，简称 T. P. N. D.)

保险有效期内，保险货物被窃走，以及货物运抵目的地以后，整件未交的损失，由保险公司负责赔偿。

2. 淡水雨淋险(Fresh Water Rain Damage，简称 F. W. R. D.)

货物在运输中，由于淡水、雨水以至雪融所造成的损失，保险公司都应负责赔偿。淡水包括船上淡水舱、水管漏水等。

3. 短量险(Risk of Shortage)

负责保险货物数量短少和重量的损失。通常包装货物的短少，保险公司必须要查清外装包是否发生异常现象，如破口、破袋、扯缝等，如属散装货物，装船和卸货重量之间的差额作为计算短量的依据。

4. 混杂、玷污险(Risk of Intermixture & Contamination)

保险货物在运输过程中，混进了杂质所造成的损换。例如矿石等混进了泥土、草屑等因而使质量受到影响。此外保险货物因为和其他物质接触而被玷污，例如布匹、纸张、食物、服装等被油类或带色的物质污染因而引起的经济损失。

5. 渗漏险(Risk of Leakage)

流质、半流质的液体物质或油类物质，在运输过程中因为容器损坏而引起的渗漏损失。如以液体装存的湿肠衣，因为液体渗漏而使肠衣发生腐烂、变质等损失，均由保险公司负责赔偿。

6. 碰损、破碎险(Risk of Clash & Breakage)

碰损主要是对金属、木质等货物来说的，破碎则主要是对易碎性物质来说的。前者是指在运输途中，因为受到震动、颠簸、挤压而造成货物本身的损失；后者是在运输途中由于装卸野蛮、粗鲁、运输工具的颠震造成货物本身的破裂、断碎的损失。

7. 串味险(Risk of Odor)

例如，茶叶、香料、药材等在运输途中受到一起堆储的皮革、樟脑等异味的影响使品质受到损失。

8. 受热、受潮险(Damage Caused by Heating & Sweating)

例如，船舶在航行途中，由于气温骤变，或者因为船上通风设备失灵等使舱内水汽凝结、发潮、发热引起货物的损失。

9. 钩损险(Hook Damage)

保险货物在装卸过程中因为使用手钩、吊钩等工具所造成的损失，例如粮食包装袋因吊钩钩坏而造成粮食外漏所造成的损失，保险公司应予赔偿。

10. 包装破裂险(Loss for Damage by Breakage of Packing)

因为包装破裂造成物资的短少、玷污等损失。此外，对于因保险货物运输过程中出于安全需要而产生的缝补包装、调换包装所支付的费用，保险公司也应负责。

11. 锈损险(Risks of Rust)

保险公司负责保险货物在运输过程中因为生锈造成的损失。不过这种生锈必须在保险期内发生，如原装时就已生锈，保险公司不负责任。

上述11种附加险，不能独立承保，它必须附属于主要险之下。也就是说，只有在投保了主要险别以后，投保人才允许投保附加险。投保“一切险”后，上述险别均包括在内。

特别附加险：

特别附加险也属附加险别，但不属于一切险的范围之内。它往往与政治、国家行政管理规章所引起的风险相关联。目前中国人民保险公司承保的特别附加险别有交货不到险(Failure to Delivery Risks)、进口关税险(Import Dulty Risk)、黄曲霉素险(Aflatoxin Risk)和出口货物到香港(包括九龙在内)或澳门存储仓火险责任扩展条款(Fire Risk Extension Clause for Storage of Cargo at Destination Hong Kong, Including Kowloon, or Macao)。此外，还包括战争险(War Risk)和罢工险(Strikes Risk)等。特别附加险也需要在投保了基本险别之一的基础上加投。

按照我国的《海洋运输货物保险条款》的规定，在海运保险中，保险责任的起讫采用“仓至仓”条款(Warehouse to Warehouse, W/W)，即保险责任自被保险货物运离保险单所载明的启运地仓库或储存处所开始，包括正常运输中的海上、陆上、内河和驳船运输在内，直至该项货物运抵保险单所载明的目的地收货人的最后仓库或储存所为止。但被保险货物在最后到达卸载港卸离海轮后，保险责任以60日为限。

当被保险货物遭受承保范围内的损失时，保险索赔时效，是从被保险货物在最后卸载港卸离海港后起算，不超过二年。

三、协会货物条款

在国际海运保险业务中，英国是一个具有悠久历史和比较发达的国家。它所制定的保险规章制度，特别是保险单和保险条款对世界各国影响很大。目前世界上大多数国家在海上保险业务中直接采用英国伦敦保险协会所制定的“协会货物条款”(Institute Cargo Clause，简称I. C. C.)。中国出口企业和保险公司对外国商人提出的按ICC投保时，可以接受。

“协会货物条款”最早制订于1912年，后来经过多次修改，最近一次的修改是在1981年完成的，从1983年4月1日起实施。伦敦保险协会新修订的保险条款一共有7种：

(1) 协会货物条款(A)(Institute Cargo Clause A，简称I. C. C. (A))；

(2) 协会货物条款(B)(Institute Cargo Clause B，简称I. C. C. (B))；

(3) 协会货物条款(C)(Institute Cargo Clause C，简称I. C. C. (C))；

(4) 协会战争险条款(货物)(Institute War Clause - Cargo)；

(5) 协会罢工险条款(货物)(Institute Strikes Clause - Cargo)；

(6) 恶意损坏条款(Malicious Damage Clause)。

(7) 偷窃、提货不着险条款(Institute Theft, Pilferage and No - delivery Clause)。

其中I. C. C. (A)承保的风险范围最大，类似于一切险；I. C. C. (B)承保的范围类似于水渍险；I. C. C. (C)类似于平安险。前五个险别可以单独投保，后2个险别不能单独投，只能在单独投保的基础上加投。

四、出口投保流程

凡是按CIP或CIF成交的货物，出口商在货物装船前要办理货物投保手续，并且按照合同或信用证的要求填制保险单，保险单也是必需的议付单据之一。

1. 出口商在开始备货时即可联系保险公司，洽谈保险费，以便使自己有充足的时间找到信誉好、保费低的保险公司，确定保险费率。

2. 货物装柜后、装船前，出口商应向保险公司正式投保。保险公司一般会让出口商填制投保单(见图表7-1)，然后根据投保单内容填制保险单(见图表7-2)，经出口商确认内容无误后打印正本。

3. 正本保险单缮制完成后，出口商按约定保险费率付费赎取正本保险单。

第二节　出口保险单证

一、保险单据的种类

(一) 保险单(Insurance Policy)

保险单俗称大保单。它是我国目前经营各类海上货物运输保险所采用的一种标准保险单。其内容分为正面与反面。正面印有该保险所需填写的基本事项。包括被保险人和保险人名称;保险标的名称、数量和包装;保险金额;保险费率与保险费;运输工具、开航日期、装运港和目的港;承保险别;检验理赔人或代理人名称;赔款偿付地点等。背面则载有保险条款。规定保险人与被保险人的各项权利和义务、保险责任范围、除外责任、责任起讫、损失处理、索赔理赔、保险争议处理、时效条款等项内容。

货物运输保险单可以由被保险人背书随物权的转移而转移,货物安全抵达目的地或保险单指定的地点后,保险单的效力即告终止。出口货物保险单一般由三份正本保单和两份副本保单组成,也可以根据投保人的要求增设正本或副本保单的份数。

(二) 保险证明书(Insurance Certificate)

保险证明书俗称“小保单”,又称保险凭证。保险凭证是保险人签发给投保人的,表明已接受其投保的证明文件,是一种简化的保险单。保险凭证上不载明保单背面保险条款,其余内容与大保单完全相同。凡保险凭证上没有列明的内容均以同类的大保单为准。小保单的法律效力与大保单相同,但不能作为对保险人提出诉讼的依据,因而在国际市场上使用不多。在实务中,小保单一般由保险人签发,也可由保险经纪人作为预约保险单代为签发。

(三) 预约保单(Open Policy)

预约保险单是指保险人或保险经纪人以承保条形式签发的,承保被保险人在一定时期内发运的以 CIF 术语出口的或以 FOB 术语进口的货物运输保险单。它载明保险货物的范围、承保险别、保险费率、每批运输货物的最高保险金额以及保险费的计算办法。凡属预约保险单规定范围内的货物,一经起运保险合同即自动按预约保险单上的承保条件生效,但要求投保人必须向保险人对每批货物运输发出起运通知书,也就是将每批货物的名称、数量、保险金额、运输工具的种类和名称、航程起讫点、开航或起运日期等通知保险人,保险人据此签发正式的保险单证。

(四) 联合凭证(Combined Certificate)

联合凭证是指国际贸易的发票与海上货物运输保险单相结合的一种特殊的保险凭证。亦称联合发票。其具体程序是:保险人在出口公司为国际贸易活动签发的出口商品发票上加注承保的保险种类、保险金额等内容,并加盖保险人的公章。至于保险单上所列明的其他项目,诸如承保货物名称、数量、包装、承运工具、装运港和目的港等,均以发票记载为准。一旦发生海上事故,保险人按有关承保险别规定的保险责任向被保险人进行赔偿。

(五) 批单(Endorsement)

批单是保险人为变更已有海上货物运输保险合同的内容而出立的补充性书面凭证,又称批改单。海上货物运输保险合同的变更,如更改险别、被保险人名称、地址、运输工具名称、保险期限、保险金额、保险权益转让等,经保险人与被保险人协商一致后,均需由保险人出立批单。批单可以是在保险单或保险凭证上进行批注,也可以另行出具变更单证。保险单一经批改,保险公司即应按批单上规定的内容承担保险责任。

二、保险单的缮制及注意事项

投保单的内容与保险单基本相似，不同的保险公司都有自己固有的保险单格式，其基本内容及缮制要点如下：

（一）被保险人(Insured)

若信用证有规定，应按规定。以 CIF 条件对外成交时，一般为进口商。

（二）发票号码(Invoice No.)

按实际号码填写。

（三）标记(MARKS & NO. S)

按信用证规定，应与发票、提单相一致。

（四）包装及数量(Quantity & Packing)

按装箱单填单件运输包装的件数及商品数量，若为散装，则应先注明“IN BULK”，再填重量。

（五）保险物资项目(Description)

填商品的名称，可与提单一致。

（六）保险金额(小写)

应为发票金额加上投保加成后的金额，一般按商业发票金额 110%投保，并注明币制，币制应与信用证规定相符，或与发票相符。

（七）总保险金额(大写)

即小写保险金额的英文翻译。

（八）装载运输工具(PER CONVEYANCE S. S)

要与运输单据一致。可填船名航次、航班号或车次，海运方式下也可填“AS PER B/L”.

（九）开行日期及起讫地点

可填提单签发日，或填“AS PER B/L”.

（十）承保险别

按合同或信用证的规定，如：COVERING ALL RISKS AS PER OCEAN MARINE CARGO CLAUSES (1981. 1. 1) OF THE PICC.

（十一）赔款偿付地点(Claim payable at)

一般为目的地，并注明使用货币的币种。

（十二）保险勘查代理人(Name Survey Agent)

由保险公司自定，但要提供其地址，以便发生损失时收货人通知其进行勘查和理赔。

（十三）签发地点和日期(Place and Date)

签发日期须早于运输单据，才能证明是在装运前办理的投保。

(十四) 保险公司签章

经签章后保险单才能生效。

(十五) 对保险单据的其他要求

信用证除了对保险单上的基本项目填写有所要求之外,对保险单据的其他方面还有规定。

首先,对保险单据种类的要求。银行将接受由保险公司或保险人或他们的代理人开立和签署的保险单;除非信用证另有规定,否则银行也将接受由他们开立的预约保单下的保险证明书或投保声明书;除非信用证另有规定,否则银行将不接受保险经纪人开立的暂保单。

其次,对保险单份数的要求。保险单可以只有一份作为全套,如果签发的正本超过一份,受益人必须提交所有的正本为全套。

由于保险单需要随着货物的运输在国际上流转,所以保险单不仅要求内容符合要求,同时形式上也必需做到清晰、正确、整洁,为此在缮制保险单据时还应做到如下几点:

1. 大小写金额只能更改一处,其他地方不能超过两处,更改处需要加盖校正章或签字确认。

2. 保险单上各个项目应按保险单提供的位置填写,不能超出格式提供的空格位置,更不能与格式上的铅字重叠。

3. 内容排列要整齐,行距要统一。

4. 被保险人名称、商品名称、大写金额、条款、地名以及月份等单词的第一个字母需要大写的不能小写,也可以全部字母大写。

5. 保险单措辞要明确,内容要和发票、提单等有关单证相符。保险条款既要明确承保的责任范围又要正确反映客户的要求。

第三节　出口信用保险

一、出口信用保险的概述

出口信用保险是由保险公司承保出口商在经营出口业务的过程中因进口商的商业风险或进口国的政治风险而遭受的损失的一种信用保险,是国家为了推动本国的出口贸易,保障出口企业的收汇安全而制定的一项由国家财政提供保险准备金的非营利性的政策性保险业务。

出口信用保险承担的风险特别巨大,且难以使用统计方法测算损失概率,一般商业性保险公司不愿意经营这种保险,所以大多数是靠政府支持来经营的。

中国出口信用保险公司(简称中国信保,英文 Sinosure)是我国唯一承办出口信用保险业务的政策性保险公司,也是我国四家政策性金融机构之一。于 2001 年 12 月 18 日正式揭牌运营,公司资本金约 300 亿,资本来源为出口信用保险风险基金,由国家财政预算安排。

二、出口信用保险的投保流程

1. 买卖双方商务洽谈过程中，涉及货物交易金额较大(100 万美元以上)，而买方坚持采用承兑交单(D/A)、远期付款交单(D/P after sight)或赊销(O/A)等付款方式，如果以这样的付款方式成交，卖方将面临货款不能收回的风险。因此，在与买方正式签订合同前，卖方可以向出口信用保险公司洽谈办理出口信用保险事宜。

2. 出口信用保险公司同卖方初步达成保险协议后，通过其设在国外的代理对买方的信用进行调查，并根据买方的信用情况向卖方提供保险信用额度(意即最大赔付额度)。

3. 卖方根据出口信用保险公司提供的额度同买方签订金额不超过信用额度的贸易合同，并按照合同的规定办理备货、发货事宜。

4. 货物装船后，卖方正式向出口信用保险公司投保，按约定缴纳保险费，出口信用保险公司正式受理卖方的投保。

5. 如果货款未能如期收回，卖方向保险公司索赔，保险公司按照约定金额赔付卖方。

6. 保险公司赔付卖方后，向买方追讨货款。

三、出口信用保险的作用

(一) 帮助出口商提高市场竞争能力，扩大贸易规模

投保出口信用保险使企业能够采纳灵活的结算方式，接受银行信用方式之外的商业信用方式(如 D/P，D/A，OA 等)。使出口商能给予其买家更低的交易成本，从而在竞争中最大程度抓住贸易机会，提高销售企业的竞争能力，扩大贸易规模。

(二) 提升出口商债权信用等级，获得融资便利

出口信用保险承保企业应收账款受国外进口商的风险的影响，从而变应收账款为安全性和流动性都比较高的资产，成为出口企业融资时对银行的一项有价值的“抵押品”，因此银行可以在有效控制风险的基础上降低企业融资门槛。

(三) 建立风险防范机制，规避应收账款风险

借助专业的信用保险机构防范风险，可以获得单个企业无法实现的风险识别、判断能力，并获得改进内部风险管理流程的协助。另外，交易双方均无法控制的政治风险可以通过出口信用保险加以规避。

(四) 通过损失补偿，确保经营安全

通过投保出口信用保险，信用保险机构将按合同规定在风险发生时对投保企业进行赔付，有效弥补企业财务损失，保障企业经营安全。同时，专业的信用保险机构能够通过其追偿能力实现企业无法实现的追偿效果。

四、中国出口信用保险公司

(一) 中国出口信用保险公司承保的风险

1. 商业风险

商业风险主要来自买方，具体包括：买方破产或实际无法偿付货款；买方拖欠货款超

过一定时间；买方蓄意违反合同拒付货款等。

2. 政治风险

政治风险又称国家风险，国家风险包括买方国家收汇管制、政府征收、国有化和战争等。

(二) 中国出口信用保险公司的主要业务

1. 短期出口信用保险

短期出口信用保险，一般情况下保障信用期限在一年以内的出口收汇风险。适用于出口企业从事以信用证(L/C)、付款交单(D/P)、承兑交单(D/A)、赊销(OA)结算方式自中国出口或转口的贸易。

(1) 承保风险

商业风险——买方破产或无力偿付债务；买方拖欠货款；买方拒绝接收货物；开证行破产、停业或被接管；单证相符、单单相符时开证行拖欠或在远期信用项下拒绝承兑。

政治风险——买方或开证行所在国家、地区禁止或限制买方或开证行向被保险人支付货款或信用证款项；禁止买方购买的货物进口或撤销已颁布发给买方的进口许可证；发生战争、内战或者暴动，导致买方无法履行合同或开证行不能履行信用证项下的付款义务；买方支付货款须经过的第三国颁布延期付款令。

(2) 损失赔偿比例

由政治风险造成损失的最高赔偿比例为95%。由破产、无力偿付债务、拖欠等其他商业风险造成损失的最高赔偿比例为95%。由买方拒收货物所造成损失的最高赔偿比例为80%。

2. 中长期出口信用保险

中长期出口信用保险旨在鼓励中国出口企业积极参与国际竞争，特别是高科技、高附加值的机电产品和成套设备等资本性货物的出口以及海外工程承包项目，支持银行等金融机构为出口贸易提供信贷融资；中长期出口信用保险通过承担保单列明的商业风险和政治风险，使被保险人得以有效规避以下风险：

(1) 出口企业收回延期付款的风险；

(2) 融资机构收回贷款本金和利息的风险。

(三) 中国出口信用保险公司经营特点

1. 保本经营为原则，不以营利为目的；

2. 政策性业务，受国家财政支持。

本章小结

本章主要讲述的是海上国际货物运输保险，通过学习，要求学生知晓海上风险和损失、海上货运保险投保的基本险别以及一般外来险和特殊外来险；要求学生学会投保和填制保险单。对于出口信用保险，则要求学生掌握其基本流程，学会使用，以便在日后商务洽谈中敢于接受风险大的付款方式，拓展业务范围。

复习思考题

1. 在海运货物保险中，保险公司承保哪些风险、损失和费用？
2. 何谓全损？何谓推定全损？请举例说明。
3. 按照我国的《海洋运输货物保险条款》，投保时有哪些基本险别？哪些附加险别？
4. 按照“协会货物条款”规定，投保时有哪些基本险别？哪些附加险别？
5. 按照第五章课后练习题所给资料，填制一份保险单。

表 7-1 货物运输保险单

中国平安保险股份有限公司

PING AN INSURANCE COMPANY OF CHINA，LTD.

NO. 1000005959

货 物 运 输 保 险 单

CARGO TRANPORTATION INSURANCE POLICY

被保险人：Insured

中国平安保险股份有限公司根据被保险人的要求及其所交付约定的保险费，按照本保险单背面所载条款与下列条款，承保下述货物运输保险，特立本保险单。

This Policy of Insurance witnesses that PING AN INSURANCE COMPANY OF CHINA，LTD. ，at the request of the Insured and in consideration of the agreed premium paid by the Insured，undertakes to insure the under mentioned goods in transportation subject to the conditions of Policy as per the clauses printed overleaf and other special clauses attached hereon.

保单号
Policy No.

赔款偿付地点
Claim Payable at

发票或提单号
Invoice No. or B/L No.

运输工具
per conveyance S. S.

查勘代理人
Survey By：

起运日期
Slg. on or abt.

自
From

至
To

保险金额
Amount Insured

保险货物项目、标记、数量及包装：
Description，Marks，Quantity & Packing of Goods：

承保条件
Conditions：

签单日期
Date：

For and on behalf of

PING AN INSURANCE COMPANY OF CHINA，LTD.

authorized
signature

第八章　国际货物运输单据

学习目标

认识海运提单、航空运单、铁路运单，知晓它们各自的性质和作用，学会填制海运提单、航空运单和铁路运单。

根据货物出口业务操作流程，出口商在办理完产地证、保险单之后，就要着手审核提单了。一般来说，重柜返场后，货代就会将提单的电子版发给出口商，让出口商审核其内容。此时出口商应该按照商业发票、装箱单、信用证等文件的内容审核提单的内容，做到单单一致、单证相符。如果有需要改动的地方，出口商最好一次提出，避免多次改动产生费用。

第一节　海运提单

一、海运提单的含义和作用

（一）含义

海运提单(Ocean Bill of Lading)，简称提单 B/L，是由船长或承运人或其代理人签发的，证明收到已收到托运货物，并将交付货物给提单持有人的物权凭证，也是承运人和托运人之间的运输合同。

（二）海运提单的作用

1. 提单是承运人签发给托运人的货物收据。

2. 提单是承运人和托运人之间的运输合同，运输合同的条款一般印在提单的背面。

3. 提单是收货人凭以提货的物权证明，承运人必须在收货人出具正本提单后才能交付货物。

4. 提单是作为收取运费的证明，承运人只有在出具提单后才能向托运人收取运费。

5. 提单是托运人向保险公司或船公司索赔的必备依据。

（三）海运提单涉及的当事人

1. 承运人(Carrier)，指船方，负责具体运输货物。承运人在货物装上船之后，要向托运人签发提单。

2. 托运人(Shipper)，指货主，一般是合同中的卖方。托运人通过货代向船公司托运货物。

3. 收货人(Consignee),提单的抬头,一般是合同中的买方。托运人在收到提单后,按照合同约定的方式寄给收货人,收货人凭提单在目的港提货。

4. 货代(Forwarder),代表承运人承揽货物运输业务,也代表托运人向承运人订舱并办理货物装船手续,有时也以自己的名义向托运人签发提单。

二、海运提单的种类

(一) 根据货物是否已装船,分为已装船提单和备运提单

已装船提单(On Board B/L)是指货物装船后签发的提单,这是比较正规的提单,买方或银行只接受已装船提单;备运提单(Received for shipment B/L)指船公司已收到货物,但货物还未装船时签发的提单。这种提单一般是托运人为了提早交单结算而要求承运人违规签发的,对承运人来说具有较大的风险,买方和银行一般不接受。

(二) 根据提单表面有无不良批注,分为清洁提单和不清洁提单

清洁提单(Clean B/L)指提单在内容上没有对其所载货物或包装做出不良批注;不清洁提单(Unclean B/L)是指提单内容上注明了货物表面状况受损或包装不良,如 One carton broken。买方或银行一般不接受不清洁提单。

(三) 根据提单的抬头,分为记名提单、不记名提单和指示提单

记名提单(Straight B/L)指提单的收货人一栏直接填写具体收货人的公司名称和地址,这种提单只能由收货人凭以提货,不能转让。尤其值得注意的是,如果该次运输合同适用美国的法律,承运人可以直接将货物放给记名提单的收货人,所以,若买方是美国客户,慎用记名提单;不记名提单(Bearer B/L)收货人一栏只写 To Bearer,很少使用;指示提单(Order B/L)是指提单的收货人一栏写 To Order 或 To Order of XX,并在提单背面背书,经过背书的提单可以转让,为收货人融资或转售提供方便,也便于发货人在买方毁约时转卖他人,所以指示提单在国际贸易中使用较多。

(四) 根据运输方式不同,分为直运提单、转运提单和联运提单

直运提单(Direct B/L)指从发货港到目的港货物不换船直达;转运提单(Transshipment B/L)是指货物运输途中停靠港口换装其他船;联运提单(Through B/L)是指货物经过两种或两种以上的运输方式来完成,如海空联运或海陆空联运,但统一签发一张提单。

(五) 根据提单内容的简繁,分为全式提单和略式提单

全式提单(Long Form B/L)指提单背面载有运输条款的提单;略式提单(Short Form B/L)提单背面没有运输条款。

(六) 按船舶的运输方式不同,分为班轮提单(Liner B/L)和租船提单(Charter Party B/L)

(七) 其他类型的提单

1. 甲板提单(On Deck B/L),又称舱面提单,指货物装在甲板上所签发的提单,这种提单除非买方或银行同意,否则一般不接受。

2. 预借提单(Advanced B/L),指托运人在货物未备妥或未装船时要求承运人或其代

理人签发的提单。这种提单的签发属于违规操作，承运人承担风险较大。

3. 过期提单(Stale B/L)，指提单晚于货物到达收货人，或者信用证付款方式下卖方交单日期晚于信用证规定。

4. 倒签提单(Anti-dated B/L)，指提单的签署日期早于实际装船日期。这种情况一般是卖方为了使自己的交货日期表面符合合同或信用证的规定而要求承运人或其代理人违规操作，如果买方追究责任，托运人和提单的签署人都将承担责任。

5. 货代提单(House B/L，or Forwarder'B/L)，指由货代签署的提单。货代签署的提单一般不具有提单的法律地位，收货人不能据此向承运人提货，而只能向提单签署人指定的货代处提货。货代提单使托运人的货物实际上置于货代的控制之下，使自己面临较大的风险。

三、海运提单的填制

(一) 托运人(Shipper)

即合同中的卖方，信用证方式下为信用证受益人，托收付款方式下为托收的委托人。

(二) 收货人(Consignee)

提单的抬头，按规定填写。记名提单直接填收货人公司名称和地址，不记名提单填"TO BEARER"，指示提单填"TO ORDER"或"TO THE ORDER OF ×××"。凡指示提单都需进行背书才能有效转让。如果买方没有要求或信用证没有特别要求，此处一般填"TO ORDER"，制为指示提单，以便于卖方和买方转让。

(三) 被通知人(Notify Party)

按照买方或信用证要求填写，如果没有要求，该栏填写买方的公司名称和地址。

(四) 收货地(Place of Receipt)

货物如需转运，填写收货的港口名称或地点，如无转运，此栏为空。

(五) 船名、航次(Ocean Vessel，Voyage No.)

填写载货的船名、航次，应与入货通知书上船名、航次一致。

(六) 装货港(Port of Loading)

要填写具体的港口，如有转运，填写中转港名称，如无转运，填写装货港名称。

(七) 卸货港(Port of Discharge)

应填写货物卸下的港口，为了防止港口重名，后面应加注国家，例如：London，UK。

(八) 交货地(Place of Delivery)

填船公司或承运人的交货地。如果交货地就是目的港，此栏空白。

(九) 提单号码(B/L NO.)

一般列在提单右上角。这个号码与装货单、大副收据或场站收据的号码是一致的。

(十) 唛头(Marks)和集装箱号码、铅封号(Container/Seal NO.)

若合同或信用证规定了唛头，则按其规定，若未规定则按双方约定或由卖方自定。无唛头则填"N/M"。集装箱货物要注明集装箱及铅封号码。

(十一) 包装与件数(NO. & Kind of Packages)

单位件数与包装都要与实际货物相符,并在大写合计数内填写英文大写文字数目,若有两种以上不同包装单位,应分别填写,再合计。散装货,只填 IN BULK。

(十二) 商品名称(Description of Goods)

按信用证规定,并与装箱单等单据一致,若货物品名较多,可用总称。

(十三) 毛重和体积(G. W. & Meas.)

若信用证无特别规定,则按装箱单规定填总毛重和总体积。

(十四) 提单按信用证规定要加注的内容可以填写在货物描述栏

例如有些信用证规定“B/L SHOW THE L/C NUMBER”,可以在这一栏下部把信用证号填上。

(十五) 运费支付(FREIGHT & CHARGES)

一般有两种:根据成交采用的贸易术语,FOB 贸易术语应填写 FREIGHT COLLECT;CIF 或 CFR 贸易术语应填 FREIGHT PREPAID 。

(十六) 签发地点与日期(Place and Date of Issue)

地点一般在装运港所在地,日期按信用证最晚装运日期的要求,一般要早于或与装运期为同一天,要避免倒签提单和预借提单。

(十七) 承运人签章

提单必须由承运人或其代理人签字才有效,并且要标明签发人的身份。一般表示方法有:CARRIER,CAPTAIN,AS AGENT FOR THE CARRIER:XXX 等。

(十八) 装船批注

货物装上船后,承运人一般在提单上加盖“SHIPPED ON BOARD”章以及装船日期章,以表明货物已装船和装船的时间。正本提单要注明 ORIGINAL。

(十九) 提单签发份数(NO. S OF ORIGINAL B/L)

信用证方式下按信用证规定,一般都是三份。

海运提单示例见表 8 - 1。

四、海运货物运杂费

提单审核完毕后,卖方应与货代结算费用。按照 CIF 或 CFR 贸易术语成交的货物,卖方要支付的海运费。除了海运费之外,不管是以何种贸易术语成交,卖方都要支付货代运杂费,不同的货代收费金额也不一样。如果是整柜货物,收费按货柜型号,通常每个 20′货柜运杂费人民币 2 000 元左右,每个 40′货柜 3 000 元左右。货代会把费用清单发给卖方,卖方要仔细核对,不明白的费用要向货代问明白。

这些杂费有些是船东收取的,有些是出货港/目的港码头收取的,还有些是货代自己立名目收取的。而且,很多费用并无明确的标准,非常灵活。除了向发货人收取外,有些费用还会向收货人收取。这就很容易产生两个陷阱:一是某些货代巧立名目多收费用,二是货代在收货人和发货人之间调节、转移部分费用。

一般地，发货人找的货代，发货人就是主顾，货代就会尽量压低费用来取悦发货人，于是少收费用，而到了目的港去多收客户（收货人）的钱，拆东墙补西墙，反之亦然。这就是为什么同样一批货物，如果按 CNF 成交，卖方自己找货代，运杂费就比较低；而按 FOB 成交的货物，由买方指定货代，卖方支付的人民币杂费就高出很多的缘故。

常见的杂费包括：

1. ORC：Origin Receiving Charge 起运港码头附加费；
2. DDC：Destination Delivery Charge 目的港提货费；
3. THC：Terminal Handling Charge 码头操作（吊柜）费；
4. BAF：Bunker Adjusted Factor 燃油附加费，或称 FAF（Fuel Adjusted Factor）；
5. CAF：Currency Adjustment Factor 货币贬值附加费；
6. DOC：Document 文件费；
7. PSS：Peak Season Sur-charge：旺季附加费；
8. AMS：America Manifest System（美国舱单系统）。

2003 年起美国出于反恐需要，规定凡是运往美国的货物，船公司必须将货物资料通过 AMS 系统报美国海关。同样的货代必须把货物资料如实报给船公司。货代因此向货主收取 AMS 附加费，通常约 25 美元/单。这些费用收取项目会根据时间和航线不同做调整，但全行业基本固定，也就是说，要收大家都会收，如果别人都不收就某个货代列名目收取，那么就有问题了。

FOB 贸易术语下，要特别注意虚高的费用项目。当然，FOB 是买方指定货代，货代服务的对象是国外客户，卖方承担的国内杂费肯定比 CNF 下要高，没办法的事情。但不能高得太离谱。各地的行情略有不同，可以根据本地情况，多找几家货代比对，以了解当地的“行规”。如果 FOB 术语下货代向卖方收取的杂费太高，卖方可以向买方反映情况，要求买方和其货代商议解决，卖方也可以借机向买方推荐于己有利的货代。

第二节　航空运单

一、航空运单概述

（一）航空运单的定义

航空运单（Airway Bill）是承运人与托运人之间签订的运输契约，也是承运人或其代理人签发的货物收据。航空运单还可作为核收运费的依据和海关查验放行的基本单据。但航空运单不是代表航空公司的提货通知单。在航空运单的收货人栏内，必须详细填写收货人的全称和地址，而不能做成指示性抬头。

（二）航空运单的性质作用

航空运单（Airway bill）与海运提单有很大不同，却与国际铁路运单相似。它是由承运人或其代理人签发的重要的货物运输单据，是承托双方的运输合同，其内容对双方均具有约束力。航空运单不可转让,持有航空运单也并不能说明可以对货物要求所有权。

1. 航空运单是发货人与航空承运人之间运输合同

航空运单不仅证明航空运输合同的存在,而且航空运单本身就是发货人与航空运输承运人之间缔结的货物运输合同,在双方共同签署后产生效力,并在货物到达目的地交付给运单上所记载的收货人后失效。

2. 航空运单是承运人签发的已接收货物的证明

航空运单也是货物收据,在发货人将货物发运后,承运人或其代理人就会将其中一份交给发货人(即发货人联),作为已经接收货物的证明。除非另外注明,它是承运人收到货物并在良好条件下装运的证明。

3. 航空运单是承运人据以核收运费的账单

航空运单分别记载着属于收货人负担的费用,属于应支付给承运人的费用和应支付给代理人的费用,并详细列明费用的种类、金额,因此可作为运费账单和发票。承运人往往也将其中的承运人联作为记账凭证。

4. 航空运单是报关单证之一

出口时航空运单是报关单证之一。在货物到达目的地机场进行进口报关时,航空运单也通常是海关查验放行的基本单证。

5. 航空运单同时可作为保险证书

如果承运人承办保险或发货人要求承运人代办保险,则航空运单也可用来作为保险证书。

6. 航空运单是承运人内部业务的依据

航空运单随货同行,证明了货物的身份。运单上载有有关该票货物发送、转运、交付的事项,承运人会据此对货物的运输做出相应安排。航空运单的正本一式三份,每份都印有背面条款,其中一份交发货人,是承运人或其代理人接收货物的依据;第二份由承运人留存,作为记账凭证;最后一份随货同行,在货物到达目的地,交付给收货人时作为核收货物的依据。

二、航空运单的种类

(一) 主运单(MAWB,Master Air Waybill)

凡由航空运输公司签发的航空运单就称为主运单。它是航空运输公司据以办理货物运输和交付的依据,是航空公司和托运人订立的运输合同,每一批航空运输的货物都有自己相对应的航空主运单。

(二) 分运单(HAWB,House Air Waybill)

集中托运人在办理集中托运业务时签发的航空运单被称作航空分运单。在集中托运的情况下,除了航空运输公司签发主运单外,集中托运人还要签发航空分运单。在这中间,航空分运单作为集中托运人与托运人之间的货物运输合同;而航空主运单作为航空运输公司与集中托运人之间的货物运输合同,当事人则为集中托运人和航空运输公司。货主与航空运输公司没有直接的契约关系。

不仅如此，由于在起运地货物由集中托运人将货物交付航空运输公司，在目的地由集中托运人或其代理从航空运输公司处提取货物，再转交给收货人，因而货主与航空运输公司也没有直接的货物交接关系。

三、航空运单的内容填写

航空运单与海运提单类似也有正面、背面条款之分，不同的航空公司也会有自己独特的航空运单格式。所不同的是，航空运单和海运提单可能千差万别，但各航空公司所使用的航空运单则大多借鉴 IATA 所推荐的标准格式，差别并不大。所以，我们这里只介绍这种标准格式，也称中性运单。下面就有关需要填写的栏目说明如下：

1. 始发站机场：需填写 IATA 统一制定的始发站机场或城市的三字代码，这一栏应该和 11 栏相一致。1A：IATA 统一编制的航空公司代码，如我国的国际航空公司的代码就是 999；1B：运单号。

2. 发货人姓名、住址(Shipper's Name and Address)：填写发货人姓名、地址、所在国家及联络方法。

3. 发货人账号：只在必要时填写。

4. 收货人姓名、住址(Consignee's Name and Address)：应填写收货人姓名、地址、所在国家及联络方法。与海运提单不同，因为空运单不可转让，所以"凭指示"之类的字样不得出现。

5. 收货人账号：同 3 栏一样只在必要时填写。

6. 承运人代理的名称和所在城市(Issuing Carrier's Agent Name and City)。

7. 代理人的 IATA 代号。

8. 代理人账号。

9. 始发站机场及所要求的航线(Airport of Departure and Requested routing)：这里的始发站应与 1 栏填写的相一致。

10. 支付信息(Accounting Information)：此栏只有在采用特殊付款方式时才填写。

11. 去往(To)：分别填入第一(二、三)中转站机场的 IATA 代码。承运人(By)：分别填入第一(二、三)段运输的承运人。

12. 货币(Currency)：填入 ISO 货币代码。

13. 收费代号：表明支付方式。

14. 运费及声明价值费(WT/VAL，weight charge/valuation charge)：

此时可以有两种情况：预付(PPD，Prepaid)或到付(COLL collect)。如预付在 14A 中填入"*"，否则填在 14B 中。需要注意的是，航空货物运输中运费与声明价值费支付的方式必须一致，不能分别支付。

15. 其他费用(Other)：也有预付和到付两种支付方式。

16. 运输声明价值(Declared Value for Carriage)：在此栏填入发货人要求的用于运输的声明价值。如果发货人不要求声明价值，则填入"NVD(No value declared)"。

17. 海关声明价值(Declared Value for Customs)：发货人在此填入对海关的声明价值，或者填入"NCV(No customs valuation)"，表明没有声明价值。

18. 目的地机场(Airport of Destination):填写最终目的地机场的全称。

19. 航班及日期(Flight/Date):填入货物所搭乘航班及日期。

20. 保险金额(Amount of Insurance):只有在航空公司提供代保险业务而客户也有此需要时才填写。

21. 操作信息(Handling Information):一般填入承运人对货物处理的有关注意事项,如"Shipper's certification for live animals(托运人提供活动物证明)"等。

22. 货物运价、运费细节。

货物件数和运价组成点(No. of Pieces RCP,Rate Combination Point):填入货物包装件数。如10包即填"10"。当需要组成比例运价或分段相加运价时,在此栏填入运价组成点机场的IATA代码。

毛重(Gross Weight):填入货物总毛重。

重量单位:可选择千克(kg)或磅(lb)。

运价等级(Rate Class):针对不同的航空运价共有6种代码,它们是M(Minimum,起码运费)、C (Specific Commodity Rates,特种运价)、S(Surcharge,高于普通货物运价的等级货物运价)、R(Reduced,低于普通货物运价的等级货物运价)、N (Normal,45公斤以下货物适用的普通货物运价)、Q(Quantity,45公斤以上货物适用的普通货物运价)。

商品代码(Commodity Item No.):在使用特种运价时需要在此栏填写商品代码。

计费重量(Chargeable Weight):此栏填入航空公司据以计算运费的计费重量,该重量可以与货物毛重相同也可以不同。

运价(Rate/Charge):填入该货物适用的费率。

运费总额(Total):此栏数值应为起码运费值或者是运价与计费重量两栏数值的乘积。

货物的品名、数量,含尺码或体积(Nature and Quantity of Goods incl. Dimensions or Volume):货物的尺码应以厘米或英寸为单位,尺寸分别以货物最长、最宽、最高边为基础。体积则是上述三边的乘积,单位为立方厘米或立方英寸。

该运单项下货物总件数。

该运单项下货物总毛重。

该运单项下货物总运费。

23. 其他费用(Other Charges):指除运费和声明价值附加费以外的其他费用。根据IATA规则各项费用分别用三个英文字母表示。其中前两个字母是某项费用的代码,如运单费就表示为AW(Air Waybill Fee)。第三个字母是C或A,分别表示费用应支付给承运人(Carrier)或货运代理人(Agent)。

24—26. 分别记录运费、声明价值费和税款金额,有预付与到付两种方式。

27—28. 分别记录需要付与货运代理人(Due Agent)和承运人(Due Carrier)的其他费用合计金额。

29. 需预付或到付的各种费用。

30. 预付、到付的总金额。

31. 发货人的签字。

32. 签单时间(日期)、地点、承运人或其代理人的签字。

33. 货币换算及目的地机场收费纪录。

以上所有内容不一定要全部填入空运单,IATA也并未反对在运单中写入其他所需的内容。但这种标准化的单证对航空货运经营人提高工作效率,促进航空货运业向电子商务的方向迈进有着积极的意义。航空运单示例见表8-2所示。

第三节 其他运输单据

一、铁路运单

(一) 铁路运单的定义

铁路运单(Railway Bill)是由铁路运输承运人签发的货运单据,是收、发货人同铁路之间的运输契约。国际铁路货物联运所使用的运单是铁路与货主间缔结的运输契约的证明。此运单正本从始发站随同货物附送至终点站并交给收货人,是铁路同货主之间交接货物、核收运杂费用和处理索赔与理赔的依据。运单副本是卖方凭以向银行结算货款的主要证件。铁路运单与海运提单不同,它不是物权凭证,所以收货人一栏不能做成指示性抬头,应做成记名抬头。

(二) 我国铁路国际货物运输的发展及局限性

目前铁路线与中国相互衔接的邻国有俄罗斯、哈萨克斯坦、蒙古、朝鲜和越南。随着中国对外开放程度的不断深入,加上周边国家的经济迅速发展,中国与周边国家之间的商贸往来日趋紧密,中国铁路口岸货物吞吐量也在以每年超过20%的高速度增长。除此之外,各国的铁路线也通过众多场站和码头等节点或枢纽与公路和海(水)运相衔接。在国际货物运输中,使用包含铁路在内的多种运输形式,以各种运输方式接力的形式将货物由出口国的启运地运至进口国的目的地的做法十分普遍。

但是,由于铁路运单没有发挥物权凭证的功能,不能像提单一样,用来进行商业性质的流通,给铁路联运的当事人造成了极大的不便。

首先,发货人面临着巨大的应收款风险。如果联运货物在转运港或者启运站装上火车发送时,货物的买卖双方还没有完成货款的结算,发货人将没有任何凭证用以控制在途货物的货权,面临无法预测和控制的应收款风险。货物到达目的站以后,收货人可以自行办理提货手续,如果在拿到货物后不按时向发货人支付货款,发货人将面对十分被动的局面。事实上中国出口商在这方面遭受损失的案例已经很多,赖账的收货人会采用种种办法拖延,为了避免被发货人追讨货款,有些企业甚至采取注销原有公司的办法,让发货人举手无措,欲哭无泪。

其次,铁路联运的货运代理人,无法实现费用到付,也面临应收款风险。与国际货物贸易所伴生的国际货物运输,货运代理人一般都会由收货人指定。也就是说,货运代理人与收货人签署货运代理合同,发货人或者出口商只需根据销售合同将货物按时在规定地点,将货物移交给收货人指定的某家货运代理公司,就等于完成了合同交付义务。如果联运货物的最后一程运输使用铁路，那么该货代将会面临要么要求客户在货物上铁路以前支付运费，要么等货物发车后向收货人催款的处境。同样，由于货物到达目的站以后，货运代理人无法对收货人自行提货的过程进行任何控制和干预，一旦收货人拒付运费和服务费，货运代理人将极其被动。

再次，阻碍了银行等机构围绕铁路联运货物提供押汇、担保和托收等金融和中介服务。众所周知，海运和多式联运提单由于其本身代表货权，出口商可以用提单向银行提供抵押，申请L/C(信用证)议付和跟单托收等，国际贸易中相互缺乏信任的买卖双方一方面可以通过银行服务改善各自的资金流，也可以通过银行和其他可信的中介机构的参与来极大降低商业风险。但是铁路运单用来发货的流转形式，使得银行等机构无法围绕铁路联运货物，开发合理的金融和信用工具，提供以上各形式的服务。

最后，不利于保护商业机密。贴牌生产(OEM)和转手贸易在国际贸易中一直占有相当大的比例，贴牌生产的委托方和转手贸易中的中间商，在绝大多数情况下不会将产品先从生产商运到自己仓库里然后再转运给下游客户，而经常是安排货运代理人直接从生产商提货，从启运地直接发送到最终收货人指定的目的地，以到达节约物流成本和简化手续的目的。在货物使用铁路联运运输出口的情况下，虽然OEM加工的委托方和中间商可以指定货运代理在办理货物托运时按照自己的指示填写运单资料，但是由于铁路运单目前也是生产企业出口退税的重要凭据之一，运单上的收货人资料会不可避免地落入生产企业之手。客户资料是OEM委托方和中间商的高度商业机密，出于使用铁路联运会造成客户资料泄漏的顾虑，OEM委托方和中间商可能放弃使用铁路联运而采用其他运输方式来完成货物运输，不利于客户积极使用铁路联运来节约物流成本，也降低了贸易的执行效率。

由此可见，铁路运单功能和形式上的不足，给众多的相关当事人造成了不便，也带来了极大风险，客观上已经成为制约我国和亚欧大陆各国之间，以及其他世界各国与亚欧大陆国家之间，使用铁路通道顺利进行货物贸易的障碍，成为急待解决的问题。国际铁路组织成员国为铁路联运量身定制合乎现代贸易发展形势需要，并方便可行的运单流转和使用规则，已成当务之急。一套为各国广泛接受、完整严密又能保留货权凭证可流通性质的通行规则，既能对当事人权利提供有效保障，也是银行和其他机构(如保理、进出口保险公司等)共同参与，为铁路联运相关方提供完善服务，促进亚欧大陆各国贸易来往和经济发展的先决条件。

但是，国际铁路联运涉及各国的铁路、海关、联运经营人、货代等众多关系方，要协同如此多不同国家的部门和行业一起来着手解决这个问题，难度很大。目前主要问题，还是由于信用体系不够完善的周边国家的官方对此事的态度不够积极。

二、多式联运单据

(一) 定义

国际多式联运(International multimodal transport)简称多式联运，是在集装箱运输的基础上产生和发展起来的，是指按照国际多式联运合同，以至少两种不同的运输方式，由多式联运经营人将货物从一国境内的接管地点运至另一国境内指定交付地点的货物运输。国际多式联运适用于水路、公路、铁路和航空多种运输方式。在国际贸易中，由于

85%～90%的货物是通过海运完成的，故海运在国际多式联运中占据主导地位。

多式联运单据(Combined Transport Documents，CTD)是指证明国际多式联运合同成立及证明多式联运经营人接管货物，并负责按照多式联运合同条款交付货物的单据。多式联运单据由承运人或其代理人签发，其作用与海运提单相似，既是货物收据也是运输契约的证明、在单据作成指示抬头或不记名抬头时，可作为物权凭证，经背书可以转让。

(二) 多式联运单据的内容

1. 货物品类、识别货物所必需的主要标志、如属危险货物，其危险特性的明确声明、包数或件数、货物的毛重或其他方式表示的数量等，所有这些事项均由发货人提供。

2. 货物外表状况。

3. 多式联运经营人的名称和主要营业所。

4. 发货人名称。

5. 如经发货人指定收货人，收货人的名称。

6. 多式联运经营人接管货物的地点和日期。

7. 交货地点。

8. 如经双方明确协议，在交付地点交货的日期或期间。

9. 表示该多式联运单据为可转让或不可转让的声明。

10. 多式联运单据的签发地点和日期。

11. 多式联运经营人或经其授权的人的签字。

12. 如经双方明确协议，每种运输方式的运费；或者应由收货人支付的运费，包括用以支付的货币；或者关于运费出收货人支付的其他说明。

13. 如在签发多式联运单据时已经确知，预期经过的路线、运输方式和转运地点。

14. 如不违背签发多式联运单据所在国的法律，双方同意列入多式联运单据的任何其他事项。

但是以上一项或者多项内容的缺乏，不影响单据作为多式联运的性质。如果多式联运经营人知道或者有合理的根据怀疑多式联运单据所列的货物品类、标志、包数或者数量、重量等没有准确地表明实际接管货物的状况，或者无适当方法进行核对的，多式联运经营人应在多式联运单据上做出保留，注明不符合之处及怀疑根据或无适当核对方法。如果不加批注，则应视为已在多式联运单据上注明货物外表状况的良好。

三、邮包收据

邮包收据(Parcel Post Receipt)是邮包运输的主要单据，它既是邮局收到寄件人的邮包后所签发的凭证，也是邮局方和发货方之间运输契约的凭证，但不能凭以提货。当邮包发生损坏或丢失时，它还可以作为索赔和理赔的依据。但邮包收据不是物权凭证，只能做成记名抬头，由经办邮局加盖日戳后成为有效凭证。

邮包按照运送方式分为三种：普通邮包、航空邮包和保价邮包。普通邮包用于海运或陆运，时间长但收费低廉。航空邮包用于空运，速度快但收费高。贵重物品还可以通过付保费而成为保价邮包。近年来，邮政特快专递服务发展较快，如 DHL、EMS 等，使邮递货物更快、更安全。

本章小结

本章主要讲述的海运提单、航空运单、铁路运单以及多式联运单据，重点是海运提单，因为国际贸易运输主要是通过海运来进行的。通过学习，要求学生了解海运提单性质及其重要性，学会填制海运提单；知晓海运提单和航空运单、铁路运单的区别，务必认识到航空运单和铁路运单没有物权凭证的作用，只要出口商办理了运输委托事宜，将失去对货物的控制权，在以后的实际工作中避免因此而陷入被动。

复习思考题

1. 提单有哪些种类？
2. 提单做成指示性抬头有什么好处？
3. 航空运单有什么作用？
4. 根据下列内容填制提单

L/C No.：894010151719

PLACE AND DATE OF ISSUE：HONG KONG MAR 04，2004

APPLICANT：BERNARD & COMPANY LIMITED

UNIT 1001－3 10/F YUE XIU BLDG

160－174 LOCKHART ROAD

WANCHAI HONG KONG

BENEFICIARY：NANJING CANTI IMPORT AND EXPORT CORP.

120 MX STREET，NANJING，CHINA

SHIPMENT：FROM SHANGHAI，CHINA TO SYDNEY，AUSTRALIA BEFORE APR. 04，2004

TRANSHIPMENT：ALLOWED

PARTIAL SHIPMENT：NOT ALLOWED

DOCUMENTS REQUIRED：

—FULL SET OF CLEAN ON BOARD FREIGHT COLLECT OCEAN BILL OF LADING，MADE OUT TO ORDER OF SHIPPER AND BLANK ENDORSED，MARKED “FREIGHT COLLECT”AND NOTIFY ID COM CO.，79—81 WALES RD，NSW，AUSTRALIA. SHOWING THE L/C NO.

DESCRIPTION OF GOODS：LUGGAGE SET OF 8 PCS

SHIPPING MARKS：N/M

GROSS WEIGHT：4000KGS

MEASUREMENT：58M^3

TOTAL PACKAGE：320CARTONS

VESSEL NAME AND VOYAGE NO.：DONGFANG /E001

表 8-1　海运提单

<table>
<tr><td colspan="2">Shipper

XIAHUA TRADING CO. ,LTD.
ADD.: 676 LIAOHE EAST ROAD, DALIAN,CHINA</td><td colspan="3" rowspan="3">B/L NO.

COSCO

OCEAN BILL OF LADING</td></tr>
<tr><td colspan="2">Consignee
TO ORDER</td></tr>
<tr><td colspan="2">Notify Party
WILLIANM OCEAN SHIPPING CO. , LTD. TEL:(001)411-3680288</td></tr>
<tr><td>Vessel Name and Voyage Number
YURONG/E244</td><td colspan="2">Port of Loading
QINGDAO PORT,CHINA</td><td colspan="2">Port of Discharge
NEW PORK,U. S. A.</td></tr>
<tr><td>Place of Receipt</td><td colspan="2">Place of Delivery</td><td colspan="2">Number of Original Bs/L
THREE</td></tr>
<tr><td colspan="5">PARTICULARS AS DECLARED BY SHIPPER—CARRIER NOT RESPONSIBLE</td></tr>
<tr><td>Container Nos/Seal Nos. Marks and/Numbers</td><td colspan="2">No. of Container / Packages / Description of Goods</td><td>Gross Weight (Kilos)</td><td>Measurement (cu-metres)</td></tr>
<tr><td>NS5698/S123
AMB
N. Y.</td><td colspan="2">SHIPPER'S LOAD,COUNT AND SEAL
WOODEN CHAIR
100CARTONS
1×20′FCL</td><td>1350
SHIPPED ON BOARD</td><td>25. 20</td></tr>
<tr><td colspan="2" rowspan="4">FREIGHT & CHARGES

FREIGHT COLLECT</td><td colspan="3">Number of Containers/Packages (in words)

SAY ONE HUNDRED CARTONS ONLY.</td></tr>
<tr><td colspan="3">Shipped on Board Date: MAY 30,2005</td></tr>
<tr><td colspan="3">Place and Date of Issue:
MAY 30,2005, QINGDAO</td></tr>
<tr><td colspan="3">In Witness Whereof this number of Original Bills of Lading stated
Above all of the tenor and date one of which being accomplished the others to stand void.</td></tr>
</table>

表 8 - 2 航空运单

Shipper's Name and Address [shipper' s Account Number]	NOT NEGOTIABLE
[illegible] [illegible] SITE 400 SHA ALAM SELANG DE MALAYSIA	Air Waybill Issued by **beijing kinte world express co., ltd.**
Consignee's Name and Address [Consignee' s Account Number] [illegible] [illegible] QINGDAO CHINA	It is agreed that the goods described herein are accepted in apparent good order and condition (except as noted) for carriage SUBJECT TO THE CONDITIONS OF CONTRACT ON THE REVERSE HEREOF, ALL GOODS MAY BE CARRIED BY ANY OTHER MEANS. INCLUDING ROAD OR ANY OTHER CARRIER UNLESS SPECIFIC CONTRARY INSTRUCTIONS ARE GIVEN HEREON BY THE SHIPPER. THE SHIPPER'S ATTENTION IS DRAWN TO THE NOTICE CONCERNING CARIER'S LIMITATION OF LIABILITY. Shipper may increase such limitation of liability by declaring a higher value of carriage and paying a supplemental charge if required.
Issuing Carrier's Agent Name and City **beijing kinte world express co., ltd.**	
Agents IATA Code / Account No.	

Airport of Departure (Add. of First Carrier) and Requested Routing K. LUMPUR, MALAYSIA						Accounting Information FREIGHT COLLECT		
to	By first carrier	to	by	to	by	Currency	Declared Value for Carriage	Declared Value for Customs
QD	KE					USD	NVD	NVD

Airport of Destination	Flight/Date	Amount of Insurance	INSURANCE-If carrier offers insurance and such insurance is requested in accordance with the conditions thereof indicate amount to be insured in figures in box marked"amount of Insurance"
QINGDAO, CHINA	KE855/17JUN -		

Handling Information

"NOTIFY PARTY-SAME AS CONSIGNEE"

No. of Pieces	Gross Weight	Rate Class	Chargeable Weight	Rate/Charge	Total	Nature and Quantity of Goods
52	510.00		211	AS ARRANGED		TV-PARTS 12.638M3

Prepaid Weight charge Collect	Other Charges
AS ARRANGED	
Valuation Charge	
Tax	
Total Other Charges Due Agent	Shipper certifies that the particulars on the face hereof are correct and that insofar as any part of the consignment contains dangerous goods, such part is properly described by name and is in proper condition for carriage by air according to the applicable Dangerous Goods Regulations.
Total Other Charges Due Carrier	________________

第九章　国际结算工具

通过学习，认知国际结算的支付工具：汇票、支票、本票，学会填写信用证付款方式和托收付款方式下的汇票。

按照出口货物业务操作流程，卖方在同货代结算完运杂费之后，货代应将全套正本提单寄给卖方。卖方在收到正本提单之后，就可以按照合同规定的付款方式同买方结算货款了。在国际贸易中，一般不使用现金或记账结算，而是采用金融票据作为结算工具。常用的结算工具有汇票、支票、本票三种，其中汇票使用较多。

第一节　汇　票

一、汇票的定义及当事人

汇票(Bill of Exchange, Draft)是由出票人签发的，要求付款人在见票时或在一定期限内，向收款人或持票人无条件支付一定款项的票据。汇票是国际结算中使用最广泛的一种信用工具。汇票是最常见的票据类型之一，我国的《票据法》第十九条规定："汇票是出票人签发的，委托付款人在见票时，或者在指定日期无条件支付确定的金额给收款人或者持票人的票据。"它是一种委付证券，基本的法律关系最少有三个人物，(1) 出票人；(2) 执票人；(3) 付款人。

出票人(Drawer)是开立票据并将其交付给他人的法人、其他组织或者个人。出票人对收款人及正当持票人承担票据在提示付款或承兑时必须付款或者承兑的保证责任。一般是出口方或债权人。

受票人(Drawee/Payer)就是"付款人"，即接受支付命令的人。进出口业务中，通常为进口人或银行。在托收支付方式下，付款人一般为买方或债务人；在信用证支付方式下，一般为开证行或其指定的付款银行。

收款人(Payee)又叫"汇票的抬头人"，是指受领汇票所规定的金额的人，即持票人。在国际结算业务中，出票人一般是托收行或议付行。

二、汇票的种类

汇票可以分为以下几种：

（一）按出票人的不同——银行汇票、商业汇票

银行汇票(Banker's draft)是出票人和付款人均为银行的汇票。

商业汇票(Commercial draft)是出票人为企业法人、公司、商号或者个人，付款人为其他商号、个人或者银行的汇票。

（二）按有无附属单据——光票汇票、跟单汇票

光票(Clean bill)汇票本身不附带货运单据，银行汇票多为光票。

跟单汇票(Documentary bill)又称信用汇票、押汇汇票，是需要附带提单、产地证、保险单、装箱单、商业发票等单据，才能进行付款的汇票，商业汇票多为跟单汇票，在国际贸易中经常使用。

（三）按付款时间——即期汇票、远期汇票

即期汇票(Sight bill, Demand bill)指持票人向付款人提示后对方立即付款，又称见票即付汇票。

远期汇票(Time bill, Usance bill)是在出票一定期限后或特定日期付款。在远期汇票中，记载一定的日期为到期日，于到期日付款的，为定期汇票，记载于出票日后一定期间付款的，为计期汇票；记载于见票后一定期间付款的，为注期汇票；将票面金额划为几份，并分别指定到期日的，为分期付款汇票。

（四）按承兑人——商业承兑汇票、银行承兑汇票

商业承兑汇票(Commercial acceptance bill)是以银行以外的任何商号或个人为承兑人的远期汇票。

银行承兑汇票(Banker's acceptance bill)承兑人是银行的远期汇票。

（五）按流通地域——国内汇票、国际汇票。

汇票有多种，就银行汇票而言也有常见的两种，一般企业间用得较多的是银行汇票和银行承兑汇票，前者是要企业在银行有全款才能申请开出相应金额的汇票(即如果企业要在开户行开 100 万元的银行汇票，它在该行账户上必须要有 100 万元以上的存款才行)；后者要看银行给企业的授信额度，一般情况是企业向银行交一部分保证金，余额可以使用抵押等手段(如开 100 万银行承兑汇票，企业向银行交 30%保证金 30 万，其他 70 万企业可以用土地、厂房、货物仓单等抵押，企业信誉好的话，也可能只要交部分保证金就可以开出全额)。对于收款人来说，如果收到别人给的银行汇票，可以立即向银行提示付款，银行即把相应的款转入收款人指定的账户。

如果企业收到的是银行承兑汇票，可以到了上面的期限向银行提示付款，也可以在期限之前向银行申请贴现(银行会扣除相应的利息)，也可以把票支付给下家。

三、汇票内容

1. 应载明“汇票”字样。
2. 无条件支付命令。
3. 一定金额。

4. 付款期限。

5. 付款地点。

6. 受票人(Drawee),又称付款人(Payer)。即接受支付命令付款的人。在进出口业务中,通常是进口人或其指定的银行。

7. 受款人(Payee)。即受领汇票所规定金额的人。在进出口业务中,通常是出口人或其指定的银行。

8. 出票日期。

9. 出票地点。

10. 出票人签字。

四、票据行为

汇票使用过程中的各种行为,都由票据法加以规范。主要有出票、提示、承兑和付款。如需转让,通常应经过背书行为。如汇票遭拒付,还需作成拒绝证书和行使追索权。

(一) 出票(Draw/Issue)

出票人签发汇票并交付给收款人的行为。出票后,出票人即承担保证汇票得到承兑和付款的责任。如汇票遭到拒付,出票人应接受持票人的追索,清偿汇票金额、利息和有关费用。

出票时有三种方式规定收款人:

1. 限制性抬头(Restrictive payee),这种汇票通常会标注“pay ABC Co. ,Ltd. only”或“pay ABC Co. ,Ltd. , not negotiable”,这种汇票不能流通转让。

2. 指示性抬头(To order),汇票常标有“pay ABC Co. Ltd. or Order”或者“pay to the order of ABC Co. Ltd. ”,这种汇票经背书后可以转让。

3. 持票人或者来人抬头(To bearer)常标注有“pay to bearer”或者“pay to ABC Co. Ltd. or bearer”。

(二) 提示(Presentation)

提示是持票人将汇票提交付款人要求承兑或付款的行为,是持票人要求取得票据权利的必要程序。提示又分付款提示和承兑提示。

(三) 承兑(Acceptance)

指付款人在持票人向其提示远期汇票时,在汇票上签名,承诺于汇票到期时付款的行为。具体做法是付款人在汇票正面写明“承兑(Accepted)”字样,注明承兑日期,于签章后交还持票人。付款人一旦对汇票作承兑,即成为承兑人以主债务人的地位承担汇票到期时付款的法律责任。

(四) 付款(Payment)

付款人在汇票到期日,向提示汇票的合法持票人足额付款。持票人将汇票注销后交给付款人作为收款证明。汇票所代表的债务债权关系即告终止。

(五) 背书(Endorsement)

票据包括汇票是可流通转让的证券。根据我国《票据法》规定,除非出票人在汇票上记载"不得转让"外，汇票的收款人可以以记名背书的方式转让汇票权利。即在汇票背面签上自己的名字，并记载被背书人的名称，然后把汇票交给被背书人即受让人，受让人成为持票人，是票据的债权人。受让人有权以背书方式再行转让汇票的权利。在汇票经过不止一次转让时，背书必须连续，即被背书人和背书人名字前后一致。对受让人来说，所有以前的背书人和出票人都是他的前手(Prior parties)，对背书人来说，所有他转让以后的受让人都是他的"后手"，前手对后手承担汇票得到承兑和付款的责任。在金融市场上，最常见的背书转让为汇票的贴现，即远期汇票经承兑后，尚未到期，持票人背书后，由银行或贴现公司作为受让人。从票面金额中扣减按贴现率结算的贴息后，将余款付给持票人。

(六) 拒付和追索(Dishonour & Recourse)

持票人向付款人提示，付款人拒绝付款或拒绝承兑，均称拒付。另外，付款人逃匿、死亡或宣告破产，以致持票人无法实现提示，也称拒付。出现拒付，持票人有追索权。即有权向其前手(背书人、出票人)要求偿付汇票金额、利息和其他费用的权利。在追索前必须按规定作成拒绝证书和发出拒付通知，用以证明持票已进行提示而未获结果，由付款地公证机构出具，也可由付款人自行出具退票理由书，或有关的司法文书、拒付通知，用以通知前手关于拒付的事实，使其准备偿付并进行再追索。

五、托收结算方式中汇票的填制

(一) 出票依据/出票条款(DRAWN UNDER)

托收项下，一般填写货物的名称、数量、合同号码。例如：" 3000PCS of wooden desks under S/C NO. 300258"。信用证付款方式中应按信用证要求填写，一般填写开证行名称、信用证号及开证日期。

(二) 年息(PAYABLE WITH INTEREST@…% PER ANNUAL)

留空不填。

(三) 出票地点及出票日期

出票地点为卖方所在地，出票日期为出口商填制汇票、到银行交单托收的日期。信用证结算时填写到议付行交单日期。

(四) 汇票编号(NO.)

填发票号码或其他有利于识别的号码。

(五) 汇票金额

即汇票上的灰色区域，分为小写和大写两部分。小写部分填货币代号和阿拉伯数字，大写部分由小写金额翻译而成。

(六) 付款期限(AT .... SIGHT)

即期汇票：填"———""…"或"＊＊＊"，不能留空；

远期汇票根据规定填写，例如30天远期可以填上"30 days after"。

（七）受款人(PAY TO THE ORDER OF /PAYEE)

在托收业务中，一般托收行为受款人(持票人)，信用证结算方式中一般填写议付行名称，通常汇票上都已经事先印好。

（八）付款人(DRAWEE/PAYER)

托收项下为进口商。信用证项下按信用证要求填写开证行或开证行指定的付款行。

（九）出票人(DRAWER)

即签发汇票的人，填写出口商公司名称、地址，并由负责人签字盖章，否则无效。

表 9-1　托收付款方式中汇票

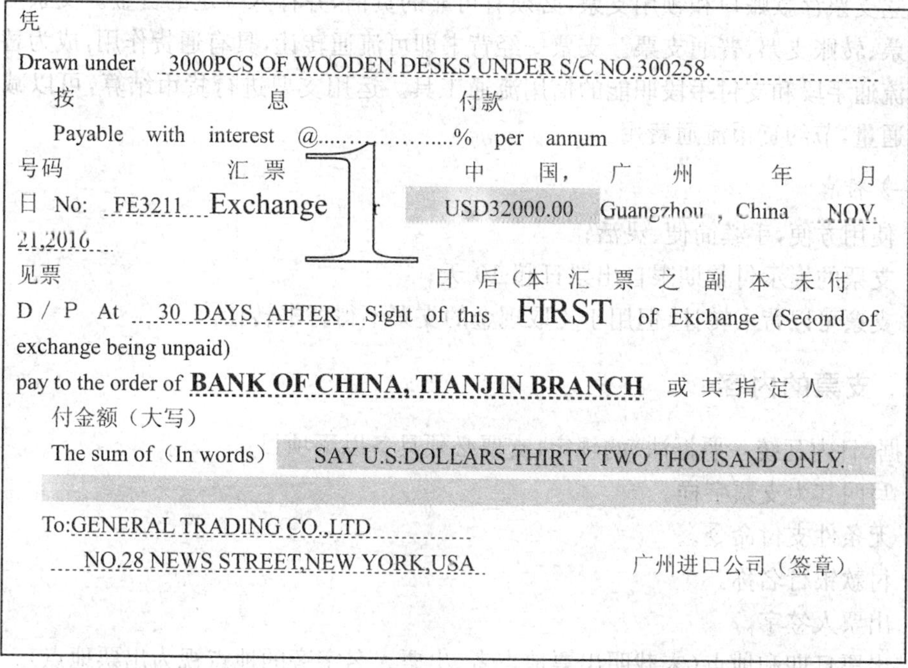

凭
Drawn under 3000PCS OF WOODEN DESKS UNDER S/C NO.300258.
按　息　付款
Payable with interest @..................% per annum
号码　汇票　中国，广州　年　月　日
No: FE3211 Exchange for USD32000.00 Guangzhou, China NOV. 21,2016
见票　日后(本汇票之副本未付)
D/P At 30 DAYS AFTER Sight of this FIRST of Exchange (Second of exchange being unpaid)
pay to the order of **BANK OF CHINA, TIANJIN BRANCH** 或其指定人
付金额(大写)
The sum of (In words) SAY U.S.DOLLARS THIRTY TWO THOUSAND ONLY.
To:GENERAL TRADING CO.,LTD
NO.28 NEWS STREET,NEW YORK,USA
广州进口公司(签章)

表 9-2　信用证付款方式中汇票

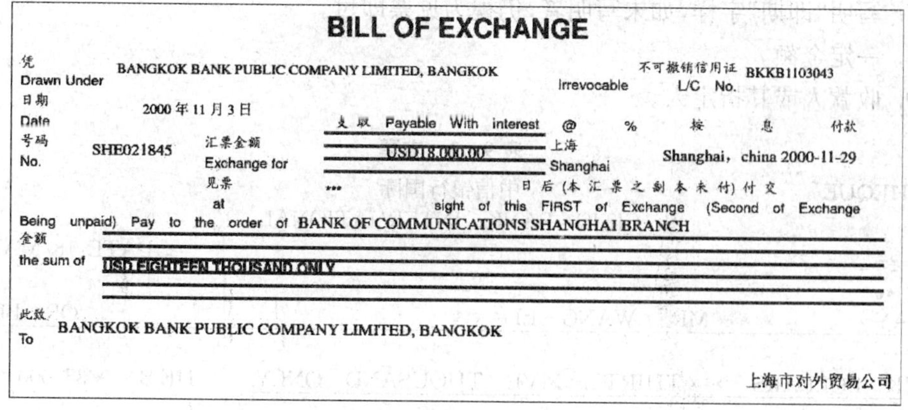

BILL OF EXCHANGE

凭
Drawn Under BANGKOK BANK PUBLIC COMPANY LIMITED, BANGKOK　不可撤销信用证 Irrevocable L/C No. BKKB1103043
日期
Date 2000年11月3日
支取 Payable With interest @ % 按息付款
号码
No. SHE021845　汇票金额 Exchange for USD18,000.00　上海 Shanghai　Shanghai，china 2000-11-29
见票 at ••• 日后(本汇票之副本未付)付交 sight of this FIRST of Exchange (Second of Exchange Being unpaid) Pay to the order of BANK OF COMMUNICATIONS SHANGHAI BRANCH
金额
the sum of USD EIGHTEEN THOUSAND ONLY
此致
To BANGKOK BANK PUBLIC COMPANY LIMITED, BANGKOK
上海市对外贸易公司

第二节　支　票

一、支票的定义及特点

(一) 定义

支票(Cheque,Check)是以银行为付款人的即期汇票,可以看作汇票的特例。支票出票人签发的支票金额,不得超出其在付款人处的存款金额。如果存款低于支票金额,银行将拒付给持票人。这种支票称为空头支票,出票人要负法律上的责任。

开立支票存款账户和领用支票,必须有可靠的资信,并存入一定的资金。支票可分为现金支票、转账支票、普通支票。支票一经背书即可流通转让,具有通货作用,成为替代货币发挥流通手段和支付手段职能的信用流通工具。运用支票进行货币结算,可以减少现金的流通量,节约货币流通费用。

(二) 特点

1. 使用方便,手续简便、灵活;
2. 支票的提示付款期限自出票日起 10 天;
3. 支票可以背书转让,但用于支取现金的支票不得背书转让。

二、支票的内容

根据《日内瓦统一票据法》的规定,支票必须具备以下项目:

1. 写明其为支票字样。
2. 无条件支付命令。
3. 付款银行名称。
4. 出票人签字。
5. 出票日期和地点(未载明出票地点者,出票人名字旁的地点视为出票地点)。
6. 付款地点(未载明付款地点者,付款银行所在地视为付款地点)。
7. 写明“即期”字样,如未写明者,仍视为见票即付。
8. 一定金额。
9. 收款人或其指定人。

表 9-3　支票

CHEQUE　　　　中信银行国际

CITIC BANK INTERNATIONAL

DATE:18/MAY/2016

PAY　　* * * MR. WANG LI * * *　　OR BEARER

HK DOLLARS * * THIRTY FIVE THOUSAND ONLY.　　HK$ * * 35,000.00 * *

(SIGNATURE)

三、支票的种类

（一）记名支票(Cheque payable to order)

是在支票的收款人一栏，写明收款人姓名，如“限付某甲”(Pay A Only)或“指定人”(Pay A Order)，取款时须由收款人签章，方可支取。

（二）不记名支票(Cheque payable to bearer)

又称空白支票，支票上不记载收款人姓名，只写“付来人”(Pay bearer)。取款时持票人无须在支票背后签章，即可支取。此项支票仅凭交付而转让。

（三）划线支票(Crossed Cheque)

是在支票正面划两道平行线的支票。划线支票与一般支票不同，划线支票非由银行不得领取票款，故只能委托银行代收票款入账。使用划线支票的目的是为了在支票遗失或被人冒领时，还有可能通过银行代收的线索追回票款。

（四）保付支票(Certified Cheque)

是指为了避免出票人开出空头支票，保证支票提示时付款，支票的收款人或持票人可要求银行对支票“保付”。保付时由付款银行在支票上加盖“保付”戳记，以表明在支票提示时一定付款。支票一经保付，付款责任即由银行承担。出票人、背书人都可免于追索。付款银行对支票保付后，即将票款从出票人的账户转入一个专户，以备付款，所以保付支票提示时，不会退票。

（五）现金支票(Cash Cheque)

是专门制作的用于支取现金的一种支票。当客户需要使用现金时，随时签发现金支票，向开户银行提取现金，银行在见票时无条件支付给收款人确定金额的现金的票据。

（六）银行支票(Banker's Cheque)

是由银行签发，并由银行付款的支票，也是银行即期汇票。银行代顾客办理票汇汇款时，可以开立银行支票。

（七）旅行支票(Traveler's Cheque)

是银行或旅行社为旅游者发行的一种固定金额的支付工具，是旅游者从出票机构用现金购买的一种支付手段。

和其他支票相比，旅行支票有以下特点：

1. 金额比较小。

2. 没有指定的付款人和付款地点。可在出票银行、旅行社的国外分支机构或代办点取款。

3. 比较安全。旅行者在购买旅行支票和取款时，须履行初签、复签手续，两者相符才能取款。

4. 汇款人同时也是收款人。其他支票只有先在银行存款才能开出支票，而旅行支票是用现金购买的，类似银行汇票，只不过旅行支票的汇款人同时也是收款人。

5. 不规定流通期限。由于发行旅行支票要收取手续费，占用资金不用付息，有利可图，所以各银行和旅行社竞相发行旅行支票。

四、支票的申办和使用

(一) 申办

1. 开立支票存款账户，申请人必须使用其本名，并提交证明其身份的合法证件；

2. 开立支票存款账户，申请人应当预留其本人的签名式样和印鉴；

3. 开立支票存款账户和领用支票，应当有可靠的资信，并存入一定的资金。

(二) 使用

1. 转账支票可以背书转让；现金支票不得背书转让。

2. 支票提示付款期为十天(从签发支票的当日起，到期日遇例假顺延)。

3. 支票签发的日期、大小写金额和收款人名称不得更改，其他内容有误，可以划线更正，并加盖预留银行印鉴证明。

4. 支票发生遗失，可以向付款银行申请挂失止付；挂失前已经支付，银行不予受理。

5. 出票人签发空头支票、印章与银行预留印鉴不符的支票，银行除将支票做退票处理外，还要按票面金额处以5%但不低于1 000元的罚款。持票人有权要求出票人赔偿支票金额2%的赔偿金。

6. 中国人民银行《支付结算办法》(银发〔1997〕393号)“第一百二十五条 出票人签发空头支票、印章与银行预留印鉴不符的支票、使用支付密码地区，支付密码错误的支票，银行应予退票，并按票面金额处以5%但不低于1 000元的罚款；持票人有权要求出票人赔偿支票金额2%的赔偿金。对于屡次签发的，银行应停止其签发支票。”《中国人民银行关于对签发空头支票行为实施行政处罚有关问题的通知》(银发〔2005〕114号)“第(一)实施处罚的主体资格：依据《中华人民共和国行政处罚法》《票据管理实施办法》的有关规定，由中国人民银行及其分支机构实施对签发空头支票、签章与预留银行欠账不符的支票的出票人的行政处罚。《支付结算办法》第125条、239条规定停止执行。”

(三) 挂失

已经签发的普通支票和现金支票。如因遗失、被盗等原因而丢失的，应立即向银行申请挂失。

1. 出票人将已经签发，内容齐备的，可以直接支取现金的支票遗失或被盗等，应当出具公函或有关证明，填写两联挂失申请书(可以用进账单代替)，加盖预留银行的签名式样和印鉴，向开户银行申请挂失止付。银行查明该支票确未支付，经收取一定的挂失手续费后受理挂失，在挂失人账户中用红笔注明支票号码及挂失的日期。

2. 收款人将收受的，可以直接支取现金的支票遗失或被盗等，也应当出具公函或有关证明，填写两联挂失止付申请书，经付款人签章证明后，到收款人开户银行申请挂失止付。其他有关手续同上。同时，依据《票据法》第15条第3款规定“失票人应当在通知挂失止付后3月内，也可以在票据丧失后，依法向人民法院申请公示催告，或者向人民法院提起诉讼。”即可以背书转让的票据的待票人在票据被盗、遗失或灭失时，须以书面形式向票据支付地(即付款地)的基层人民法院提出公示催告申请。在失票人向人民法院提交的申请书上，应写明票据类别、票面金额、出票人、付款人、背书人等票据主要内容，并说明票据丧失的情形，同时提出有关证据，以证明自己确属丧失的票据的持票人，有权提出申请。

3. 失票人在向付款人挂失止付之前，或失票人在申请公示催告以前，票据已经由付款人善意付款的，失票人不得再提出公示催告的申请，付款银行也不再承担付款的责任。由此给支票权利人造成的损失，应当由失票人自行负责。

按照规定，已经签发的转账支票遗失或被盗等，由于这种支票可以直接持票购买商品，银行不受理挂失，所以失票人不能向银行申请挂失止付。但可以请求收款人及其开户银行协助防范。如果丧失的支票超过有效期或者挂失之前已经由付款银行支付票款的，由此所造成的一切损失，均应由失票人自行负责。

第三节 本 票

一、本票的定义

本票(Promissory Note)是一项书面的无条件的支付承诺，经制票人签名承诺，即期或定期或在可以确定的将来时间，支付一定数目的金钱给一个特定的人或其指定人或来人。

我国《票据法》对本票的定义，指的是银行本票，指出票人签发的，承诺自己在见票时无条件支付确定金额给收款人或者持票人的票据。

根据《日内瓦统一票据法》和《英国票据法》规定，允许企业和个人签发本票，称为一般本票。但在国际贸易中使用的本票，均为银行本票。银行本票都是即期的。一般本票可以是即期的或远期的。而狭义的外汇的本票仅指银行本票，不包括商业本票、个人本票。本票的出票人必须具有支付本票金额的可靠资金来源，并保证支付。

二、本票的内容

根据《日内瓦统一票据法》规定，本票必须具备以下项目：
1. 表明“本票”的字样。
2. 无条件支付的承诺。
3. 确定的金额。
4. 收款人名称。
5. 出票日期。
6. 出票人签章。

表 9-4 本票

THE BANK OF ASIA
SHANGHAI BRANCH
Promissory Note

Date: JUL. 18, 2016

We promise to pay WANXIN FURNITURE CO., LTD. or order the sum of U. S. DOLLARS FIFTY THOUSAN ONLY.

US$50,000.00

For THE BANK OF ASIA
JOHN (signature)

三、本票的付款

1. 提示付款：本票的出票人在持票人提示本票时，必须承担付款的责任。

2. 付款期限最长不超过 2 个月。

3. 与提示付款相关的权利。第一次向出票人提示本票是行使第一次请求权，它是向本票的其他债务人行使追索的必经程序，没有按期提示的本票，持票人就不能向其前手追索。

本章小结

本章主要讲述了国际结算中常用的三种支付工具：汇票、本票、支票，其中汇票应用得较多。通过学习，要求学生了解汇票的种类，学会汇票的使用方法、内容填制；了解支票的使用方法以及支票的风险性；了解本票与汇票的区别，学会使用本票。

复习思考题

1. 简述汇票的定义、种类以及当事人之间的关系。

2. 简述汇票和本票的区别。

3. 根据下列材料填制一张汇票。

ISSUING BANK：DEUTSCHE BANK (ASIA) HONGKONG

L/C NO. AND DATE：756/05/1495988，NOV. 20，2004

AMOUNT：USD19,745.00

APPLICANT：MELCHERS (H. K) LTD.，RM. 1210，SHUNTAK CENTRE，200 CONNAUGHT ROAD，CENTRAL，HONGKONG

BENEFICIARY：CHINA NATIONAL ARTSAND CRAFTS IMP. & EXP. CORP. GUANG DONG (HOLDINGS) BRANCH.

WE OPENED IRREVOCABLE DOCUMENTS CREDIT AVAILABLE BY NEGOTIATION AGAINST PRESENTATION OF THE DOCUMENTS DETAILED HEREIN AND OF BENEFICIARY'S DRAFTS IN DUPLICATE AT SIGHT DRAWN ON OUR BANK.

INV. NO.：ITBE001121

DATE OF NEGOTIATION：DEC. 20，2004

第十章　汇付方式下的国际结算

学习目标

了解汇付的相关知识，掌握汇付的操作流程，学会汇付方式下卖方如何同买方进行结算。

在国际贸易中，买卖双方进行货款结算的方式主要有三种，即汇付、托收、信用证。在不同的结算方式下，卖方准备单证的依据和种类也不尽相同，单据的流转的程序也各不相同，本章首先介绍在汇付这种付款方式中，卖方如何同买方进行结算。

第一节　汇付的概述

一、汇付(Remittance)的定义及当事人

(一) 汇付的定义

汇付即汇款，是付款人通过银行，将货款汇交收款人的一种结算方式。国际贸易中的汇付，一般是由买方按合同约定的条件(如收到单据或货物)和时间，将货款通过银行，汇交给卖方。

(二) 汇付业务中的当事人

1. 汇款人(Remitter)

汇出款项的人，通常为进口人。

2. 收款人(Payee or Beneficiary)

收取款项的人，通常为出口人。

3. 汇出行(Remitting Bank)

受汇款人委托汇出款项的银行，通常为进口人所在地银行。

4. 汇入行(Paying Bank)

受汇出行委托解付汇款的银行，又称解付行，通常为出口人所在地银行。

二、汇付的种类及操作流程

(一) 电汇(Telegraphic Transfer，简称 T/T)

汇出行应汇款人的申请，拍发加押电报(Tested cable)、电传(Telex)给国外汇入行，指示付款给指定收款人的一种汇款方式。此方式的优点是收款人可迅速收到货款，但汇

款人要负担较高的费用。随着世界范围内电信业的发展,电汇已成为汇付中最常用的一中付款方式。电汇结算业务的流程图如下:

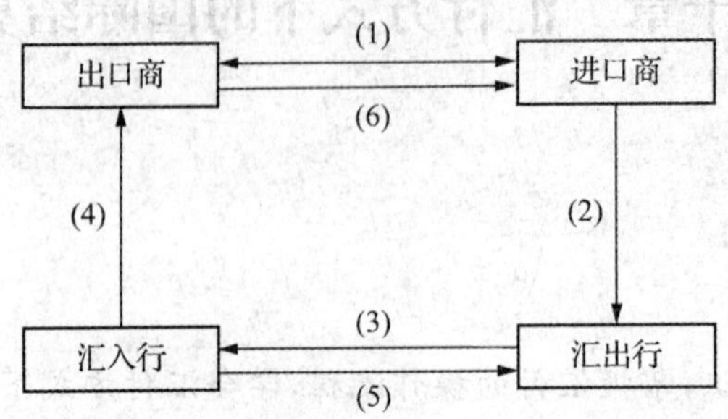

(1) 买卖双方签订合同,在合同中规定使用电汇作为付款方式。
(2) 进口商到当地银行(汇出行)申请汇款给出口商。
(3) 汇出行接受进口商的申请后,向汇入行发出电报或电传,请求汇入行解付一定金额的外汇给出口商。
(4) 汇入行收到汇出行的电报或电传后,按规定的金额拨交给出口商。
(5) 汇入行向汇出行寄送付讫通知书并索偿。
(6) 出口商收到货款后将全套正本单据寄给进口商。

(二) 信汇(Mail Transfer,简称 M/T)

汇出行应汇款人的申请,将信汇委托书(汇出行向汇入行发出的付款委托)寄给汇入行,授权汇入行付款给指定收款人的一种汇款方式。此方式优点是费用低廉,但收款人收到汇款的时间较迟,资金可被银行短期占用。由于信汇的速度较慢,且信函邮寄所需的时间难以掌握,所以现代国际贸易中较少使用。

(三) 票汇(Demand Draft, 简称 D/D)

进口人向本地银行申请开立银行汇票,寄给出口人,出口人凭以向汇票上指定的银行取款的汇付方式。

票汇与信汇、电汇的不同在于:票汇的汇入行无须通知收款人,而由收款人自行持票上门取款;票汇除有限制转让和流通的规定外,经收款人背书,可转让流通,而信汇委托书则不能转让流通。

采用票汇方式时,银行利用汇款资金的时间较长,因此票汇为银行提供较多的利润,对银行最为有利。由于汇票在邮寄的过程中存在不可预知的风险,故现代国际贸易中使用较少。

三、汇付方式的特点

从上面所讲的汇付的种类中可以看出,汇付付款方式具有如下特点:

(一) 商业信用

汇付虽然是以银行为媒介进行国际结算的,但银行在此过程中仅承担收付委托款项的责任,而对买卖双方在履行合同中的义务并不提供任何担保。汇付的实现,取决于进口商的信用。

(二) 风险大

对于货到付款的卖方或对于预付货款的买方来说,能否按时收汇或能否按时收货,完全取决于对方的信用。如果对方信用不好，则可能钱货两空。因此，买卖双方必定有一方要承担较大的风险，这就要求经营者加强信用风险管理。

（三）资金负担不平衡

对于货到付款的卖方或对于预付货款的买方来说，资金负担较重，整个交易过程中需要的资金，或者由买方，或者由卖方承担，资金负担极为不平衡。

四、汇付在国际贸易中的应用

基于上述汇付付款方式的特点，在国际贸易中，如果采用汇付作为付款方式，应注意如下几点：

（一）金额较大的贸易合同中，不采用汇付作为付款方式。因为在大金额的贸易合同中，如果卖方让买方预付定金，定金金额太小，对卖方的保障意义不大；定金金额太大，买方将面临很大风险且难以接受。为了平衡买卖双方的风险的资金负担，大金额的贸易合同中可以采用信用证作为付款方式，如果金额超过100万美元且利润可观，可以考虑D/P并国际保理方式。

（二）小额贸易可以采用汇付作为付款方式。在我国的出口贸易中，小额贸易所占的比重较大，汇付也是较为常用的一种付款方式。一般来说，按照国际惯例，卖方可以先让买方电汇合同金额的30%作为定金，余额在发货后收到提单的副本后付清。卖方在收清全额货款后，把全套正本单据寄给买方。

（三）在出口鲜活商品时，由于商品的特性不易储藏，一般情况下，卖方可以要求买方先付定金，发货前再付清余额，卖方再收齐全部货款后发货，以免货到港后联系不到收货人致使货物变质失去使用价值。

（四）在运输方式是空运或铁路运输的贸易中，空运单或铁路运单都不具备物权凭证的作用，一旦货物装上运输工具，卖方就失去了对货物的控制权，所以卖方可以要求买方先付定金，发货前再付清余额，卖方再收齐全部货款后发货。

总而言之，汇付这种付款方式，无法兼顾买卖双方的共同利益，作为卖方，如果同意货到后付款，自己就会承担买方不付款提货或延迟付款提货的风险；作为买方，如果预付了定金，就会承担卖方不发货或延迟发货的风险。所以，大额贸易不采用汇付这种付款方式，以免使自己承担太大的风险。小额贸易中，卖方一定要先行收取定金后再备货、发货，以免使自己陷入备货后联系不到买方的被动局面，这也是国际贸易中一种惯例。而作为买方，应根据本公司的实际情况，将预付定金的金额控制在自己风险承担能力之内。

第二节　汇付方式下的结算单证

根据汇付的操作流程，卖方在收齐买方的货款后应将全套正本单据寄给买方。卖方应该给买方寄哪些单据呢？基本的单据有四种：商业发票、装箱单、提单、产地证明。除此之外，不同的国家对进口不同的货物可能会要求卖方提供其他单据，例如澳大利亚对进口的木制品、草制品要求提供给熏蒸证明（Certificate of Fumigation），美国对含有木制包装材料的进口货物也要求提供熏蒸证明，多数国家对进口食品要求提供卫生证明

(Certificate of Health)等。这就要求卖方在同买方谈判时，一定要确认买方需要的单据有哪些，有些单据卖方未必能提供，有些即使能提供，也会增加费用、耗费工时，这将直接影响到产品的报价。

下面将根据贸易合同讲述汇付方式下进行结算所需要的基本单证。

销 售 合 同
S ALES CONTRACT

卖方(Seller)：XINHU CRAFT CO. ,LTD. 合同号(Contract No.)：161208

地址(Address)：NO. 168 BEIJING RD. , QINGDAO,CHINA 合同日期(Date)：DEC. 08,2016

签约地点(Place)：QINGDAO

买方(Buyer)：A. E. DISTRIBUTORS

地址(Address)：5 COULSON WAY, WA 1558,AUSTRALIA

双方同意按下列条款由卖方出售、买方购进下列货物：

The seller agree to sell and the buyer agree to buy the following goods according to the terms and conditions stipulated below：

(1) 唛头 Marks	(2) 名称 Name of Commodity	(3) 数量 Quantity	(4) 单价 Unit Price	(5) 金额 Amount
N/M	STRAW BASKET LH01 LH03	 500SETS 600SETS	FOB QINGDAO USD8. 00 USD9. 00	 USD4000. 00 USD5400. 00
	Total：	1100SETS		USD9400. 00

5 % more or less allowed.

(6) 货物总值(Total Amount)：SAY U. S. DOLLARS NINE THOUSAND FOUR HUNDRED ONLY.

(7) 付款方式(Terms of Payment)：30% PAID IN DEPOSIT BY T/T, BALANCE PAID UPON THE RECEIPT OF COPY B/L.

买方须于____年____月____日前开出本批交易的信用证(或通知售方进口许可证号码)，否则，售方有权不经过通知取消本合同，并有权提出索赔。

The buyers shall establish the covering Letter of Credit (or notify the Import License Number) before DEC. 20, 2016, falling which the Seller reserves the right to lodge a claim.

(8) 装运期限(Time of Shipment)：WITHIN 45DAYS AFTER THE RECEIPT OF DEPOSIT.

(9) 装运港/目的港(Port of Loading & Port of Destination)：

SHIPMENT FROM QINGDAO PORT,CHINA TO SYDNEY,AUSTRALIA

(10) 分批及转船(Partial Shipment and Transshipment)：ALLOWED

(11) 品质及检验(Quality & Inspection)：QUALITY AS CONFIRMED SAMPLES AND INSPECTION EFFECTED BY CHINA CIQ.

(12) 包装(Packing)：PACKED IN PLASTIC BAGS PER SETS，THEN 4SETS/CARTON

(13) 买方所需单据(Documents Required)：1 ORIGINAL PLUS 2 COPIES OF COMMERCIAL INVOICE，PACKING LIST AND GSP FORM A；FULL SET OF B/L，1 ORIGINAL CERTIFICATE OF FUMIGATION.

(13) 品质/数量异议：如买方提出索赔，凡属品质异议须于货到目的____日内提出，凡属数量异议须于货到目的口岸至____日内提出，对所装货物所提任何异议属于保险公司，船公司等其他有关运输或邮递机构，卖方不负任何责任。

Quality/Quantity Discrepancy：In case of quality discrepancy，claim should be filed by the Buyer within 30 days after the arrival of the goods at port of destination；while for quantity discrepancy，claim should be filed by the Buyer within 15 days after the arrival of the goods at port of destination. It is under stood that the seller shall mot be liable for any discrepancy of the goods shipped due to causes for which the Insurance Company，Shipped Company other transportation organization/ or Post Office are liable.

(14) 本确认书内所述全部或部分商品，如因人力不可抗拒的原因，以致不能履行或延迟交货，卖方概不负责。

The Seller shall not be held liable for failure of delay in delivery of the entire lot or a portion of the goods under this Sales Confirmation in consequence of any Force Major incidents.

(15) 仲裁(Arbitration)：本合同在执行过程中若发生争议，双方应通过友好协商方式解决；如果协商不成，则应提交北京中国国际经济贸易仲裁委员会裁决。裁决是终局的，对双方均有约束力。仲裁费用由败诉方承担。

All disputes arising from the execution of the contract shall be settled by friendly negotiation，falling which the case should be submitted to the China International Economic & Trade Arbitration Commission，Beijing. The Decision is final and binding upon both parties. The fee shall be borne by the losing party.

(16) 买方收到本售货确认书后请立即签回一份，如买方对本确认书有异议，应于收到后五天内提出，否则认为买方已同意接受本确认书所规定的各项条款。

The buyer is requested to sign and return one copy of the Sales Confirmation immediately after the receipt of same. Objection，if any，should be raised by the Buyer within five days after the receipt of this Sales Confirmation，in the absence of which it is understood that the Buyer has accepted the terms and condition of the sales confirmation.

The Seller：　　　　The Buyer：

根据上面合同，卖方在收到定金后即可备货、发货。发货后应向买方提供商业发票、装箱单、提单、产地证、熏蒸证明5类单证。卖方在货物装柜后，按照实际的发货数量及各单证制作、申领的时间要求，逐一备齐，备齐后应先通过电子邮件把单证发给买方确认，并提示买方按合同要求及时支付剩余货款，待买方付清货款后，卖方把全套正本单证通过正规的快寄公司寄给买方，买方凭以报关、提货。下面将逐一讲述根据合同如何制作这5类单证。

一、商业发票（Commercial Invoice）

在汇付付款方式下，商业发票制作的主要依据是合同，货物名称、唛头、单价、买卖双方应与合同完全一致，数量则应体现实际发货数量，可以根据合同的规定和实际装柜情况多于或少于合同中的货物数量，如果买方对商业发票有其他附加要求，卖方把买方要求的内容填写在商业发票的下部就可以了。

<table>
<tr><td colspan="2">SELLER（卖方）：
XINHUA CRAFT CO.，LTD.
ADD.：NO. 168 BEIJING RD.
QINGDAO, CHINA</td><td colspan="3" rowspan="2">COMMERCIAL INVOICE

商业发票</td></tr>
<tr><td colspan="2">BUYER（买方）：
A. E. DISTRIBUTORS
5 COULSON WAY， WA 1558，
AUSTRALIA</td></tr>
<tr><td colspan="2">S/C NO.（合同号）： 161208</td><td colspan="3">INVOICE NO（发票号）： XA001
DATE（发票日期）： DEC. 20, 2016</td></tr>
<tr><td colspan="5">运输路线和方式：
SHIPMENT FROM QINGDAO PORT, CHINA TO SYDNEY，AUSTRALIA BY SEAWAY.</td></tr>
<tr><td>唛头
MARK</td><td>货物名称
DESCRIPTION OF GOODS</td><td>数量
QUANTITY</td><td>单价
UNIT PRICE</td><td>金额
AMOUNT</td></tr>
<tr><td>

N/M</td><td>STRAW BASKET
LH01
LH03</td><td>
500SETS
600SETS</td><td>FOB QINGDAO

USD8. 00
USD9. 00</td><td>

USD4000. 00
USD5400. 00</td></tr>
<tr><td></td><td>TOTAL：</td><td>1100SETS</td><td></td><td>USD9400. 00</td></tr>
<tr><td colspan="5">TOTAL AMOUNT（金额大写）：SAY U. S. DOLLARS NINE THOUSAND FOUR HUNDRED ONLY.</td></tr>
</table>

XINHUA CRAFT CO.，LTD.
（法人代表签字章）

二、装箱单(Packing List)

装箱单制作的主要依据是商业发票货物的实际情况。装箱单一般要有个标头,标头就是商业发票的卖方。一般情况下,装箱单上可以不体现买方的公司名称。装箱单制作过程中应注意如下问题:

1. 发票号和日期:按商业发票的号码和日期填写。

2. 货物名称:与商业发票一致即可。

3. 装箱单的货物运输路线:与商业发票一致。

4. 唛头:与商业发票一致。

5. 数量:装箱单所列的数量应该有 2 项,一项是货物的数量,应与商业发票中的数量一致;另一项是包装数量,应根据货物的实际包装情况,填写每一型号货物的实际包装数量。例如在本合同中,货物的包装是"4SETS/CARTONS",所以 LH01 的包装数量应该是 125 箱,LH03 的包装数量应该是 150 箱。

6. 净重:货物的实际重量,一定要实际称量后填写。在本合同中,如果 LH01 每套实际称重为 3 千克,那么 500 套总的净重应为 1 500 千克;LH03 每套实际称重为 4 千克,那么 600 套总的净重应为 2 400 千克。

7. 毛重:毛重=净重+包装材料的重量。在本合同中,如果 LH01 每个包装箱重量为 2 千克,那么 LH01 总的毛重应该是 1 500+125×2=1 750 千克;如果 LH03 每个包装箱重量为 3 千克,那么 LH03 总的毛重应该是 2 400+150×3=2 850 千克。当然,毛重也可以在货物包装好后直接称一下每箱货物的重量,然后乘以箱数即可。

8. 尺码:货物的体积,单位为立方米。货物的体积一定要在实际测量货物包装尺寸后计算得出,填写货物的体积时为了精确,一般保留小数点后两位数。在本合同中,如果 LH01 包装箱尺寸测量后为 60×50×40CM,那么一箱的体积应为 0.6×0.5×0.4=0.12 立方米,总的体积为 0.12×125=15 立方米。如果 LH03 包装箱尺寸测量后为 50×40×40CM,那么一箱的体积应为 0.5×0.4×0.4=0.08 立方米,总的体积为 0.08×150=12 立方米。

9. 包装数量大写:对货物总的包装数量大写。

10. 如果买方还有其他要求需要在装箱单上体现,卖方填写在装箱单的下部即可。

XINHUA CRAFT CO.,LTD.

ADD.:NO.168 BEIJING RD. QINGDAO,CHINA

PACKING LIST

INVOICE NO.: XA001　　　　DATE:DEC.20,2016

SHIPMENT FROM QINGDAO PORT,CHINA TO SYDNEY, AUSTRALIA BY SEAWAY.

MARKS	NAME OF GOODS	QUANTITY		N. W.	G. W.	MEAS.
N/M	STRAW BASKET LH01 LH03	500SETS 600SETS	125CTNS 150CTNS	1500KGS 2400KGS	1750KGS 2850KGS	15.00CBM 12.00CBM
	TOTAL:	1100SETS	275CTNS	3900KGS	4600KGS	27.00CBM

SAY TWO HUNDRED AND SEVENTY FIVE CARTONS ONLY.

XINHUA CRAFT CO., LTD.
(法人代表签字章)

三、原产地证明(Certificate of Origin)

原产地证明分为一般原产地证明和普惠制产地证明。普惠制产地证明适用于同我国签订关税优惠协议的国家(详见第六章),需要出口商到当地进出口检验检疫主管部门办理;一般原产地证明适用于未和我国签订关税优惠协议的国家,根据客户的要求,可以到进出口检验检疫主管部门办理,也可以到贸促会办理。原产地证明办理的时间一般要求在货物装船前的5天,如果装船后办理,需要签发“后发证书”(签往日本的除外),出口商还要提交以下单据:

1. 解释迟交申请原因的函件。
2. 正常签证所需要的资料。
3. 提单或运单,证明货物确实已发运。

原产地证明的办理,无论由进出口检验检疫主管部门办理还是由贸促会办理,都需要现在网上录入信息,信息的内容必需商业发票和装箱单一致,出证机构网上审核合格后,出口商要到出证机构现场交单、缴费,所交的单据主要包括一般原产地证明/普惠制产地证明申请书、商业发票、装箱单、产品成本明细表、打印好的原产地证明书。因为合同中的进口国是澳大利亚,澳大利亚和我国签有关税优惠协议,根据协议规定,出口商应给进口商办理普惠制产地证明A格式(G. S. P. Form A),证书的详细内容见下一页,录入各栏信息时应注意下列问题:

1. 按照商业发票填写出口商公司名称、地址,要具体到国家。
2. 按照商业发票填写进口商的公司名称、地址,要具体到国家。
3. 运输方式及路线应同商业发票一致。
4. 官方填写栏免填。
5. 该栏主要用于填写商品的序号,若产地证所载的商品名称不同,应分别列明。
6. 该栏填写唛头,同商业发票一致。
7. 该栏按装箱单填写货物的名称、总的包装数量。
8. 按要求填写产品原产地种类,出口到澳大利亚的产品本栏可以留空。

9. 按装箱单填写货物总的数量或毛重。

10. 按照商业发票填写号码、日期。

11. 该栏由商检据审核合格后签字盖章。

12. 出口商在该栏签字盖章，并填写货物出口的目的国、申请产地证的日期、地点。

四、提单(Bill of Lading, B/L)

在第二章国际货物出口贸易流程中我们讲过，重柜返场后，货代会发一份提单样式让卖方确认内容。提单格式里货代已经根据卖方订舱时的货运委托书内容填制了，卖方要认真审核其中的内容是否有误，审核提单的主要依据是商业发票和装箱单，审核时应注意如下问题：

(一) 托运人(Shipper)

应和商业发票卖方一致，填写卖方的公司名称、地址。

(二) 收货人(Consignee)

若买方无特殊要求，此处填 TO ORDER(凭指示)，以利于提单转让。

普惠制产地证 A 格式

<table>
<tr><td colspan="3">1. goods consigned from (Exporter's name, address, country)XINHUA CRAFT CO., LTD.
ADD.: NO. 168 BEIJING RD. QINGDAO, CHINA</td><td colspan="3" rowspan="2">Reference No.
GENERALIZED SYSTEM OF PREFERENCES CERTIFICATE ORIGIN
(combined declaration and certificate)
FORM A
Issued in THE PEOPLE'S REPUBLIC OF CHINA
(COUNTRY)</td></tr>
<tr><td colspan="3">2. good consigned to (Consignee's name, address, country) A. E. DISTRIBUTORS
5 COULSON WAY, WA 1558,
AUSTRALIA</td></tr>
<tr><td colspan="3">3. Means of transport and route(as far as known)
SHIPMENT FROM QINGDAO PORT, CHINA TO SYDNEY, AUSTRALIA BY SEAWAY.</td><td colspan="3">4. For official use</td></tr>
<tr><td>5. Item Number
1</td><td>6. Marks and numbers
N/M</td><td>7. Number and kind of packages; description of goods
TWO HUNDRED AND SEVENTY FIVE (275) CARTONS OF STRAW BASKETS</td><td>8. Origin criterion</td><td>9. Gross weight or other Quantity
1100SETS</td><td>10. Number and date of invoices
XA001
DEC. 20, 2016</td></tr>
</table>

（续表）

11. **Certification** It is hereby certified, on the basis of control out, that the declaration by the exporter is correct. QINGDAO,CHINA. DEC. 30,2016 Place and date, signature and stamp of certifying authority	12. **Declaration by the exporter** The undersigned hereby declares that the above details and statements are correct; that all the goods were produced in **CHINA** and that they comply with the origin requirements specified for those goods in the generalized system of preferences for goods exported to…AUSTRALIA(importing country) QINGDAO,CHINA. DEC. 30,2016 Place and date, signature and stamp of certifying authority

（三）通知人(Notify Party)

按买方的要求填写，如果买方没有特别要求，按商业发票填写买方的公司名称、地址。

（四）收货地(Place of Receipt)

货物如需转运，填写收货的港口名称或地点，如无转运，此栏为空。

（五）船名、航次(Ocean Vessel, Voyage No.)

填写载货的船名、航次，应与入货通知书上船名、航次一致。

（六）装货港(Port of Loading)

同商业发票一致。

（七）卸货港(Port of Discharge)

同商业发票一致。

（八）交货地(Place of Delivery)

填船公司或承运人的交货地。如果交货地就是目的港，此栏空白。

（九）提单号码(B/L NO.)

一般列在提单右上角。这个号码与装货单、大副收据或场站收据的号码是一致的。

（十）唛头(Marks)和集装箱号码、铅封号(Container/Seal NO.)

同商业发票一致，集装箱号码、铅封号应与实际装柜时所记录的箱号、封号一致。

（十一）包装与件数(NO. & Kind of Packages)

单位件数与包装都要与实际货物相符，与装箱单一致，并在大写合计数内填写英文大写文字数目，若有两种以上不同包装单位，应分别填写，再合计。散装货，只填 IN BULK。

（十二）商品名称(Description of Goods)

与商业发票、装箱单等单据一致，若货物品名较多，可用总称。

（十三）毛重和体积(G. W. & Meas.)

按装箱单规定填总毛重和总体积。

（十四）运费支付(FREIGHT & CHARGES)

一般有两种：根据成交采用的贸易术语，FOB 贸易术语应填写 FREIGHT COLLECT；CIF 或 CFR 贸易术语应填 FREIGHT PREPAID。

（十五）签发地点与日期(Place and Date of Issue)

按实际装船日期填写，地点为签署提单的地点。

（十六）承运人签章

提单必须由承运人或其代理人签字才有效，并且要标明签发人的身份。一般表示方法有：CARRIER，CAPTAIN，AS AGENT FOR THE CARRIER：XXX 等。

（十七）装船批注

货物装上船后，承运人一般在提单上加盖"SHIPPED ON BOARD"章以及装船日期章，以表明货物已装船和装船的时间。正本提单要注明 ORIGINAL。

（十八）提单签发份数(NO. S OF ORIGINAL B/L)

一般都是三份正本，三份副本。

<table>
<tr><td colspan="2">Shipper

XINHUA CRAFT CO.，LTD.
ADD.：NO. 168 BEIJING RD.
QINGDAO，CHINA</td><td colspan="2" rowspan="3">B/L NO.

COSCO

OCEAN BILL OF LADING</td></tr>
<tr><td colspan="2">Consignee
TO　ORDER</td></tr>
<tr><td colspan="2">Notify Party
A. E. DISTRIBUTORS
5 COULSON WAY，　WA 1558，
AUSTRALIA</td></tr>
<tr><td>Vessel Name and Voyage Number
YURONG/E244</td><td>Port of Loading

QINGDAO　PORT，CHINA</td><td colspan="2">Port of Discharge

SYDNEY，AUSTRALIA</td></tr>
<tr><td>Place of Receipt</td><td>Place of Delivery</td><td colspan="2">Number of Original Bs/L
THREE</td></tr>
<tr><td colspan="4">**PARTICULARS AS DECLARED BY SHIPPER—CARRIER NOT RESPONSIBLE**</td></tr>
<tr><td>Container Nos/Seal Nos.
Marks and/Numbers</td><td>No. of Container / Packages / Description of Goods</td><td>Gross Weight
(Kilos)</td><td>Measurement
(cu-metres)</td></tr>
<tr><td>NS5698/S1234

N/M</td><td>**SHIPPER'S LOAD，COUNT AND SEAL**

TWO HUNDRED AND SEVENTY FIVE(275) CARTONS OF STRAW BASKETS
1×20′FCL</td><td>4 600
SHIPPED ON BOARD</td><td>27.00</td></tr>
</table>

（续表）

<table>
<tr><td rowspan="4">FREIGHT & CHARGES

FREIGHT COLLECT</td><td>Number of Containers/Packages (in words)

SAY TWO HUNDRED AND
SEVENTY FIVE CARTONS ONLY.</td></tr>
<tr><td>Shipped on Board Date：
DEC. 31,2016</td></tr>
<tr><td>Place and Date of Issue：
DEC. 31,2016,QINGDAO</td></tr>
<tr><td>In Witness Whereof this number of Original Bills of Lading stated
Above all of the tenor and date one of which being accomplished the others to stand void.</td></tr>
</table>

本章小结

本章重点介绍了在汇付这种付款方式下，卖方如何同买方结算货款以及使用这种付款方式时应该注意的问题、需要准备的单证、单证的制作依据等。通过本章的学习，要求学生掌握汇付这种付款方式的运用，学会在汇付这种付款方式下制作买方需要的单证。

1. 什么是汇付？汇付有哪些种类？
2. 电汇付款方式的流程是什么？
3. 使用汇付付款方式时，应注意哪些问题？
4. 在汇付付款方式的结算中，卖方一般应给买方准备那些单据？备单时应注意哪些问题？

第十一章　托收付款方式下的国际结算

学习目标

了解托收的相关知识，掌握托收的操作流程，学会托收方式下卖方如何同买方进行结算。

第一节　托收付款方式概述

一、托收的含义

托收(Collection) 是指债权人(出口人)出具债权凭证(汇票等)委托银行向债务人(进口人)收取货款的一种支付方式。

托收一般都通过银行办理，故又叫银行托收。银行托收的基本做法是：出口人根据买卖合同先行发运货物，然后开立汇票(或不开汇票)连同商业单据，向出口地银行提出托收申请，委托出口地银行(托收行)通过其在进口地的代理行或往来银行(代收行)向进口人收取货款。

二、托收付款方式的基本当事人

托收涉及四个主要当事人，即委托人、付款人、托收行和代收行。

(一) 委托人(Principal)

是指委托银行办理托收业务的一方。在国际贸易实务中一般是出口商，出口商开具汇票，委托银行向国外进口人(债务人)收款。

(二) 托收行(Remitting Bank)

又称寄单行，指受委托人的委托办理托收业务的银行，通常为出口人所在地的银行。

(三) 代收行(Collecting Bank)

是指接受托收行委托，向付款人收款的银行，通常是托收行在付款人所在地的分行、代理行或有经常性业务往来的关系行。

(四) 付款人(Payer or Drawee)

是银行根据托收指示书的指示提示单据的对象。托收业务中的付款人，一般是商务合同中的买方、托收汇票中的受票人。

三、托收的种类

(一) 按照银行向买方收取货款时是否提供单据,可以分为光票托收和跟单托收

1. 光票托收

光票托收(Clean Collection) 指卖方或债权人仅向托收行提交汇票、本票、支票等金融单据,委托其代为收款。一般情况下,在对外承包工程或服务贸易中,债权人通常采用光票托收的方式。

2. 跟单托收

跟单托收(Documentary Collection)是指卖方或债权人向托收行提交发票、提单等商业单据,可提交也可不提交金融单据,委托其代为收款的结算方式。在货物贸易中,一般采用跟单托收的结算方式。

(二) 在跟单托收中,按照银行交给买方单据的条件不同,可分为付款交单和承兑交单

1. 付款交单(Documents against Payment,简称 D/P)

所谓付款交单,是指银行的交单是以买方的付款为条件,提示行在向买方提示汇票和单据后,只有在收到买方付款后方能把单据交给他。

在付款交单这种结算方式中,根据买方付款的时间不同,又分为即期付款交单(D/P at sight)和远期付款交单(D/P after sight)。

即期付款交单是指出口商开具即期汇票,通过银行向买方提示,买方在见到汇票及随附单据后立即付款,付款后从银行取得货物相关单据。

远期付款交单是指出口商根据合同开具远期汇票(一般有 30 天、60 天、90 天远期),通过银行向买方提示,买方在见到汇票及随附单据后不是立即付款,而是先行承兑汇票,并在汇票到期日履行付款责任,在付清货款后从银行取得货物相关单据。

2. 承兑交单(Documents against Acceptance,简称 D/A)

是银行的交单以进口人在汇票上承兑为条件。即出口人在装运货物后开具远期汇票,连同商业单据,通过银行向进口人提示,进口人见到汇票及随附单据后不是立即付款,而是承兑汇票,代收行在进口人承兑汇票后即将商业单据交给进口人,进口人在汇票到期时,方履行付款义务。由于承兑交单是进口人只要在汇票上办理承兑之后,即可取得商业单据,凭以提取货物,所以承兑交单方式只适用于远期汇票的托收。

四、托收方式下结算的业务流程

(一) 付款交单结算方式的业务流程

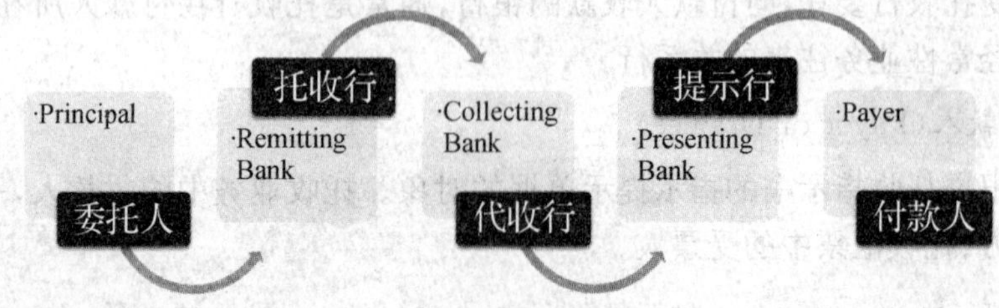

1. 即期付款交单的业务流程

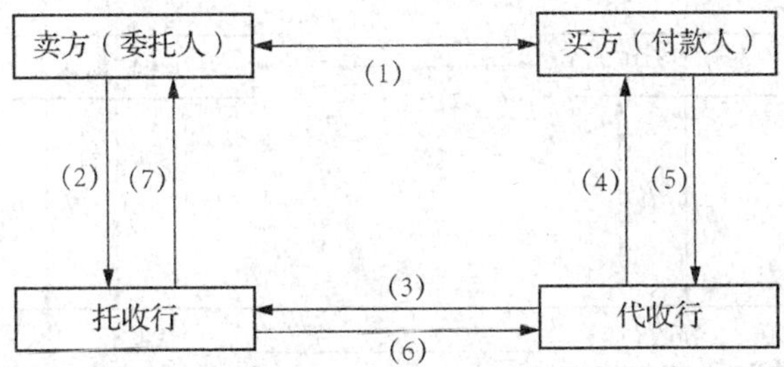

(1) 买卖双方签订合同,合同中规定使用 D/P at sight 作为付款方式。

(2) 卖方发货后按照买方的要求备齐单据,交单至当地银行(托收行)托收。

(3) 托收行让卖方填写托收委托书,并按照卖方在委托书上的指示寄单给代收行。

(4) 代收行收到托收行寄来的单据和汇票后,向买方提示。

(5) 买方审核单据无误后付款,领取单据。

(6) 代收行将货款汇给托收行。

(7) 托收行收到货款后,扣除手续费,将余额拨交给卖方。

2. 远期付款交单的业务流程

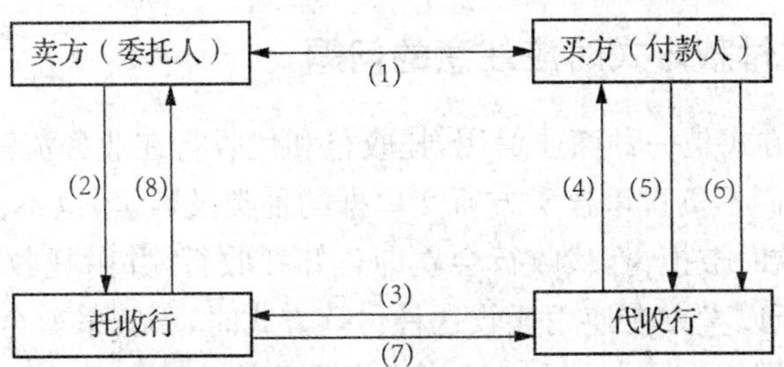

(1) 买卖双方签订合同,合同中规定使用 D/P after sight 作为付款方式。

(2) 卖方发货后按照买方的要求备齐单据,交单至当地银行(托收行)托收。

(3) 托收行让卖方填写托收委托书,并按照卖方在委托书上的指示寄单给代收行。

(4) 代收行收到托收行寄来的单据和汇票后,向买方提示。

(5) 买方审核单据无误后承兑汇票。

(6) 买方在汇票到期日之后到代收行付款,代收行收到付款后交单给买方。

(7) 代收行将货款汇给托收行。

(8) 托收行收到货款后,扣除手续费,将余额拨交给卖方。

（二）承兑交单的业务流程

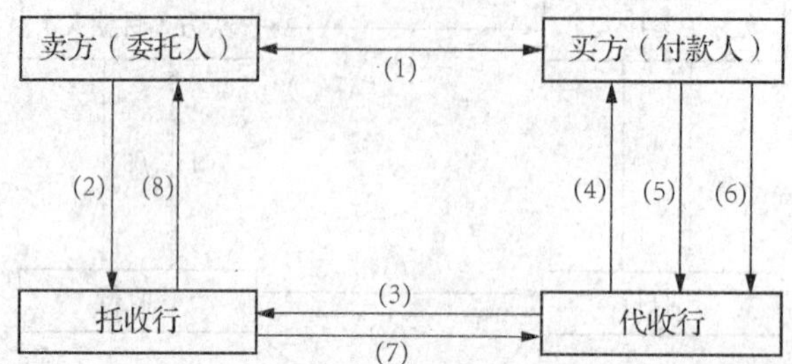

(1) 买卖双方签订合同，合同中规定使用 D/A after sight 作为付款方式。

(2) 卖方发货后按照买方的要求备齐单据，交单至当地银行(托收行)托收。

(3) 托收行让卖方填写托收委托书，并按照卖方在委托书上的指示寄单给代收行。

(4) 代收行收到托收行寄来的单据和汇票后，向买方提示。

(5) 买方审核单据无误后承兑汇票，代收行交单给买方。

(6) 买方在汇票到期日之后到代收行付款。

(7) 代收行将货款汇给托收行。

(8) 托收行收到货款后，扣除手续费，将余额拨交给卖方。

五、使用托收付款方式时应注意的问题

（一）托收付款方式是一种商业信用，托收行和代收行在业务流程中仅是按照卖方委托书的指示操作，他们不负责审核卖方所交单据的种类及数量，也不保证货款的收回。如果代收行向买方收款时被拒付，代收行会立即告知托收行，并由托收行联系卖方，由卖方决定下一步行动。所以卖方在使用托收这种付款方式时，不宜采取全额托收，可以先让买方支付定金，余额采用托收的方式。从上述业务流程中也可以看出，卖方在没有任何定金保障的情况下就直接备货发货，承担的风险是很大的。

（二）根据国际商会颁布的《托收统一规则》简称 URC522 之规定，“托收不应含有远期汇票而又同时规定商业单据要在付款后才交付”，所以不提倡使用 D/P 远期。因为在现代国际贸易中，随着航运技术的进步，从发货港到目的港的时间大大缩短，再行使用远期付款交单已无多大意义，还可能导致货已到港而汇票未到期的后果，买方未及时付款赎单提货而产生滞港费、箱使费等。更有甚者，买方可能会向银行借单提货，增加了卖方回收货款的风险。有些国家法律规定远期 D/P 视为 D/A，买方承兑汇票后可以直接得到单据。

（三）全额托收的付款方式多用于大金额合同。如果交易金额较大，买方为了不占用己方资金，一般会要求以 D/A 远期付款方式成交。这时卖方可以通过国际保理公司或出口信用保险公司调查买方资信，并签订保险合同，以转移风险。

第二节　托收付款方式下的结算单证

根据上一节内容可知，在对托收这一付款方式的结算时，卖方向托收行递交的单据是由卖方自己决定的，银行并不负责审核单据的种类和份数。所以，在使用托收付款方式时，买卖双方在合同中应该列明卖方应提交哪些单据给托收行。一般来说，和汇付付款方式一样，卖方应提交给买方商业发票、装箱单、提单、产地证4种基本单据，如果买方还要求卖方提供其他单据，卖方首先要考虑该单据自己是否能够提供，其次还要考虑提供该单据是否会增加额外的费用，如果增加额外费用，卖方在报价时应该高一些。

和汇付付款方式一样，托收付款方式中结算用的单证的制作也主要是依据合同、货物的实际情况以及买方的要求。下面依据托收的议付流程，以一份销售合同为例介绍托收付款方式中结算用的单证。

销 售 合 同

S ALES CONTRACT

卖方(Seller)：YONGXIN FURNITURE CO. LTD.　　合同号(Contract No.)：170907
地址(Address)：NO. 32 NANJING STREET SHANGHAI, CHINA　　合同日期(Date)：SEP. 20, 2017
签约地点(Place)：SHANGHAI
买方(Buyer)：SUNNY FLOWER SRL
地址(Address)：CUYRQINA ROAD, NAPOLI, ITALY

双方同意按下列条款由卖方出售、买方购进下列货物：

The seller agree to sell and the buyer agree to buy the following goods according to the terms and conditions stipulated below:

(1) 唛头 Marks	(2) 名称 Name of Commodity	(3) 数量 Quantity	(4) 单价 Unit Price	(5) 金额 Amount
SUNNY PO#170907 C/NO. 1 - UP	WOOD DESK YF17 - 08(WHITE) YF17 - 10(BROWN)	 1000PCS 800PCS	CIF NAPOLI USD20. 00 USD30. 00	 USD20,000. 00 USD24,000. 00
	Total:	1800PCS		USD44,000. 00

5 % more or less allowed.

(6) 货物总值(Total Amount)：SAY U. S. DOLLARS FORTY FOUR THOUSAND ONLY.

(7) 付款方式(Terms of Payment)：30% PAID IN DEPOSIT BY T/T, BALANCE PAID BY D/P AT SIGHT. THE SELLER SHOULD SEND ALL DOCUMENTS REQUIRED TO THE BANK OF ITALIA, NAPOLI BRANCH FOR COLLECTING

BALANCE PAYMENT.

买方须于____年____月____日前开出本批交易的信用证(或通知售方进口许可证号码),否则,售方有权不经过通知取消本合同,并有权提出索赔。

The buyers shall establish the covering Letter of Credit (or notify the Import License Number) before OCT. 05, 2017__________, falling which the Seller reserves the right to lodge a claim.

(8) 装运期限(Time of Shipment): WITHIN 60 DAYS AFTER THE RECEIPT OF DEPOSIT.

(9) 装运港/目的港(Port of Loading & Port of Destination):

SHIPMENT FROM SHANGHAI PORT, CHINA TO NAPOLI, ITALY

(10) 分批及转船(Partial Shipment and Transshipment): ALLOWED

(11) 品质及检验(Quality & Inspection): QUALITY AS CONFIRMED SAMPLES AND INSPECTION EFFECTED BY CHINA CIQ.

(12) 包装(Packing): 1PC/CTN, NO WOOD PACKING MATERIALS WILL BE USED

(13) 保险(Insurance): TO BE EFFECTED BY THE SELLER COVERING ALL RISKS AND WAR RISKS FOR 110% INVOICE VALUE.

(14) 买方所需单据(Documents Required): 3 ORIGINAL OF COMMERCIAL INVOICE, PACKING LIST AND 1 ORIGINAL GSP FORM A; FULL SET OF B/L, 1 ORIGIAL INSURANCE POLICY. ALL THE DOCUMENTS SHOULD STATE THAT THERE IS NO WOOD PACKING MATERIALS USED.

(15) 品质/数量异议:如买方提出索赔,凡属品质异议须于货到目的____日内提出,凡属数量异议须于货到目的口岸至____日内提出,对所装货物所提任何异议属于保险公司,船公司等其他有关运输或邮递机构,卖方不负任何责任。

Quality/Quantity Discrepancy: In case of quality discrepancy, claim should be filed by the Buyer within __30__ days after the arrival of the goods at port of destination; while for quantity discrepancy, claim should be filed by the Buyer within __15__ days after the arrival of the goods at port of destination. It is under stood that the seller shall mot be liable for any discrepancy of the goods shipped due to causes for which the Insurance Company, Shipped Company other transportation organization/ or Post Office are liable.

(16) 本确认书内所述全部或部分商品,如因人力不可抗拒的原因,以致不能履行或延迟交货,卖方概不负责。

The Seller shall not be held liable for failure of delay in delivery of the entire lot or a portion of the goods under this Sales Confirmation in consequence of any Force Major incidents.

(17) 仲裁(Arbitration):本合同在执行过程中若发生争议,双方应通过友好协商方式解决;如果协商不成,则应提交北京中国国际经济贸易仲裁委员会裁决。裁决是终局的,对双方均有约束力。仲裁费用由败诉方承担。

All disputes arising from the execution of the contract shall be settled by friendly negotiation, falling which the case should be submitted to the China International Economic & Trade Arbitration Commission, Beijing. The Decision is final and binding upon both parties. The fee shall be borne by the losing party.

(18) 买方收到本售货确认书后请立即签回一份，如买方对本确认书有异议，应于收到后五天内提出，否则认为买方已同意接受本确认书所规定的各项条款。

The buyer is requested to sign and return one copy of the Sales Confirmation immediately after the receipt of same. Objection, if any, should be raised by the Buyer within five days after the receipt of this Sales Confirmation, in the absence of which it is understood that the Buyer has accepted the terms and condition of the sales confirmation.

The Seller:　　　　　　　　　　The Buyer:

买卖双方签订上述合同后，卖方首先要根据合同中约定的付款方式催买方支付定金，在收到买方的定金后，卖方便可以开始备货发货了。发完货后卖方按照合同约定备齐单据送至当地银行托收。根据流程，卖方应制作如下单证。

一、商业发票

托收中商业发票的制作要求和上一章讲过的汇付付款方式一样，制作的主要依据是合同，货物名称、唛头、单价、买卖双方应与合同完全一致，数量则应体现实际发货数量，可以根据合同的规定和实际装柜情况多于或少于合同中的货物数量，如果买方对商业发票有其他附件要求，卖方把买方要求的内容填写在商业发票的下部就可以。

由于合同中单据要求有规定“ALL THE DOCUMENTS SHOULD STATE THAT THERE IS NO WOOD PACKING MATERIALS USED”.所以要在商业发票的下面按合同的要求写一句声明。

YONGXIN FURNITURE CO. LTD.

NO. 32 NANJING STREET, SHANGHAI, CHINA

COMMERCIAL INVOICE

TO: SUNNY FLOWER SRL　　　　　　　　INVOICE NO.: Y17IT020

CUYRQINA ROAD, NAPOLI, ITALY　　　　　　DATE: NOV. 30, 2017

SHIPMENT FROM SHANGHAI PORT, CHINA TO NAPOLI, ITALY BY SEAWAY

SHIPPING MARKS	NAME OF GOODS	Q'TY	UNIT PRICE	AMOUNT
SUNNY PO＃170907 C/NO. 1 - UP	WOOD DESK YF17 - 08(WHITE) F17 - 10(BROWN)	 900PCS 800PCS	CIF NAPOLI USD20. 00 USD30. 00	 USD18,000. 00 USD24,000. 00
	TOTAL:	1700PCS		USD42,000. 00

SAY U. S. DOLLARS FORTY TWO THOUSAND ONLY.

WE HEREBY STATE THAT THERE IS NO WOOD PACKING MATERIALS USED.

YONGXIN FURNITURE CO. LTD.
（法人代表签字章）

二、装箱单

装箱单的要求和上一章汇付付款方式中要求的一样，内容不再赘述，看下面示例，装箱单的下面也要和商业发票一样，加一句非木质包装声明。

YONGXIN FURNITURE CO. LTD.

NO. 32 NANJING STREET, SHANGHAI, CHINA

PACKING LIST

INVOICE NO.：Y17IT020　　DATE：NOV. 30, 2017

SHIPMENT FROM SHANGHAI PORT, CHINA TO NAPOLI, ITALY BY SEAWAY.

MARKS	NAME OF GOODS	QUANTITY		N. W. (KGS)	G. W. (KGS)	MEAS. CBM
SUNNY PO＃170907 C/NO. 1 - UP	WOOD DESK YF17 - 08(WHITE) YF17 - 10(BROWN)	900PCS 800PCS	900CTNS 800CTNS	18000 20000	22500 24000	90. 00 96. 00
	TOTAL:	1700PCS	1700CTNS	38000	46500	186. 00

YOUNGXIN FURNITURE CO., LTD.
（法人代表签字章）

SAY ONE THOUSAND SEVEN HUNDRED CARTONS ONLY.

WE HEREBY STATE THAT THERE IS NO WOOD PACKING MATERIALS USED.

三、产地证明

根据合同要求，意大利是给惠国，卖方需要给买方办理 GSP Form A，按照商业发票、装箱的内容，填制 Form A 如下：

普惠制产地证 A 格式

<table>
<tr><td colspan="3">1. goods consigned from (Exporter's name, address, country)
YONGXIN FURNITURE CO. LTD.
NO. 32 NANJING STREET, SHANGHAI, CHINA</td><td colspan="3" rowspan="2">Reference No.
GENERALIZED SYSTEM OF PREFERENCES
CERTIFICATE ORIGIN
(combined declaration and certificate)
FORM A
Issued in THE PEOPLE'S REPUBLIC OF CHINA
(COUNTRY)</td></tr>
<tr><td colspan="3">2. good consigned to (Consignee's name, address, country)
SUNNY FLOWER SRL
CUYRQINA ROAD, NAPOLI, ITALY</td></tr>
<tr><td colspan="3">3. Means of transport and route(as far as known)
SHIPMENT FROM SHANGHAI PORT, CHINA TO NAPOLI, ITALY BY SEAWAY</td><td colspan="3">4. For official use</td></tr>
<tr><td>5. Item Number
1</td><td>6. Marks and numbers
SUNNY
PO
#170907
C/NO. 1 - UP</td><td>7. Number and kind of packages; description of goods
ONE THOUSAND SEVEN HUNDRED (1700) CART - ONS OF WOOD DESK
WE HEREBY STATE THAT THERE IS NO WOOD PACKING MATERIALS USED.</td><td>8. Origin criterion "P"</td><td>9. Gross weight or other Quantity
1700PCS</td><td>10. Number and date of invoices
Y17IT020 NOV. 30, 2017</td></tr>
<tr><td colspan="3">11. Certification
It is hereby certified, on the basis of control out, that the declaration by the exporter is correct.

SHANGHAI, CHINA. DEC. 1, 2017
Place and date, signature and stamp of certifying authority</td><td colspan="3">12. Declaration by the exporter
The undersigned hereby declares that the above details and statements are correct; that all the goods were produced in CHINA and that they comply with the origin requirements specified for those goods in the generalized system of preferences for goods exported to E. U. (importing country)
SHANGHAI, CHINA. DEC. 1, 2017
Place and date, signature and stamp of certifying authority</td></tr>
</table>

四、提　单

<table>
<tr><td colspan="2">Shipper

YONGXIN FURNITURE CO. LTD.
NO. 32 NANJING STREET, SHANGHAI, CHINA</td><td colspan="3" rowspan="3">B/L NO.

COSCO

OCEAN BILL OF LADING</td></tr>
<tr><td colspan="2">Consignee
TO ORDER</td></tr>
<tr><td colspan="2">**Notify Party**
SUNNY FLOWER SRL
CUYRQINA ROAD, NAPOLI, ITALY</td></tr>
<tr><td>Vessel Name and Voyage Number
YURONG/E244</td><td>Port of Loading
SHANGHAI PORT, CHINA</td><td colspan="3">Port of Discharge
NAPOLI, ITALY</td></tr>
<tr><td>Place of Receipt</td><td>Place of Delivery</td><td colspan="3">Number of Original Bs/L
THREE</td></tr>
<tr><td colspan="5">**PARTICULARS AS DECLARED BY SHIPPER—CARRIER NOT RESPONSIBLE**</td></tr>
<tr><td>Container Nos/Seal Nos.
Marks and/Numbers</td><td>No. of Container / Packages /
Description of Goods</td><td>Gross Weight
(Kilos)</td><td colspan="2">Measurement
(cu-metres)</td></tr>
<tr><td>NS5698/S1234
SUNNY
PO#170907
C/NO. 1-UP</td><td>**SHIPPER'S LOAD, COUNT AND SEAL**

ONE THOUSAND SEVEN HUNDRED (1700) CARTONS OF WOOD DESK
3X40'FCL
WE HEREBY STATE THAT THERE IS NO WOOD PACKING MATERI-ALS USED.</td><td>46500

SHIPPED ON BOARD</td><td colspan="2">186. 00</td></tr>
<tr><td rowspan="4">FREIGHT & CHARGES

FREIGHT COLLECT</td><td colspan="4">Number of Containers/Packages (in words)

SAY ONE THOUSAND SEVEN HUNDRED CARTONS ONLY.</td></tr>
<tr><td colspan="4">Shipped on Board Date:
DEC. 3, 2017</td></tr>
<tr><td colspan="4">Place and Date of Issue:
DEC. 3, 2017, SHANGHAI</td></tr>
<tr><td colspan="4">In Witness Whereof this number of Original Bills of Lading stated
Above all of the tenor and date one of which being accomplished the others to stand void.</td></tr>
</table>

五、保险单

中国平安保险股份有限公司
PING AN INSURANCE COMPANY OF CHINA,LTD.

保单号 Policy No.:1000005959

货物运输保险单

CARGO TRANPORTATION INSURANCE POLICY

被保险人(Insured):TO ORDER

中国平安保险股份有限公司根据被保险人的要求及其所交付约定的保险费,按照本保险单背面所载条款与下列条款,承保下述货物运输保险,特立本保险单。

This Policy of Insurance witnesses that PING AN INSURANCE COMPANY OF CHINA,LTD.,at the request of the Insured and in consideration of the agreed premium paid by the Insured,undertakes to insure the under mentioned goods in transportation subject to the conditions of Policy as per the clauses printed overleaf and other special clauses attached hereon.

MARKS 唛头	DESCRIPTION OF GOODS 货物名称	QUANTITY &PACKING 货物包装、数量	AMOUNT INSURED 保险金额
SUNNY PO#170907 C/NO. 1 - UP	WOOD DESK	1700 CARTONS	USD46200.00

承保条件

Conditions:ALL RISKS AND WAR RISKS

发票或提单号　Y17IT020　运输工具　YURONG/E244

Invoice No. or B/L No. ______ per conveyance S. S.: ______

起运日期　DEC. 3, 2017　自　SHANGHAI PORT, CHINA　至　NAPOLI, ITALY

Slg. on or abt.　From　To

赔款偿付地点

Claim Payable at　NAPOLI, ITALY

签单日期 Date:DEC. 1,2017

For and on behalf of

PING AN INSURANCE COMPANY OF CHINA,LTD. (authorized signature)

六、汇　票

在托收付款方式下，卖方备齐买方需要的单据后，交到银行去托收时还要填制一张汇票，汇票是由银行印制的，各银行的格式有所不同，但主要内容是一样的。卖方一般将单据交给自己有业务关系的银行托收，并填制好该银行的汇票、托收委托单交单托收。

BILL OF EXCHANGE

凭
Drawn under 1700PCS OF WOOD DESKS UNDER S/C NO.170907.

按　息　付款
Payable with interest @..................% per annum

号码　汇票　中　国，上海　年　月　日
No: 170907 Exchange for USD30000.00 Shanghai, China DEC. 5, 2017

见票　日　后（本 汇 票 之 副 本 未 付
D / P At ****** Sight of this FIRST of Exchange (Second of exchange being unpaid)

pay to the order of **BANK OF CHINA, SHANGHAI BRANCH** 或 其 指 定 人

付金额（大写）
The sum of（In words） SAY U.S.DOLLARS THIRTY THOUSAND ONLY.

To: SUNNY FLOWER SRL
CUYRQINA ROAD, NAPOLI, ITALY

YONGXIN FURNITURE CO. LTD.
（法人代表签字章）

七、托收委托单

托收行在接受卖方的托收委托之前，会让卖方填制一份托收委托单，填上托收的种类、代收行的名称地址、所交单据的种类数量等，以便据此履行职责。下面是一份中国银行的托收委托书，如果卖方到当地中国银行托收货款，应填制如下：

托 收 委 托 书

COLLECTION ORDER

致：中国银行上海分行　　　　日期：2017 年 12 月 5 日

托收行（Remitting Bank）： 中国银行上海分行， 上海市人民大道 170 号	**代收行**（Collecting Bank）： 名称：BANK OF ITALIA，NAPOLI BRANCH 地址：NO. 132 ROMAN ST. NAPOLI， ITALY. TEL：0039 77843210
委托人（Principal）： 永鑫家具有限公司 上海市南京路 32 号	**付款人**（Drawee）： SUNNY FLOWER SRL CUYRQINA ROAD，NAPOLI，ITALY

付款交单 D/P ✓　承兑交单 D/A	国外费用承担：付款人✓　委托人
发票号：Y17IT020	国内费用承担：付款人　委托人✓
托收金额：USD30000.00	

单据种类	汇票	商业发票	装箱单	提单	原产地证	保险单	质量证书	卫生证书	动植物检疫证书	普惠制产地证	
数量	1	3	3	3		1				1	

付款指示：请将收汇款原币划入我公司下列账户上：
开户行：中国银行上海分行
账号：610098000100
联系人：
电话：

银行签章：　　　　　　　　　　委托人签章：

本章小结

本章重点介绍了在托收这种付款方式下，卖方如何同买方结算货款以及使用这种付款方式时应该注意的问题、需要准备的单证、单证的制作依据等。通过本章的学习，要求学生掌握托收这种付款方式的运用，尤其是要警惕托收付款方式给卖方带来的潜在风险，在实际工作中要慎用。学生也应学会在托收这种付款方式下制作买方需要的单证。

复习思考题

1. 什么是托收？托收有哪些种类？
2. D/P AT SIGHT 付款方式的流程是什么？
3. 使用托收付款方式时，应注意哪些问题？
4. 在托收付款方式的结算中，卖方一般应给买方准备那些单据？备单时应注意哪些问题？

第十二章　信用证付款方式下的国际结算单证

在了解了第三章信用证相关知识的基础上，学会阅读信用证，能够读懂信用证，并且能够按照信用证的要求制作出各种议付单据。

如果买卖双方在合同中签订的付款方式是信用证，那么卖方在收到信用证后首先要认真审核，审核没问题后再安排备货、发货。信用证的审核涉及很多方面，本书第三章已经介绍过，本章主要详细讲解信用证各条款的含义以及如何做单证才能体现出来信用证的要求。

第一节　读懂信用证

下面是一份信用证样：

Issue of a Documentary Credit　开证行（买方当地银行，买方签订合同后，应按照合同相关条款的要求，向当地银行申请开立信用证给卖方）

KOEXKRSEXXX MESSAGE TYPE：700

KOREA EXCHANGE BANK

SEOUL

178.2 KA，ULCHI RO，CHUNG－KO

Destination Bank　通知行（通知行一般由卖方指定其当地银行，在买卖双方签订合同时，卖方应及时将自己的银行信息告知买方）

BKCHCNBJA08E SESSION：000 ISN：000000

BANK OF CHINA

LIAONING

NO. 5 ZHONGSHAN SQUARE

ZHONGSHAN DISTRICT

DALIAN

CHINA

Type of Documentary Credit 40A　IRREVOCABLE

跟单信用证的类型：不可撤销，如果此处未注明是否可撤销，则该信用证是不可撤销的。

Letter of Credit Number 20 LC84E0081

信用证号码

Date of Issue 31G　170116

开证日期 2017 年 1 月 16 日

Date and Place of Expiry 31D 170315 CHINA

信用证的到期日和到期地点：此处对卖方提出的要求是必须在到期日之前将单据交至到期地点所在的银行。如果到期地点是受益人所在地，卖方只要在到期日之前将单据交至当地议付行就可以了，这样的信用证叫国内到期信用证；如果到期地点是开证申请人所在地或者开证行所在地，则单据必须在到期日之前寄至信用证所指定的付款行，这样的信用证叫国外到期信用证。在使用国外到期信用证时，可能会由于快寄公司的耽搁使单据未能按时到达付款行，使卖方承担了信用证过期的风险。所以应慎重接受国外到期信用证。

Applicant 50 SANGYONG CORPORATION

CPO BOX 118，SEOUL，KOREA

开证申请人，一般应为合同中的买方。

Beneficiary 59 DALIAN WEIDA TRADING CO.，LTD.

NO. 180 RENMIN ROAD，DALIAN，CHINA.

受益人，一般为合同中的卖方。

Currency Code，Max. Amount 32B USD 334000.00

货币币种、金额、最大付款金额。此处金额、币种应与合同相符，卖方要注意审核金额是否少于合同。此处标明了最大付款金额，意即卖方提交的议付单据中金额不应超过此金额。在实际操作中，卖方需要注意即使合同中规定了发货数量允许有 5%增减，由于信用证的该条款也不能多发货。

Available with... by... 41D ANY BANK BY NEGOTIATION

通过任何银行议付有效。该条款规定受益人可以将单据交到任何银行议付，此规定说明该信用证是自由议付信用证。如果此处标明的是具体的银行名称，则该证是限制议付信用证，受益人应看看自己到该议付行交单是否方便。

Drafts at 42C 45 DAYS AFTER SIGHT

汇票：45 天远期。该条款说明该信用证是远期信用证。卖方在审核该条款时要看其是否与合同一致，因为这是买卖双方在签订合同时谈判的结果。

Drawee 42D KOREA EXCHANGE BANK

受票人：此条款告诉卖方在填写汇票时，受票人应填写 KOREA EXCHANGE BANK

Partial Shipments 43P NOT ALLOWED

分批发货：不允许。此条款要求卖方在制作单据时，金额和数量不能少于信用证要求，在实际操作中不能少发货。

Transhipment 43T NOT ALLOWED

转船：不允许。该条款要求就是各单据中不允许出现中转港、二程船名等意即转船运输的字样，实际操作中卖方应先联系货代确认该批货物的运输是否为直达，若没有直达船，则卖方必须要求买方修改此条款。

Shipping on Board/Dispatch/Packing in Charge at/ from

44A ANY PORT IN CHINA 装运港：中国任何港口。该条款要求各单据中的发货港必

须是中国的具体港口，要写明具体港口的名称，并后缀中国。例如 QINGDAO PORT，CHINA，

Transportation to 44B BUSAN，KOREA

目的港：韩国釜山

Latest Date of Shipment 44C 170301

最晚装船日期：2017 年 3 月 1 日。此条款要求所提交提单的签署日期必须是在 2017 年的 3 月 1 日之前的日期。在实际操作中卖方须及早联系货代，落实好船期，必须在信用证的最晚装船日期之前装货上船。

Description of Goods or Services：45A

FROZEN YELLOWFIN SOLE WHOLE ROUND (WITH WHITE BELLY) USD770/MT CFR BUSAN QUANTITY：200MT

ALASKA PLAICE (WITH YELLOW BELLY) USD600/MT CFR BUSAN QUANTITY：300MT

货物/服务描述：此条款若载有货物的名称、数量、价格等内容，必须与合同一致。卖方交单议付时，所有单据所载的货物信息必须和信用证相符。根据 UCP600 的规定，信用证该条款下所有的内容必须全部体现在商业发票上。

Documents Required：46A

要求提交的单据：

1. SIGNED COMMERCIAL INVOICE IN 5 COPIES SHOWING THE L/C NUMBER AND FULL NAME AND ADDRESS OF THE MANUFACTUER.

5 份手签的商业发票，发票上要显示信用证号码和货物制造商的公司全称和地址。

2. PACKING LIST/WEIGHT MEMO IN 4 COPIES INDICATING QUANTITY/GROSS AND NET WEIGHTS OF EACH PACKAGE AND PACKING CONDITIONS AS CALLED FOR BY THE L/C.

4 份装箱单/重量单，单据上应注明每一包装所装货物的数量、毛重和净重，并注明包装方式和信用证要求的一致。

3. FULL SET OF CLEAN ON BOARD OCEAN BILLS OF LADING MADE OUT TO ORDER AND BLANK ENDORSED, MARKED “FREIGHT PREPAID” NOTIFYING SANSCO TANSPORTING COMPANY, NO. 265 SCAL ROAD, SEOUL，KOREA。

全套清洁已装船海运提单，提单的收货人做成“凭指示(TO ORDER)”，提单要空白背书，标注上“运费预付”，通知人 SANSCO TANSPORTING COMPANY, NO. 265 SCAL ROAD, SEOUL，KOREA。

4. CERTIFICATE OF QUALITY IN 3 COPIES ISSUED BY PUBLIC RECOGNIZED SURVEYOR.

3 份由公众认可的机构签发的质量证明。质量证明一般由检验检疫局签发，卖方应到当地检验检疫机构报检，检验检疫局在检验货物合格后，可以签发该证明。

5. CERTIFICATE OF ORIGIN IN 3 COPIES ISSUED BY AUTHORIZED INSTITUTION.

3份由授权机构签发的产地证明。

6. CERTIFICATE OF HEALTH IN 3 COPIES ISSUED BY AUTHORIZED INSTITUTION.

3份由授权机构签发的卫生(健康)证明。

7. BENEFICIARY'S CERTIFIED COPY OF FAX DISPATCHED TO THE ACCOUNTEE WITH 3 DAYS AFTER SHIPMENT ADVISING NAME OF VESSEL, DATE, QUANTITY, WEIGHT, VALUE OF SHIPMENT, L/C NUMBER AND CONTRACT NUMBER.

受益人证明的传真复印件。该传真的内容应该包含船名航次、开船日期、所发货物的数量、重量、金额、信用证号码和合同号码。该传真卖方必须在开船后3天内发给付款人(买方)。

8. CERTIFICATE OF INSPECTION SIGNED BY WILLIANM LEE.

由威廉·李签发的验货证明。

ADDITIONAL INSTRUCTIONS: 47A

附加条款:

1. CHARTER PARTY B/L AND THIRD PARTY DOCUMENTS ARE ACCEPTABLE.

租船提单和第三方单据可以接受。

2. SHIPMENT PRIOR TO L/C ISSUING DATE IS ACCEPTABLE.

在信用证开证日期之前发货可以接受。

3. BOTH QUANTITY AND AMOUNT 10 PERCENT MORE OR LESS ARE ALLOWED.

数量和金额增减10%可以接受。

Charges 71B ALL BANKING CHARGES OUTSIDE THE OPENNING BANK ARE FOR BENEFICIARY'S ACCOUNT.

费用:开证行以外的费用由受益人承担。

Period for Presentation 48 DOCUMENTS MUST BE PRESENTED WITHIN 15 DAYS AFTER THE DATE OF ISSUANCE OF THE TRANSPORT DOCUMENTS BUT WITHIN THE VALIDITY OF THE CREDIT.

交单期限:所有的单据必须在运输单据日期后的15天内交至银行议付,但必须在信用证的有效期内。

Confimation Instructions 49 WITHOUT

保兑条款:无

Instructions to the Paying/Accepting/Negotiating Bank: 78

给付款行/承兑行/议付行的通知:

1. ALL DOCUMENTS TO BE FORWARDED IN ONE COVER, UNLESS OTHERWISE STATED ABOVE.

除非上面另有规定,所有单据应装在一个信封里寄送。

2. DISCREPANT DOCUMENT FEE OF USD 50.00 OR EQUAL CURRENCY WILL BE DEDUCTED FROM DRAWING IF DOCUMENTS WITH DISCREPANCIES ARE ACCEPTED.

如果单据中有不符点，这些不符点能够被接受，受益人将被扣掉 50 美元或其他等值货币。

第二节　信用证结算中单证的制作

在读懂了上一节的信用证后，卖方在发货后就可以根据信用证的要求制作单据了。与汇付、托收付款方式不同的是，信用证付款方式单证的制作依据是信用证，凡是信用证中提及的内容，如果需要在某个单据上体现出来，那么该单据必须先满足信用证的要求。因为在第三章中讲过信用证的特点，它是独立于合同之外的自足性文件，所以只要卖方接受了信用证，就等于接受了信用证的所有条款，当信用证条款与合同条款冲突时，要按照信用证要求来制作单据，单据中信用证没有提及的内容，可以参照合同，但不能与信用证相关条款冲突。下面就根据第一节信用证及买卖双方所签的售货确认书要求制作如下单据：

SALES CONFIRMATION

THE SELLER：　DALIAN WEIDA TRADING CO.，LTD.　　NO.：CK170108

NO. 180 RENMIN ROAD，DALIAN，CHINA.　　DATE：JAN. 8，2017

THE BUYER：SANGYONG CORPORATION

CPO BOX 118，SEOUL，KOREA

MARKS	NAME OF GOODS	Q'TY	UNIT PRICE	AMOUNT
S. Y. BUSAN C/NO. 1 - UP	FROZEN YELLOWFIN SOLE ALASKA PLAICE	 200MT 300MT	CFR BUSAN USD770/MT USD600/MT	 USD154000.00 USD180000.00
	TOTAL：	500MT		USD334000.00

5% MORE OR LESS ALLOWED

1. TOTAL AMOUNT：SAY U. S. DOLLARS THREE HUNDRED AND THIRTY FOUR THOUSAND ONLY.
2. TIME OF DELIVERY：WITH 45DAYS AFTER THE RECEIPT OF L/C.
3. TERMS OF PAYMENT：BY IRREVOCABLE L/C AT SIGHT.
4. SHIPMENT FROM DALIAN PORT. CHINA TO BUSAN，KOREA.

一、商业发票

信用证付款方式中商业发票的制作，和其他付款方式中的不同之处在于：根据《跟单信用证统一惯例》UCP600 的规定，信用证 Description of Goods or Services：45A 项下所有的内容必须全部体现在商业发票上。此外，信用证还可能要求受益人在发票上标注上合同号、信用证或其他的一些声明、证明字句。

DALIAN WEIDA TRADING CO.，LTD.

NO. 180 RENMIN ROAD，DALIAN，CHINA.

COMMERCIAL INVOICE

TO：SANGYONG CORPORATION　　INVOICE NO.：CSC1701

CPO BOX 118，SEOUL，KOREA　　DATE：MAR. 2，2017

SHIPMENT FROM DALIAN PORT，CHINA TO BUSAN，KOREA

SHIPPING MARKS	NAME OF GOODS	Q'TY	UNIT PRICE	AMOUNT
S. Y. BUSAN C/NO. 1 - UP	FROZEN YELLOWFIN SOLE WHOLE ROUND（WITH WHITE BELLY）USD770/MT CFR BUSAN QUANTITY：200MT ALASKA PLAICE（WITH YELLOW BELLY）USD600/MT CFR BUSAN QUANTITY：300MT			USD154，000.00 USD180，000.00
	TOTAL：	500MT		USD334，000.00

SAY U. S. DOLLARS THREE HUNDRED AND THIRTY FOUR THOUSAND ONLY.

THE L/C NUMBER：LC84E0081

FULL NAME AND ADDRESS OF THE MANUFACTUER：

DALIAN WEIDA TRADING CO.，LTD.

NO. 180 RENMIN ROAD，DALIAN，CHINA.

DALIAN WEIDA TRADING CO.，LTD.

（法人代表签字章）

从上面商业发票可以看出，根据信用证做商业发票时，如果信用证中货物描述非常详细，而且又不是按照商业发票中的数量、单价分开来写的，在做商业发票时可以把货物名称、单价、数量合起来写，这样易于银行审核单据，也可以使受益人减少遗漏内容的可能性。根据信用证的要求，向银行交单时应当提交 5 份商业发票。

二、装箱单

装箱单的制作除了和其他结算方式下一样的内容以外，还要看信用证有无其他额外要求。该信用证规定 PACKING LIST/WEIGHT MEMO IN 4 COPIES INDICATING QUANTITY/GROSS AND NET WEIGHTS OF EACH PACKAGE AND PACKING CONDITIONS AS CALLED FOR BY THE L/C.（4 份装箱单/重量单，单据上应注明每一包装所装货物的数量、毛重和净重，并注明包装方式和信用证要求的一致）。根据这一规定，出口商在制作装箱单时，必须在装箱单上体现出来"每一包装所装货物的数量、毛重和净重，并注明包装方式和信用证要求的一致"这一内容。装箱单上的货物描述不必和商业发票完全一样，只要反映出货物的名称即可，但这一名称必须是商业发票货物描述中的一部分。

DALIAN WEIDA TRADING CO., LTD.
NO. 180 RENMIN ROAD, DALIAN, CHINA.

PACKING LIST

INVOICE NO.:CSC1701　　　　DATE: MAR. 2,2017

SHIPMENT FROM DALIAN PORT, CHINA TO BUSAN, KOREA.

MARKS	NAME OF GOODS	QUANTITY		N. W. (KGS)	G. W. (KGS)	MEAS. CBM
S. Y. BUSAN C/NO. 1 - UP	FROZEN YELLOWFIN SOLE ALASKA PLAICE	200MT 300 MT	20000CTNS 30000CTNS	200000 300000	240000 260000	600.00 900.00
	TOTAL:	500MT	50000CTNS	500000	600000	1500.00

SAY FIFTY THOUSAND CARTONS ONLY.

QUANTITY/GROSS AND NET WEIGHTS OF EACH CARTON:

FROZEN YELLOWFIN SOLE　10KGS/12KGS　10KGS

ALASKA PLAICE　10KGS/12KGS　10KGS

THIS IS TO STATE THAT PACKING CONDITIONS ARE AS CALLED FOR BY THE L/C.

DALIAN WEIDA TRADING CO., LTD.
（法人代表签字章）

当信用证中的文句用 PACKAGE 时，受益人在制作单据时必须把 PACKAGE 这个词用具体的包装种类来替代，如 CARTON, DRUM, BALE 等。对于信用证中没有做具体要求的内容，受益人按实际发货情况结合商业发票填制就可以了。

三、提　单

根据信用证填制提单时，首先要看懂信用证对提单的内容提出了几项要求，然后按要求填制。信用证没有提及的内容，则按商业发票、装箱单填制即可。该信用证对提单的要求是 FULL SET OF CLEAN ON BOARD OCEAN BILLS OF LADING MADE OUT TO ORDER AND BLANK ENDORSED, MARKED "FREIGHT PREPAID" NOTIFYING SANSCO TANSPORTING COMPANY, NO. 265 SCAL ROAD, SEOUL, KOREA。通过阅读该段文句，可以得出如下几点信用证对填制提单的要求：

1. FULL SET（全套），指受益人交单时必须按照提单 Number of Original Bs/L 项下所载的正本提单的份数全部交到银行，例如如果该项下写的是 THREE，受益人需要交 3 张正本提单到银行。

2. CLEAN（清洁），意指提单上不能有任何关于货物或包装不良批注的字样。

3. ON BOARD（已装船），意指提单上要有 SHIPPED ON BOARD 字样，银行审单

时主要看提单上是否盖有 SHIPPED ON BOARD 章。

4. MADE OUT TO (签发给……)，其后面所接的词句应为提单的收货人一栏所填的内容。后面接的词句一般有 ORDER, ORDER OF SHIPPER, ORDER OF ISSUING BANK,或 ORDER OFXXX (具体的银行名称) 等,受益人直接根据信用证的要求填在提单的收货人一栏即可。

5. BLANK ENDORSED(空白背书),所谓空白背书,即由提单提示人在背面签章即可。

6. MARKED "FREIGHT PREPAID",要求受益人在提单上必须标注上"FREIGHT PREPAID"字样,意即运费预付。

7. NOTIFYING SANSCO TANSPORTING COMPANY, NO. 265 SCAL ROAD, SEOUL,KOREA。意即提单的"Notify Party"项必须按照信用证的要求填写 SANSCO TANSPORTING COMPANY, NO. 265 SCAL ROAD, SEOUL,KOREA 公司名址。

找出上述几点要求后,制作提单如下:

<table>
<tr><td colspan="2">Shipper
DALIAN WEIDA TRADING CO., LTD.
NO. 180 RENMIN ROAD, DALIAN, CHINA.</td><td colspan="2" rowspan="3">B/L NO.

COSCO

OCEAN BILL OF LADING</td></tr>
<tr><td colspan="2">Consignee
TO ORDER</td></tr>
<tr><td colspan="2">Notify Party
SANSCO TANSPORTING COMPANY, NO. 265 SCAL ROAD, SEOUL,KOREA</td></tr>
<tr><td>Vessel Name and Voyage Number
YURONG/E244</td><td colspan="2">Port of Loading
DALIAN PORT,CHINA</td><td>Port of Discharge
BUSAN,KOREA</td></tr>
<tr><td>Place of Receipt</td><td colspan="2">Place of Delivery</td><td>Number of Original Bs/L
THREE</td></tr>
<tr><td colspan="4">PARTICULARS AS DECLARED BY SHIPPER—CARRIER NOT RESPONSIBLE</td></tr>
<tr><td>Container Nos/Seal Nos.
Marks and/Numbers</td><td>No. of Container / Packages /
Description of Goods</td><td>Gross Weight
(Kilos)</td><td>Measurement
(cu-metres)</td></tr>
<tr><td>S. Y.
BUSAN
C/NO. 1 - UP</td><td>FIFTY THOUSAND(50000)
CARTONS OF FROZEN
YELLOWFIN SOLE AND
ALASKA PLAICE

25X40'FCL</td><td>600000</td><td>1500. 00</td></tr>
</table>

（续表）

<table>
<tr><td rowspan="4">FREIGHT & CHARGES

FRIEGHT PREPAID
FREIGHT COLLECT</td><td>Number of Containers/Packages (in words)

SAY FIFTY THOUSAND CARTONS ONLY.</td></tr>
<tr><td>Shipped on Board Date：
FEB. 25，2017</td></tr>
<tr><td>Place and Date of Issue：
FEB. 25，2017，DALIAN</td></tr>
<tr><td>In Witness Whereof this number of Original Bills of Lading stated
Above all of the tenor and date one of which being accomplished the others to stand void.</td></tr>
</table>

四、质量证明

该信用证要求提交的第四个单据是 CERTIFICATE OF QUALITY(质量证明)，而且要求质量证明必须是由公众认可的机构签发的。在我国，签发质量证明的官方机构是国家质检总局或其下属的各地检验检疫机构。因此，要取得这份证明，受益人在发货前就要求当地检验检疫机构报检，并联系机构人员验货后取得该证明。证明的格式是由国家质检总局统一制定的，无须受益人自己填写。

五、产地证明

信用证要求的第五个单据是 CERTIFICATE OF ORIGIN(产地证明)且必须由授权机构签发。在我国，有权签发产地证明的机构有 2 个——贸促会和检验检疫局，所以受益人在发货之前要去办理产地证明，去上面 2 个机构中的任何一个办理都可以。产地证明的格式是由各机构统一印制的，但内容需要受益人在网上申报时自己填写，填写的主要依据是商业发票和装箱单。

<table>
<tr><td>1. Exporter
DALIAN WEIDA TRADING CO.，LTD.
NO. 180 RENMIN ROAD，DALIAN，CHINA.</td><td rowspan="2">Certificate No.

CERTIFICATE OF ORIGIN
OF
THE PEOPLE'S REPUBLIC OF CHINA</td></tr>
<tr><td>2. Consignee
SANGYONG CORPORATION
CPO BOX 118，SEOUL，KOREA</td></tr>
<tr><td>3. Means of transport and route
SHIPMENT FROM DALIAN PORT，CHINA TO BUSAN，KOREA.</td><td rowspan="2">5. For certifying authority use only</td></tr>
<tr><td>4. Country/region of destination
KOREA</td></tr>
</table>

（续表）

6. Marks and numbers	7. Number and kind of packages; description of goods	8. H. S code	9. Quantity	10. Number and date of invoices
1.	TWENTY THOUSAND (20000) OF FROZEN YELLOWFIN SOLE	03034300	200MT	
2.	THIRTY THOUSAND (30000) OF ALASKA PLAICE	03033900	300MT	CSC1701 MAR. 2,2017
S. Y. BUSAN C/NO. 1 - UP				

11. Declaration by the exporter	12. Certification
The undersigned hereby declares that the above details and statements are correct; that all the goods were produced in china and that they comply with the rules of origin of the people's republic of china. ………………………………………… Place and date, signature and stamp of certifying authority	It is hereby certified that the declaration by the exporter is correct. ………………………………………… Place and date, signature and stamp of certifying authority

如果信用证对产地证明还有其他要求，受益人在填制产地证明时可以把那些要求添加的内容加在第 7 栏的下部。

六、健康证明

信用证要求提交的第六个单据是由被授权机构签发的健康检疫证明。在我国，签署健康检疫证明的机构是国家质检总局及其在各地的下属检验检疫局。受益人要取得这个证明，在发货前就要向当地检验检疫局报检，并经检疫局相关人员检疫合格后，领取健康证明。信用证若无特殊要求，健康证明的内容和格式由检疫当局填写，无须受益人填写。在该信用证项下有两个证明需要检验检疫局出具，受益人可以就这两个证明同时向检验检疫局报检。

七、受益人证明的传真复印件

很多信用证中都有要求该类单据。该类单据一般是要求受益人在某段时间内必须发传真告知某事，并把所发传真的复印件一并交至银行议付，以此来证明受益人确实已经做了这件事。这个单据可以这样制作。

DALIAN WEIDA TRADING CO. , LTD.
NO. 180 RENMIN ROAD, DALIAN, CHINA.

TO：SANGYONG CORPORATION　　　　DATE：FEB. 26,2017
CPO BOX 118,SEOUL,KOREA
FAX NO.：0082 5378932

WE HERE BY CERTIFY THAT THE FOLLOWING INFORMATION HAVE BEEN SENT TO YOU BY FAX WITHIN 3 DAYS AFTER SHIPMENT.
NAME OF VESSEL：YURONG/E244
DATE：FEB. 25，2017
QUANTITY：
FROZEN YELLOWFIN SOLE：200MT/ 20000CTNS
ALASKA PLAICE：300MT/30000CTNS
WIGHT：
FROZEN YELLOWFIN SOLE：200MT
ALASKA PLAICE：300MT
VALUE OF SHIPMENT：USD334000.00 CFR BUSAN
L/C NUMBER：LC84E0081
CONTRACT NUMBER：CK170108

DALIAN WEIDA TRADING CO.，LTD.
（法人代表签字章）

制作这类单据时，受益人首先要按照信用证的要求把该写的内容先写上，有一些内容如果信用证未要求，受益人可以根据实际情况添加上。信用证要求的类似证明性文件，将在下一节内容进一步阐述。

八、验货证明

信用证要求提交的第八个单据是验货证明，该证明不是由受益人来制作的，而是由WILLIANM LEE 来制作并签署。这类文件一般被称作信用证中的软条款，因为受益人能否及时得到该文件是由验货人决定的，有时候买方为了维护自己的利益、取得主动权可能会在信用证中加上这样的条款，使卖方陷入被动地位，加大了卖方不能按时交单议付的风险。该类证明卖方能否接受？主要看买方的信誉度及买卖双方的合作情况。一般来说，像 WAL-MART 这样的大公司有自己的规定，对于任何进口货物，也不管何种付款方式，都必须实施装运前检验，买方凭沃尔玛公司指定人员出具的验货报告付款。如果买方是这样的大公司，信用证中有验货证明可以考虑接受。如果买方并非知名大公司，且成交金额不大，如果信用证中有验货证明要求，应当慎重接受。

九、汇　票

按照信用证的要求准备好这八份单据后，受益人还需要按照信用证的要求填制一张汇票。根据信用证的条款，汇票的受票人、汇票金额、付款期限信用证都做出了相应的规定，受益人在填制汇票时首先要满足信用证的这些要求，未做要求的内容，受益人根据发票填写就可以了。

凭	信用证号
Drawn under KOREA EXCHANGE BANK	L/C NO. LC84E0081

日期　按　息　付款
Dated JAN.16,2017 Payable with interest @..................% per annum
号码　汇票　中　国，大　连　年　月　日
No: CSC1701 Exchange for USD334,000.00 Guangzhou , China MAR. 1,2017
见票　日　后（本　汇　票　之　副　本　未　付
At 45 DAYS AFTER Sight of this FIRST of Exchange (Second of exchange being unpaid)
pay to the order of **BANK OF CHINA, DALIAN BRANCH** 或其指定人
付金额（大写）
The sum of (In words) SAY U.S.DOLLARS THREE HUNDRED THIRTY FOUR THOUSANDONLY
To: KOREA EXCHANGE BANK

DALIAN WEIDA TRADING CO., LTD.
（法人代表签字章）

填制好汇票后，受益人可以带着信用证、汇票及单据到当地银行交单议付了，由于该信用证是自由议付信用证，受益人可以到当地任何银行交单议付。

第三节　信用证结算中其他单据

信用证中对单据的要求因进口国不同、开证申请人不同而不同。一般来说，欧洲国家银行开出的信用证对单据的要求比较少，而来自中东国家、美国的信用证对单据种类的要求比较多。除了本章第一节信用证中所提到的单据外，以下几种单据也会出现在信用证中。有些单据可能不在“DUCUMENTS REQUIRED”项下，而是出现在“ADDITIONAL CONDITIONS” 项下。

一、装运通知(Shipping Advice)

（一）装运通知的含义和作用

装运通知又称 declaration of shipment 或 notice of shipment，系出口商向进口商发出货物已于某月某日或将于某月某日装运某船的通知。装运通知的作用在于方便买方购买保险或准备提货手续，其内容通常包括货名、装运数量、船名、装船日期、契约或信用证号码等。装运通知的作用在于方便买方投立保险、准备提货手续或转售；出口商作此项通知时，有时附上或另行寄上货运单据副本，以便进口商明了装货内容。

在实际业务操作中，由于保险单承保的起讫地点为 W/W(仓至仓)，所以在 FOB 或 CFR 贸易术语下，由于投保方是买方，卖方应于货物运至保险单所载起运地点仓库之前将装船通知发给买方，提醒买方及时投保。在 CIF 贸易术语中，卖方也应于装船前办理投保手续，以便在货物装船时遇到损失可以得到赔偿。

（二）装运通知的内容

在信用证付款方式中，信用证可能对装船通知的内容有详细规定，所以如果是根据信用证要求做装船通知，首先要把要求的内容写进去。除此之外，装运通知应包括货物名称、唛头、包装及数量、金额、船名、航次、发货港、目的港、发票号、提单号、预计到港日期等。

（三）信用证中的装运通知举例

INSURANCE COVERED BY BUYER. SHIPPING ADVICE MUST BE SENT TO SWISS INSURANCE CO.，LTD. P. O. BOX NO. 397，ZURICH BY REGISTERED AIRMAIL IMMEDIATELY AFTER SHIPMENT. ADVISING FULL DETAILED SHIPPING PARTICULARS, SUCH COPY OF SHIPPING ADVICE TO ACCOMPANY THE DOUCMENTS FOR NEGOTIATION.

该条款规定保险由买方办理。卖方必须在发货后立即通过航空挂号将装运通知寄给 SWISS INSURANCE CO.，LTD. P. O. BOX NO. 397，ZURICH。装运通知必须列明货物的详细信息，并把装运通知的复印件和其他单据一并交至银行议付。

根据该项要求，卖方需要制作一份装运通知，并按指定的地址寄走，装运通知的复印件则要交至银行议付。装运通知没有固定的格式，但制作时应包括以下内容：

1. 出口商的公司名称。

2. 标题。按信用证要求，一般为 SHIPPING ADVICE，DECLARATION OF SHIPMENT 等。

3. 装运通知抬头。按信用证要求填写，通常为买方、保险公司、或信用证指定的公司。

4. 日期。按照信用证要求的日期范围填写。

5. 合同号、信用证号、商业发票号。

6. 船、货明细。

7. 声明文句。

8. 发货人签章。

SHANGHAI INTERNATIONAL COMPANY

ADD. 22NANJING ROAD, SHANGHAI,CHINA

SHIPPING ADVICE

TO：SWISS INSURANCE CO.，LTD. DATE：JUL. 10，2017

P. O. BOX NO. 397，ZURICH INVOICE NO：AB17010

L/C NO.：LC089E12 S/C NO.：CBN171210

NAME OF GOODS：WOODEN DESKS

QUANTITY：1000PCS

PACKING：1000CARTONS

SHIPPING MARKS：N/M

AMOUNT：USD15000.00

VESSEL NAME：HUAHAI E/39

B/L NO.：DS908723879

PORT OF LOADING：SHANGHAI PORT，CHINA

PORT OF DESTINATION：LONDON，UK

ETD.：JUL. 12，2017

ETA.：AUG. 10，2017

SHANGHAI INTERNATIONAL COMPANY （法人代表签字章）

二、受益人证明（Beneficiary's Certificate）

受益人证明是信用证中规定由受益人自己签发的证明文件，证明自己已经履行某项义务，例如证明自己交货的品质符合合同的要求、证明自己已经按期寄给买方单据等。

（一）信用证中受益人证明/声明条款示例

1. Beneficiary's declaration that one complete set of non-negotiable shipping documents set directly to the applicant by express airmail within 2 days after shipment.

2. Beneficiary's certificate certify that each package to be marked with "MADE IN CHINA".

（二）受益人证明/声明的缮制

1.

SHANGHAI INTERNATIONAL COMPANY

ADD. 22NANJING ROAD，SHANGHAI，CHINA

BENEFICIARY'S DECLARATION

TO：WHOM IT MAY CONCERN　　　DATE：JUL. 12，2017

WE HEREBY DECLARE THAT ONE SET OF NOE-NEGOTIABLE SHIPPING DOCUMENTS HAS BEEN SET DIRECTLY TO THE APPLICANT BY EXPRESS AIRMAIL WITHIN 2 DAYS AFTER SHIPMENT.

SHANGHAI INTERNATIONAL COMPANY （法人代表签字章）

制作此证明要注意以下几点：

(1) 证明文件要有标头，即受益人公司名址。

(2) 证明文件要有标题，标题要和信用证的要求一致。

(3) 证明文件内容的时态要用一般完成时，意即该事件已经做了。

(4) 若证明文件有时间要求，则证明文件中的时间要符合逻辑。如上述证明中，要求时间是货物装船后 2 天，那么该证明的制作时间应该是提单日期后的 2 天内。

(5) 证明文件最后要求受益人的签章。

2.

SHANGHAI INTERNATIONAL COMPANY

ADD. 22NANJING ROAD, SHANGHAI,CHINA

BENEFICIRY'S CERTIFICATE

TO: WHOM IT MAY CONCERN　　DATE:JUL. 12,2017

WE HEREBY CERTIFY THAT EACH CARTON HAS BEEN MARKED WITH " MADE IN CHINA".

SHANGHAI INTERNATIONAL COMPANY
(法人代表签字章)

该证明制作的要点：

(1) 证明文件要有标头，即受益人公司名址。

(2) 证明文件要有标题，标题要和信用证的要求一致。

(3) 证明文件内容的时态要用一般完成时，意即该事件已经做了。

(4) 信用证中的证明文件的"PACKAGE"要换成具体的包装名称。

三、船公司证明(Shipping Company's Certificate)

船公司证明也是信用证要求提交的单据中常见的文件，多见于中东国家开来的信用证。这类证明文件一般要求承运人或其代理证明船籍、船龄、航行路线等。

(一) 信用证中的船公司证明条款示例

A certificate from the shipping company or their agent certifying that the goods are shipped on vessels that are allowed by Arab authorities to call at Arabian ports and not scheduled to call at any Israeli port during its voyage to the UAE.

(二) 船公司证明的缮制

缮制该类证明文件时，一般是由受益人将证明文件打印好，然后寄给承运人或货代，由其签字盖章后再寄回，受益人将其交至银行议付。缮制时需注意如下几点：

1. 证明文件无须标头，也就是说无须写受益人的公司名址。

2. 证明文件要有标题，标题要和信用证的要求一致。

3. 证明文件中的英语时态一般用一般现在时即可，也就是说和信用证中的时态一般是一致的。

4. 证明文件最后的签章必须是和提单上的签章一致的。

CERTIFICATE

TO WHOM IT MAY CONCERN　　　DATE：JUL. 12，2017

WE HEREBY CERFIFY THAT THE CARRYING VESSEL（HUAHAI E/39）THAT ARE ALLOWED BY ARAB AUTHORITIES TO CALL AT ANY ARABIAN PORTSAND NOT SCHEDULED TO CALL AT ANY ISRAELI PORTS DURING ITS VOYAGE TO THE UAE.

CHINA SHIPPING COMPANY （法人代表签字章）

本章小结

本章主要讲述了信用证的主要条款及各条款要求受益人应注意的问题、信用证结算中各种单据的制作。通过本章的学习，要求学生能够读懂信用证，在实际工作中能够独立的按照信用证的要求制作各种单据，并学会灵活运用各种单据。

根据下列信用证，缮制一套议付单据。

34127 B BOCSH CN

6229

1705 03/25 04803089 TCH0063

0325004658

ZCZC

FROM：Commercial Bank of London

OUR REF：LD980520004658001T01

TO：BANK OF CHINA DALIAN BRANCH

50 HUQIU ROAD，DALIAN

PEOPLE'S REP. OF CHINA

TEST：FOR USD/200，000.00 ON DATE14/03/2016

PLEASE ADVICE BENEFICIARY OF THE FOLLOWING IRREVOCABLE LETTER OF CREDIT

ISSUED BY US IN THEIR FAVOR SUBJECT TO UCP 500：
DOCUMENTARY CREDIT NUMBER：DRG-LDLC01
DATE AND PLACE OF EXPIRY：May 10th 2016，IN U. S. A.
APPLICANT：ADAM INDUSTRY CO.，LTD.
21 GUARD STREET LONDON，PA4561，UK.
BENEFICIARY：DALIAN CHEM IMP. & EXP. CO.，LTD.
Add：CHEM BLDG.，No. 61 RENMIN ROAD，DALIAN 116001，CHINA
AMOUNT：USD200，000. 00
AVALIABLE WITH：ANY BANK
BY：NEGOTIATIN OF BENEFICIARY'S DRAFT(S) AT 30 DAYS' SIGHT DRAWN ON COMMERCIAL BANK OFLONDON ACCOMPANIED BY THE DOCUMENTS INDICATED HEREIN.
DESCRIPTION OF COMMODITY：MUFFLER AS PER CONTRACT
NO.：AD018

ART NO.	QUANTITY	UNIT PRICE
MUFFLER－2	1000DOZS	USD80. 00
MUFFLER－4	1200 DOZS	USD100. 00

SHIPPING TERMS：CIF LONDON，UK
SHIPPING MARK：
LD－DRGSC01
ADAM INDUSTRY
LONDON/NO. 1－UP
DOCUMENTS REQUIRED：
—3 COPIES OF COMMERCIAL INVOICE INDICATING L/C NUMBER AND DATE.
—2COPIES OF PACKING LIST SHOWING GROSS/NET WEIGHT AND MEASUREMENT OF EACH CARTON.
—1 ORIGINAL PLUS ONE COPY OF GSP FORM A ISSUED BY AUTHORITIED BUREAU.
—2 COPIES OF INSURANCE POLICY OR CERTIFICATE ENDORSED IN BLANK FOR THE INVOICE VALUE OF THE GOODS PLUS 10% COVERING ALL RISKS AND WAR RISK AS PER AND SUBJECT TO OCEAN MARINE CARGO CLAUSES OF THE PEOPLE'S INSURANCE COMPANY OF CHINA DATED 1/1/1981.
—3/3 SET AND ONE COPY OF CLEAN ON BOARD OCEAN BILLS OF LADING MADE OUT TO ORDER AND BLANK ENDORSED MARKED FREIGHT PREPAID AND NOTIFY APPLICANT.
PARTIAL SHIPMENTS： PERMITTED
TRANSSHIPMENTS： PERMITTED

SHIPMENT FROM:　　DALIAN, CHINA　　TO: LONDON
NOT LATER THAN:　　APRIL 30, 2016
DOCUMENTS MUST BE PRESENTED WITHIN 15DAYS AFTER SHIPMENT, BUT
WITHIN VALIDITY OF THE LETTER OF CREDIT.

INSTRUCTIONS TO THE PAYING/ACCEPTING /NEGOTIATING BANK
NEGOTIATING BANK IS TO FORWARD ALL DOCUMENTS IN ONE AIRMAIL TO CHEMICAL BANK NEW YORK, 55 PETER STREET, ROOM 1702, LONDON, LONDON 10041 UK ATTN: LETTER OF CREDIT DEPARTMENT
END OF MESSAGE
NN/
62814 CBC VW
(WRU)
34127 8B BOCSH CN

其他材料:

货物型号	包装	净重	毛重	包装尺寸
MUFFLER－2	10DOZS/CTN	15KGS/CTN	17KGS/CTN	50X40X25CM
MUFFLER－4	10DOZS/CTN	20KGS/CTN	23KGS/CTN	50X40X25CM

装船日期:2016年4月25日
船名/航次:CHANGFENG/V.89E
受益人于2016年4月20号申办产地证明,货物完全国产。

第十三章 进口单证

学习目标

通过本章学习，要求学生能够掌握进口的基本流程，重点是学会申请开立信用证，并能够根据信用证的要求审核单据。

作为进口商，买方自己不需要制作单证，但买方要知道办理进口货物的通关手续所需要的单证。在签订合同之前，买方就要向检验检疫局、海关问清楚进口货物的手续及必需的单证，在跟卖方签合同时就要在合同中列明，只有在卖方提供了必需的单据后才能付款。如果付款方式是信用证，买方可以在申请开证时把所需要的单据写在信用证里，要求卖方交单议付。

第一节 进口货物的基本流程

一、交易前的准备

进口商在进口货物之前，应做好如下几项准备工作：

(一) 寻找可靠的供货商

进口商可以通过参加专业的国际展销会、国际知名的商务平台联系卖家。如果进口货物的金额较大，买方还应到卖方生产地进行实际考察，货比三家，最后和质优价廉、诚信度较高的供应商签合同。

(二) 联系货代

如果买方打算以 FOB 贸易术语购货，就要签订合同之前联系好货代，确定运费，以便于在同卖方谈判时核算成本，同时也便于及时把货代资料告知卖方。

(三) 备好购货资金，安排好仓储

一般来说，买方在签订购货合同之前应该预留资金，以便支付定金或者交付开证保证金，以免签订合同后资金不到位而影响合同的执行进度。

二、签订购货合同

选定好卖家后，买方应积极同卖方进行洽谈，以争取对己方有利的条件。如果购货金额较小，买方可以依次提出采用 D/P、T/T、L/C 付款方式。如果购货金额较大，买方可以要求采用 D/A 付款方式，尽可能地减少己方风险。

在签订购货合同时，买方还应把自己需要的单证写进去，以免货到时由于单证不全而影响办理进口手续。

三、支付订金或开立信用证

合同签订以后，买方应根据合同规定的付款方式，及时支付订金或开证。申请开立信用证时应注意如下几个问题：

（一）选择开证行

进口商在选择开证行时，一般选择与自己关系较为密切、信誉度较好的银行。选择这样的银行，一方面可以简化手续，另一方面易于被受益人接受。

（二）与银行谈妥保证金比例

开证行在给申请人开立信用证时，会根据申请人的信誉度以及与己方的关系收取一定比例的保证金。对于金额较小、信誉度一般的开证申请人，银行一般按开证金额收取100%的保证金；对于金额较大、信誉度较好的申请人，银行可以根据实际情况与其谈判，确定保证金收取的比例。

（三）递交有关合同的副本及附件

进口商在申请开证时，需向银行递交合同的副本及所需的附件，如进口许可证、相关部门的批文等。

（四）填写开证申请书

信用证中的条款，一般由申请人决定，申请人在申请书中要详细列明自己需要的单据，银行审核申请书后，附加上自身要求的条款，开立信用证。

（五）备妥相关文件交银行审验

银行一旦开出信用证，只要单证相符，就承担了不可撤销的付款责任。因此，为了避免日后付款时，因为有关文件不具备而导致银行付汇与国家政策相矛盾的情况发生，国家外汇管理局规定，申请人在申请开证时，必须备妥相关文件。如果进口属于我国许可证管辖范围内的，应提供许可证；申请人属于国家外汇管理局需要进行"真实性审查"的企业，或不在国家外汇管理局公布的"进口单位名录"里的企业，需要提供国家外汇管理局或其分支机构出具的备案表等。

（六）缴付保证金

（七）支付进口开证手续费

进口人在申请开证时，必须按照规定支付一定金额的开证手续费。

四、租船订舱

按照FOB贸易术语成交的合同，买方需要租船订舱。买方应在合同签订后及时落实船期，联系货代，并同货代签订运输委托合同，然后及早让货代联系卖方商定发货事宜。

五、投　保

以 FOB 或 CFR 成交的合同，买方要负责办理货物海上运输保险事宜。买方应及时联系卖方，让卖方在货物装船前发装船通知，以便及时投保。

六、审单付汇

卖方通过电子邮件或银行发来的单证，买方务必认真审核，确认单据符合自己的进口清关要求后，买方应及时付款赎取正本单据。

七、报关、验收、拨交货物

货物运抵目的地后，由进口企业或其代理人向海关办理申报手续，并配合海关查验货物；需要经进出口检验检疫主管部门检验方能进口的货物，要及时报检。验货时若发现货物数量短缺或质量与合同不符，应保留检验证据以供将来索赔时用。货物清关后，进口商可与实际用货单位结算货款并办理拨交手续。

八、进口索赔

进口商发现货物数量短缺或质量与合同不符合时，应按合同索赔期限的规定，及时向卖方提出索赔。如果是由于保险范围内自然灾害或意外事故造成的货物损失，应及时凭相关单证向保险公司提出索赔。

第二节　开证申请书的填制

开证申请书填制的主要依据是合同，一把来说，开证申请书中的条款不能与合同条款相抵触，所以买方在填制开证申请书时，应按照合同的条款，以免产生不必要的改证费。

填制开证申请书应注意如下问题：

1. DATE(申请开证日期)。在申请书右上角填写实际申请日期。

2. TO(致)。银行印制的申请书上事先都会印就开证银行的名称、地址，银行的 SWIFT CODE、TELEX NO 等也可同时显示。

3. PLEASE ISSUE ON OUR BEHALF AND/OR FOR OUR ACCOUNT THE FOLLOWING IRREVOCABLE LETTER OF CREDIT(请开列以下不可撤销信用证)。如果信用证是保兑或可转让的，应在此加注有关字样。开证方式多为电开(BY TELEX)，也可以是信开、快递或简电开立。

4. L/C NUMBER(信用证号码)。此栏由银行填写。

5. APPLICANT(申请人)。填写申请人的全称及详细地址，有的要求注明联系电话、传真号码等。

6. BENEFICIARY(受益人)。填写受益人的全称及详细地址。

7. ADVISING BANK(通知行)。受益人在签订合同时告知申请人己方的银行资料，由申请人据此填写。

8. AMOUNT(信用证金额)。分别用数字和文字两种形式表示,并且表明币制。如果允许有一定比率的上下浮动,要在信用证中明确表示出来。

9. EXPIRY DATE AND PLACE(到期日期和地点),填写信用证的有效期及到期地点。

10. PARTIAL SHIPMENT(分批装运)、TRANSHIPMENT(转运)。根据合同的实际规定打"×"进行选择。

11. LOADING IN CHARGE、FOR TRANSPORT TO、LATEST DATE OF SHIPMENT(装运地/港、目的地/港的名称,最迟装运日期)。按实际填写,如允许有转运地/港,也应清楚标明。

12. CREDIT AVAILABLE WITH/BY(付款方式)。在所提供的即期、承兑、议付和延期付款四种信用证有效兑付方式中选择与合同要求一致的类型。

13. BENEFICIARY'S DRAFT(汇票要求)。金额应根据合同规定填写为:发票金额的一定百分比;发票金额的100%(全部货款都用信用证支付);如部分信用证,部分托收时按信用证下的金额比例填写。付款期限可根据实际填写即期或远期,如属后者必须填写具体的天数。信用证条件下的付款人通常是开证行,也可能是开证行指定的另外一家银行。

14. DOCUMENTS REQUIRED(单据条款)。各银行提供的申请书中已印就的单据条款通常为十几条,从上至下一般为发票、运输单据(提单、空运单、铁路运输单据及运输备忘录等)、保险单、装箱单、质量证书、装运通知和受益人证明等,最后一条是 OTHER DOCUMENTS,IF ANY(其他单据),如要求提交超过上述所列范围的单据就可以在此栏填写,比如有的合同要求 CERTIFICATE OF NO SOLID WOOD PACKING MATERIAL(无实木包装材料证明)、CERTIFICATE OF FREE SALE(自由销售证明书)、CERTIFICATE OF CONFORMITY(合格证明书)等。申请人填制这部分内容时应依据合同规定,不能随意增加或减少。选中某单据后对该单据的具体要求(如一式几份、要否签字、正副本的份数、单据中应标明的内容等)也应如实填写,如申请书印制好的要求不完整应在其后予以补足。

15. COVERING/EVIDENCING SHIPMENT OF(商品描述)。所有内容(品名、规格、包装、单价、唛头)都必须与合同内容相一致,价格条款里附带"AS PER INCOTERMS2000"、数量条款中规定"MORE OR LESS"或"ABOUT"、使用某种特定包装物等特殊要求必须清楚列明。

16. ADDITIONAL INSTRUCTIONS(附加指示)。该栏通常体现为以下一些条款:

＋ALL DOCUMENTS MUST INDICATE CONTRACT NUMBER(所有单据加列合同号码)。

＋ALL BANKING CHARGES OUTSIDE THE OPENING BANK ARE FOR BENEFICIARY'S ACCOUNT(所有开证行以外的银行费用由受益人承担)。

＋BOTH QUANTITY AND AMOUNT FOR EACH ITEM % MORE OR LESS ALLOWED(每项数量与金额允许 %增减)。

＋THIRD PARTY AS SHIPPER IS NOT ACCEPTABLE(第三方作为托运人是不能接受的)。

＋DOCUMENTS MUST BE PRESNTED WITHIN xxx DAYS AFTER THE DATE OF ISSUANCE OF THE TRANSPORT DOCUMENTS BUT WITHIN THE

VALIDITY OF THIS CREDIT(单据必须在提单日后 xxx 天送达银行并且不超过信用证有效期)。

＋ SHORT FORM/BLANK BACK/CLAUSED/CHARTER PARTY B/L IS UNACCEPTABLE(银行不接受略式/不清洁/租船提单)。

＋ ALL DOCMENTS TO BE FORWARDED IN ONE COVER, UNLESS OTHERWISE STATED ABOVE(除非有相反规定,所有单据应一次提交)。

＋ PREPAID FREIGHT DRAWN IN EXCESS OF L/C AMOUNT IS ACCEPTABLE AGAINST PRESENTATION OF ORIGINAL CHARGES VOUCHER ISSUED BY SHIPPING CO. /AIR LINE OR ITS AGENT(银行接受凭船公司/航空公司或其代理人签发的正本运费收据索要超过信用证金额的预付运费)。

＋DOCUMENT ISSUED PRIOR TO THE DATE OF ISSUANCE OF CREDIT NOT ACCEPTABLE(不接受早于开证日出具的单据)。

如需要已印就的上述条款,可在条款前打"×",对合同涉及但未印就的条款还可以做补充填写。

17. NAME, SIGNATURE OF AUTHORISED PERSON, TEL NO., FAX, ACCOUNT NO.(授权人名称、签字、电话、传真、账号等内容)。

IRREVOCABLE DOCUMENTARY CREDIT APPLICATION

<table>
<tr><td colspan="2">TO:</td><td>DATE:</td></tr>
<tr><td colspan="2">□Issue by airmail
□With brief advice by teletransmission
□Issue by express delivery
□Issue by teletransmission (which shall be the operative instrument)</td><td>Credit No.

Date and place of expiry</td></tr>
<tr><td colspan="2">Applicant</td><td>Beneficiary (Full name and address)</td></tr>
<tr><td colspan="2">Advising Bank</td><td>Amount</td></tr>
<tr><td>Partial shipments
□allowed
□not allowed</td><td>Transhipment
□allowed
□not allowed</td><td rowspan="3">Credit available with

By
□sight payment □acceptance
□negotiation
□deferred payment at against the documents detailed herein
□and beneficiary's draft(s) for ____ % of invoice value at ________________ sight
drawn on</td></tr>
<tr><td colspan="2">Loading on board/dispatch/taking in charge at/from not later than
For transportation to:</td></tr>
<tr><td colspan="2">□FOB □CFR □CIF
□or other terms</td></tr>
</table>

（续表）

Documents required:（marked with X）
1. (　) Signed commercial invoice in ____ copies indicating L/C No. and Contract No.
2. (　) Full set of clean on board Bills of Lading made out to order and blank endorsed, marked "freight [　] to collect / [　]
prepaid [　] showing freight amount" notifying ________________________.
(　) Airway bills/cargo receipt/copy of railway bills issued by ________________________
showing "freight [　] to collect/[　] prepaid [　] indicating freight amount" and consigned to ____.
3. (　) Insurance Policy/Certificate in ______ copies for ______ % of the invoice value showing claims payable in ________________________ incurrency of the draft, blank endorsed, covering All Risks, War Risks and ________________________.
4. (　) Packing List/Weight Memo in _______ copies indicating quantity, gross and weights of each package.
5. (　) Certificate of Quantity/Weight in _______ copies issued by ________________________.
6. (　) Certificate of Quality in ______ copies issued by [　] manufacturer/[　] public recognized surveyor ________________________.
7. (　) Certificate of Origin in ________ copies.
8. (　) Beneficiary's certified copy of fax / telex dispatched to the applicant within ________ days after shipment advising L/C No. , nameof vessel, date of shipment, name, quantity, weight and value of goods.

Other documents, if any

Description of goods:

Additional instructions:
1. (　) All banking charges outside the opening bank are for beneficiary's account.
2. (　) Documents must be presented within ____ days after date of issuance of the transport documents but within the validity of this credit.
3. (　) Third party as shipper is not acceptable, Short Form/Blank back B/L is not acceptable.
4. (　) Both quantity and credit amount _______ % more or less are allowed.
5. (　) All documents must be sent to issuing bank by courier/speed post in one lot.
(　) Other terms, if any

第三节　主要进口单证

进口单证由卖方提供，买方一定要认真审核，以免影响办理进口通关手续。买方应在签订合同之前就向相关部门问清楚进口通关所需要的单证，在同卖方签订合同时把所需的单证写进合同里。

一、进口货物的商务单据

进口货物的相关单证是买方付款的主要依据和支付货款的唯一依据。主要包括：发票、装箱单、提单、品质与质量证明、原产地证明等。

（一）发票

它是国外卖方或厂商对货物出具的明细账单。它的作用主要是作为办理托运和结算上的一种重要单证，是买方办理通关手续的必备单证之一。

（二）提单

它是代表货物所有权的物权或运输契约。买方的付款以见到提单原件或副本为前提。

（三）装箱单

它是辅助发票说明不足之处，并详细说明包装的内容或货物的数量，以供买方办理货运、仓储参考，也是买方办理通关手续的必备单据之一。

（四）原产地证明

主要是证明货物的产地，是进口国海关征收关税的主要依据之一，也是买方办理通关手续的必备单据之一。

（五）保险单证

进口商如果采用的 CIF 贸易术语成交，出口商应提供保险单给买方，如果货物在运输途中遭遇损失，买方可以据此向保险公司索赔。

二、进口接货单证

（一）进口许可证

进口许可证是进口国采用的行政管理手续，它要求进口商向有关行政管理机构呈交申请书或其他文件，作为货物进口至海关边境的先决条件。即进口商进口商品必须凭申请到的进口许可证进行，否则一律不予进口的贸易管理制度。

1. 进口许可证的发放

进口许可证管理实行“一证一关”管理。一般情况下进口许可证为“一批一证”，如果要实行“非一批一证”，应当同时在进口许可证备注栏打印“非一批一证”字样。“一证一关”指进口许可证只能在一个海关报关；“一批一证”指进口许可证在有效期内一次报关使用；“非一批一证”是指进口许可证在有效期内可以多次报关使用，但最多不超过十二次，由海关在许可证背面“海关验放签注栏”内逐批签注核减进口数量。

2. 进口许可证的有效期

进口许可证的有效期为一年。进口许可证应当在进口管理部门批准文件规定的有效期内签发。进口许可证当年有效。特殊情况需要跨年度使用时，有效期最长不得超过次年 3 月 31 日。进口许可证应当在有效期内使用，逾期自动失效，海关不予放行。

（二）进口货物报关单

进口货物报关单是进口货物的收货人或其代理人向海关申请货物进口的凭证，也是海关验收进口货物的主要依据。

本章小结

本章介绍了进口的基本程序，以及在进口业务中所用到的单据。通过本章的学习，要求学生掌握货物进口的基本程序，学会填制开证申请书，学会审核卖方所提供的单据。

复习思考题

1. 申请开立信用证的基本程序有哪些？
2. 如何填制开证申请书？
3. 在进口程序中主要涉及哪些单据？

第十四章 信用证结算实训

学习目标

通过本章学习，要求学生在总结前面所学章节的基础上，融会贯通信用结算中单证的制作。读懂信用证、知晓信用证单证制作的相关技巧。

下面是中国出口商收到的一个信用证。阅读信用证，找出信用证要求提交的单据、单据制作的要求，并准确地制作单据。

MSGACK DWS765I AUTH OK, KEY B198081689580FC5, BKCHCNBJ RJHISARI RECORO		
BASIC HEADER		F 01 BKCHCNBJA940 0588 550628
APPLICATION HEADER		0 700 1057 010320 RJHISARIAXXX 7277 977367 020213 1557 ALRAJHI BANKING AND INVESTMENT CORPORATION * RIYADH * (HEAD OFFICE)
USER HEADER		SERVICE CODE 103: BANK. PRIORITY 113:MSG USER REF. 108: INFO. FROM CI 115:
SEQUENCE OF TOTAL	* 27	1 / 1
FORM OF DOC. CREDIT	* 40 A	IRREVOCABLE
DOC. CREDIT NUMBER	* 20	0011LC123756
DATE OF ISSUE	31 C	010320
DATE/ PLACE EXP.	* 31 D	DATE 010505 PLACE CHINA
APPLICANT	* 50	NEO GENERAL TRADING CO. P. O. BOX 99552, RIYADH 22766, KSA TEL: 00966 - 1 - 4659220 FAX: 00966 - 1 - 4659213
BENEFICIARY	* 59	DESUN TRADING CO., LTD. HUARONG MANSION RM2901 NO. 85 GUANJIAQIAO, NANJING 210005, CHINA TEL: 0086 - 25 - 4715004 FAX: 0086 - 25 - 4711363
AMOUNT	* 32 B	CURRENCY USD AMOUNT 13260

（续表）

AVAILABLE WITH/BY	*41 D	ANY BANK IN CHINA, BY NEGOTIATION
DRAFTS AT...	42 C	SIGHT
DRAWEE	42 A	RJHISARI * ALRAJHI BANKING AND INVESTMENT * CORPORATION * RIYADH *（HEAD OFFICE）
PARTIAL SHIPMTS	43 P	NOT ALLOWED
TRANSSHIPMENT	43 T	NOT ALLOWED
LOADING ON BRD	44 A	CHINA MAIN FORT, CHINA
FOR TRANSPORT TO	44 B	DAMMAM PORT, SAUDI ARABIA
LATEST SHIPMENT	44 C	010430
GOODS DESCRIPT	45 A	ABOUT 1700 CARTONS CANNED MUSRHOOM PIECES & STEMS 24 TINS X 425 GRAMS NET WEIGHT AT USD7. 80 PER CARTON CIF DAMMAM ROSE BRAND.
DOCS REQUIRED	46 A	DOCUMENTS REQUIRED: + SIGNED COMMERCIAL INVOICE IN TRIPLICATE ORIGINAL AND MUST SHOW BREAK DOWN OF THE AMOUNT AS FOLLOWS: FOB VALUE, FREIGHT CHARGES AND INSURANCE PREMIUM. + FULL SET CLEAN ON BOARD BILL OF LADING MADE OUT TO THE ORDER OF AL RAJHI BANKING AND INVESTMENT CORP, MARKED FREIGHT PREPAID AND NOTIFY APPLICANT, INDICATING THE FULL NAME, ADDRESS AND TEL NO. OF THE CARRYING VESSEL'S AGENT AT THE PORT OF DISCHARGE. + PACKING LIST IN ONE ORIGINAL PLUS 5 COPIES, ALL OF WHICH MUST BE MANUALLY SIGNED. + CERTIFICATE OF ORIGIN DULY CERTIFIED BY C. C. P. I. T. STATING THE NAME OF THE MANUFACTURERS OR PRODUCERS AND THAT GOODS EXPORTED ARE WHOLLY OF CHINESE ORIGIN. + THE PRODUCTION DATE OF THE GOODS NOT TO BE EARLIER THAN HALF MONTH AT TIME OF SHIPMENT. BENEFICIARY MUST CERTIFY THE SAME. + SHIPMENT TO BE EFFECTED BY CONTAINER AND BY REGULARE LINE. SHIPMENT COMPANY'S CERTIFICATE TO THIS EFFECT SHOULD ACCOMPANY THE DOCUMENTS.

（续表）

		＋INSURANCE POLICY OR CERTIFICATE IN 1 ORIGINAL AND 1 COPY ISSUED OR ENDORSED TO THE ORDER OF AL RAJHI BANKING AND INVESTMENT CORP FOR THE INVOICE PLUS 10 PERCENT COVERING INSTITUTE CARGO CLAUSES(A)，INSTITUTE STRIKES. ADDITIONAL CONDITION： ＋A DISCREPANCY FEE OF USD50.00 WILL BE IMPOSED ON EACH SET OF DOCUMENTS PRESENTED FOR NEGOTIATION UNDER THIS L/C WITH DISCREPANCY. THE FEE WILL BE DEDUCTED FROM THE BILL AMOUNT. PAYMENT UNDER THE GOODS WERE APPROVED BY SAUDI GOVERNMENT LAB. ＋SHIPPING ADVICE GIVING FULL DETAILS OF SHIPMENT INCLUDING CONTAINER NO. SEAL NO. INVOICE AMOUNT TOTAL QUANTITY TO BE SENT TO M/S. NEO GENERAL TRADING CO. FAX：00966－1－4659213 WITHIN THREE DAYS AFTER SHIPMENT，COPY OF THE SHIPPING ADVICE SHOULD BE ACCOMPANIED WITH THE DOCUMENTS. ＋EACH PACKAGE MUST SHOW ON BOTH OUTSIDE MADE IN CHINA，PACKING LIST SHOULD CERTIFY THE SAME. ＋A CERTIFICATE FROM THE SHIPPING COMPAY，CARRIER OR ITS AGENT REQUIRED STATING THAT THE CARRYING VESSEL（INDICATE NAME OF THE VESSEL）IS ISM（INTERNATIONAL SAFETY MANAGEMENT）CODE CETIFIED. ＋SHIPPING MARKS： NEO DAMMAM NO.1－UP
CHARGES	71 B	ALL CHARGES AND COMMISSIONS OUTSIDE KSA ON BENEFICIARIES' ACCOUNT INCLUDING REIMBURSING， BANK COMMISSION，DISCREPANCY FEE（IF ANY）AND COURIER CHARGES.
CONFIRMAT INSTR	＊49	WITHOUT
REIMBURS. BANK		AL RAJHI BANKING AND INVESTMENT CORP RIYADH（HEAD OFFICE）
INS PAYING BANK		DOCUMENTS TO BE DESPATCHED IN ONE LOT BY COURIER. ALL CORRESPONDENCE TO BE SENT TO ALRAJHI BANKING AND INVESTMENT COPRORATION RIYADH（HEAD OFFICE）
SEND REC INFO	72	REIMBURSEMENT IS SUBJECT TO ICC URR 525

（续表）

TRAILER	ORDER IS＜MAC:＞＜PAC:＞＜ENC:＞＜CHK:＞＜TNG:＞＜PDE:＞ MAC:E55927A4　CHK:7B505952829A　HOB:

一、确定信用证要求的单据

信用证要求提交的单据，除了在 DOCUMENTS REQUIRED 项下外，ADDITIONAL CONDITIONS 项下有时也有要求，卖方在阅读信用证是一定要注意不要遗漏。通过阅读该信用证，我们可以确定信用证要求如下单据及各单据的份数。

种　类	商业发票	装箱单	提单	保险单	产地证明	受益人证明	船公司证明 1	船公司证明 2	装船通知
正本份数	3	1	全套	1	1	1	1	1	1
副本份数		5		1					

二、确定信用证对各种单据内容的要求

（一）商业发票 COMMERCIAL INVOICE

首先要明确根据信用证制作商业发票时，信用证 DESCRIPTION OF GOODS 项下所有的内容必须体现在商业发票上。其次，要读懂该信用证对商业发票提出了要求"MUST SHOW BREAK DOWN OF THE AMOUNT AS FOLLOWS: FOB VALUE, FREIGHT CHARGES AND INSURANCE PREMIUM."意即商业发票必须分别显示出如下分解的金额:FOB 金额、运费、保险费。

（二）装箱单 PACKING LIST

该信用证 DOCUMENTS REQUIRED 项下对装箱单的内容没有提出额外要求，但是在 ADDITIONAL CONDITIONS 项下，对装箱单提出了要求"EACH PACKAGE MUST SHOW ON BOTH OUTSIDE MADE IN CHINA, PACKING LIST SHOULD CERTIFY THE SAME."意即在装箱单上需要显示证明事件的语句，证明"外包装两面有 MADE IN CHINA 字样"。

（三）提单 BILL OF LADING

该信用证对提单的内容提出的要求很多，主要包括如下几点：

1. CLEAN(清洁)，意即提单上不允许有任何关于货物或包装不良批注。

2. ON BOARD(已装船)，要求提单上盖有 SHIPPED ON BOARD 章。

3. 提单收货人要求"MADE OUT TO THE ORDER OF AL RAJHI BANKING AND INVESTMENT CORP,"意即提单的收货人一栏要按照信用证的要求填写 TO THE ORDER OF AL RAJHI BANKING AND INVESTMENT CORP。

4. MARKED FREIGHT PREPAID，要求在提单上标注上 FREIGHT PREPAID(运

费预付)。

5. NOTIFY APPLICANT,要求提单的通知人一栏按照信用证的要求填写申请人,要具体填写申请人的公司名址。

6. INDICATING THE FULL NAME, ADDRESS AND TEL NO. OF THE CARRYING VESSEL'S AGENT AT THE PORT OF DISCHARGE.要求在提单上标注出承运人在目的港代理的公司名称、地址和电话。这个需要受益人在和货代核对提单时要求货代直接把他们在目的港代理的公司名称、地址和电话填在提单上。

(四) 产地证明 CERTIFICATE OF ORIGIN

要求产地证明必须由贸促会签发,而且产地证明上必须加注两个内容:

1. THE NAME OF THE MANUFACTURERS OR PRODUCERS,意即在产地证明书上标注上货物制造商的公司名称。

2. GOODS EXPORTED ARE WHOLLY OF CHINESE ORIGIN,在产地证明上标注该证明语句,意即出口的货物完全原产自中国。

(五) 保险单 INSURANCE POLICY

内容要求如下3点:

1. 被保险人:按照信用证要求应填写 TO THE ORDER OF AL RAJHI BANKING AND INVESTMENT CORP。

2. 保险金额:按照发票金额的110%投保。

3. 承保险别:投保协会保险条款(A)以及协会战争险。

(六) 受益人证明

按照信用证要求证明的事件写一份证明,证明货物的生产日期是在开船前的一个月。

(七) 船公司证明

受益人按照信用证的要求写好证明,然后由船公司或其代理签章。

(八) 装船通知复印件

按照信用证要求的内容制作装船通知,通过传真发给申请人后,再把复印件连同其他单据一起交单议付。

三、具体制作信用证要求的单据

明确了信用证对各种单据要求后,就可根据实际发货情况和货物的具体信息制作单据了。具体发货信息如下:

(一) 装船日期

2001年4月25号。

(二) 货物毛重

每箱12千克,包装箱尺寸:50×40×20 cm。

(三) 发货港

上海。

（四）提单号

EFK239801。

（一）商业发票

DESUN TRADING CO.，LTD.

HUARONG MANSION RM2901 NO. 85 GUANJIAQIAO,
NANJING 210005，CHINA
TEL：0086 - 25 - 4715004 FAX：0086 - 25 - 4711363

COMMERCIAL INVOICE

TO：NEO GENERAL TRADING CO. INVOICE NO.：DT0102
P. O. BOX 99552，RIYADH 22766，KSA DATE：APR. 25，2001
TEL：00966 - 1 - 4659220 FAX：00966 - 1 - 4659213
SHIPMENT FROM SHANGHAI PORT，CHINA TO DAMMAM PORT，SAUDI ARABIA

SHIPPING MARKS	NAME OF GOODS	Q'TY	UNIT PRICE	AMOUNT
NEO DAMMAM NO. 1 - UP	ABOUT 1700 CARTONS CANNED MUSRHOOM PIECES & STEMS 24 TINS X 425 GRAMS NET WEIGHT AT USD7. 80 PER CARTON CIF DAMMAM ROSE BRAND. FOB VALUE：USD11200. 00 FRIEIGHT CHARGES：USD2000. 00 INSURANCE PREMIUM：USD60. 00			USD13260. 00
	TOTAL：	1700CTNS		USD13260. 00

SAY U. S. DOLLARS THIRTEEN THOUSAND TWO HUNDRED AND SIXTY ONLY.

DESUN TRADING CO., LTD.
（法人代表签字章）

（二）装箱单

DESUN TRADING CO.，LTD.

HUARONG MANSION RM2901 NO. 85 GUANJIAQIAO,
NANJING 210005，CHINA
TEL：0086 - 25 - 4715004 FAX：0086 - 25 - 4711363

PACKING LIST

INVOICE NO.：DT0102 DATE：APR. 25，2001
SHIPMENT FROM SHANGHAI PORT，CHINA TO DAMMAM PORT，SAUDI ARABIA

MARKS	NAME OF GOODS	QUANTITY	N. W. (KGS)	G. W. (KGS)	MEAS. CBM
NEO DAMMAM NO. 1 - UP	CANNED MUSRHOOM PIECES & STEMS	1700CARTONS	17340	20400	68.00
	TOTAL:	1700CARTONS	17340	20400	68.00

SAY SEVENTEEN THOUSAND CARTONS ONLY.
WE HERBY CERTIFY THAT EACH CARTON HAS SHOWN ON BOTH OUTSIDE MADE IN CHINA.

DESUN TRADING CO., LTD.
（法人代表签字章）

（三）提单

Shipper DESUN TRADING CO., LTD. HUARONG MANSION RM2901 NO. 85 GUANJIAQIAO, NANJING 210005, CHINA TEL: 0086 - 25 - 4715004 FAX: 0086 - 25 - 4711363	B/L NO. ***COSCO*** **OCEAN BILL OF LADING**		
Consignee TO THE ORDER OF AL RAJHI BANKING AND INVESTMENT CORP			
Notify Party NEO GENERAL TRADING CO. P. O. BOX 99552, RIYADH 22766, KSA TEL: 00966 - 1 - 4659220 FAX: 00966 - 1 - 4659213			
Vessel Name and Voyage Number ZHONGHUA/E198	Port of Loading SHANGHAI PORT, CHINA	Port of Discharge DAMMAM PORT, SAUDI ARABIA	
Place of Receipt	Place of Delivery	**Number of Original Bs/L** THREE	
PARTICULARS AS DECLARED BY SHIPPER—CARRIER NOT RESPONSIBLE			
Container Nos/Seal Nos. Marks and/Numbers	No. of Container / Packages / Description of Goods	Gross Weight (Kilos)	Measurement (cu-metres)

（续表）

NEO DAMMAM NO. 1－UP	SEVENTEENTHOUSAND(1700) CARTONS OF CANNED MUSRHOOM PIECES & STEMS 1X40′HFCL THE FULL NAME，ADDRESS AND TEL NO. OF THE CARRYING VESSEL'S AGENT AT THE PORT OF DISCHARGE.： THF LOGISTICS CO. P. O. BOX 289，DAMMAM. TEL：00966－3－5987253	20400	68.00
FREIGHT & CHARGES FRIEGHT PREPAID	Number of Containers/Packages (in words) SAY SEVENTEEN THOUSAND CARTONS ONLY.		
	Shipped on Board Date： APR. 25，2001		
	Place and Date of Issue： APR. 25，2001，SHANGHAI		
	In Witness Whereof this number of Original Bills of Lading stated Above all of the tenor and date one of which being accomplished the others to stand void.		

（四）产地证

1. Exporter DESUN TRADING CO.，LTD. HUARONG MANSION RM2901 NO. 85 GUANJIAQIAO，NANJING 210005，CHINA TEL：0086－25－4715004 FAX：0086－25－4711363	Certificate No.
2. Consignee NEO GENERAL TRADING CO. P. O. BOX 99552，RIYADH 22766，KSA TEL：00966－1－4659220 FAX：00966－1－4659213	**CERTIFICATE OF ORIGIN OF THE PEOPLE'S REPUBLIC OF CHINA**
3. Means of transport and route SHIPMENT FROM SHANGHAI PORT，CHINA TO DAMMAM PORT，SAUDI ARABIA BY SEAWAY	5. For certifying authority use only
4. Country/region of destination SAUDI ARABIA	

（续表）

6. Marks and numbers NEO DAMMAM NO. 1 - UP	7. Number and kind of packages; description of goods SEVENTEENTHOUSAND(1700) CARTONS OF CANNED MUSRHOOM PIECES & STEMS GOODS EXPORTED ARE WHOLLY OF CHINESE ORIGIN THE NAME OF MANUF ACTURER: DESUN TRADING CO., LTD.	8. H. S code 06029010	9. Quantity 20 400 KG	10. Number and date of invoices DT0102 APR. 25, 2001

11. Declaration by the exporter	12. Certification
The undersigned hereby declares that the above details and statements are correct; that all the goods were produced in china and that they comply with the rules of origin of the people's republic of china. .... Place and date, signature and stamp of certifying authority	It is hereby certified that the declaration by the exporter is correct. .... Place and date, signature and stamp of certifying authority

（五）保险单

中保财产保险有限公司

The People's Insurance (Property) Company of China, Ltd

发票号码 保险单号次

Invoice No. DT0102 Policy No. 019832589

海洋货物运输保险单

MARINE CARGO TRANSPORTATION INSURANCE POLICY

被保险人：

Insured: TO THE ORDER OF AL RAJHI BANKING AND INVESTMENT CORP

中保财产保险有限公司(以下简称本公司)根据被保险人的要求,及其所缴付约定的保险费,按照本保险单承担险别和背面所载条款与下列特别条款承保下列货物运输保险,特签发本保险单。

This policy of Insurance witnesses that the People's Insurance (Property) Company of China, Ltd. (hereinafter called "The Company"), at the request of the Insured and in consideration of the agreed premium paid by the Insured, undertakes to insure the undermentioned goods in transportation subject to conditions of the Policy as per the Clauses printed overleaf and other special clauses attached hereon.

保险货物项目 Descriptions of Goods	包装 Packing 单位 Unit 数量 Quantity	保险金额 Amount Insured
CANNED MUSRHOOM PIECES & STEMS	1 700CARTONS	USD14586.00

承保险别　　　　　　　　　　　　　　　　　　　货物标记
Conditions　　　　　　　　　　　　　　　　　　Marks of Goods
INSTITUTE CARGO CLAUSES(A),　　　　　　　　NEO
INSTITUTE STRIKES.　　　　　　　　　　　　　DAMMAM
NO. 1 - UP

总保险金额：
Total Amount Insured: SAY U. S. DOLLARS FORTEEN THOUSAND FIVE HUNDRED AND EIGHTY SIX ONLY.

保费　　　　　　　载运输工具　　　　　　　开航日期 APR. 25,2001
Premium AS ARRANGED Per conveyance S. S ZHONGHUA/E198 Slg. on or abt ____

起运港　　　　　　　　　　　　　　目的港
From SHANGHAI PORT, CHINA　　　TO DAMMAM PORT, SAUDI ARABIA

赔款偿付地点　　　　　　　　　　　理赔公司名址：
Claim payable at ____________　　Claim to: ____________

（六）受益人证明

DESUN TRADING CO. , LTD.

HUARONG MANSION RM2901 NO. 85 GUANJIAQIAO,
NANJING 210005, CHINA
TEL:0086 - 25 - 4715004　FAX: 0086 - 25 - 4711363

BENEFICIARY'S CERTIFICATE

DATE: APR. 20,2001

WE HEREBY CERTIFY THAT THE PRODUCTION DATE OF THE GOODS IS APR. 20,2001,NOT EARLIER THAN HALF MONTH AT TIME OF SHIPMENT.

DESUN TRADING CO., LTD.
（法人代表签字章）

（七）船公司证明 1

SHIPPING COMPANY'S CERTIFICATE

DATE: APR. 26,2001

WE HEREBY CERTIFY THAT THE SHIPMENT HAS BEEN EFFECTED BY CONTAINER AND BY REGULARE LINE.

COSCO
（法人代表签字章）

（八）船公司证明 2

SHIPPING COMPANY'S CERTIFICATE

DATE：APR. 26，2001

WE HEREBY CERTIFY THAT THE CARRYING VESSEL（VESSEL NAME：ZHONGHUA/E198）IS ISM （INTERNATIONAL SAFETY MANAGEMENT）CODE CETIFIED.

COSCO
（法人代表签字章）

（九）装船通知

DESUN TRADING CO.，LTD.

HUARONG MANSION RM2901 NO. 85 GUANJIAQIAO，

NANJING 210005，CHINA

TEL：0086－25－4715004 FAX：0086－25－4711363

SHIPPING ADVICE

DATE：APR. 25，2001

TO M/S. NEO GENERAL TRADING CO.

FAX：00966－1－4659213

WE HEREBY CERTIFY THAT THE SHIPPING ADVICE WITH THE FOLLOWING FULL DETAILS OF SHIPMENT HAS BEEN SET TO M/S. NEO GENERAL TRADING CO. FAX：00966－1－4659213 WITHIN 3 DAYS AFTER SHIPMENT.

NAME OF GOODS：CANNED MUSRHOOM PIECES & STEMS

INVOICE AMOUNT：USD13260.00

TOTAL QUANTITY：1700CARTONS

VESSEL NAME：ZHONGHUA/E198

SHIPMENT FROM SHANGHAI PORT，CHINA TO DAMMAM PORT，SAUDI ARABIA

CONTAINER NO. / SEAL NO.：TESU25782/S24578

ETD.：APR. 25，2001 ETA.：MAY 25，2001

DESUN TRADING CO., LTD.
（法人代表签字章）

本章小结

本章主要是在结合前面所学章节的基础上，让学生做信用证结算方式中单证的模拟操作实训。通过实训，要求学生能够在实际工作中根据信用证准确地制作要求的单据。

复习思考题

根据下列信用证及其他材料制作单据。

FROM: THE MASHREQ BANK PSC. P. O. BOX9271. DUBAI, U. A. E.
TO: SHANGHAI BANKING CORP., SHANGHAI
SEQUENCE OF TOTAL　1/1
FORM OF DOC. CREDIT　IRREVOCABLE
DOC. CREDIT NUMBER　DBS 268330
DATE OF ISSUE　090205
EXPIRY　DATE 090520 PLACE IN COUNTRY OF BENEFICIARY
APPLICANT　SALAM　CO.,
P. O. BOX 3472, DUBAI, U. A. E.
BENEFICIARY　HANGZHOU ART IMP. &EXP. CO. LTD.
191 BAOCHU ROAD, HANGZHOU, CHINA
CURRENCY AMOUNT　USD AMOUNT 21,000. 00
AVAILABLE WITH/BY　ANY BANK BY NEGOTIATION
DRAFT AT　AT SIGHT
PARTIAL SHIPMENT　ALLOWED
TRANSSHIPMENT　NOT ALLOWED
PORT OF LOADING　ANY ASIAN PORT
FOR TRANSPORT TO　DUBAI, U. A. E.
LATEST DATE OF SHIP.　090505
DESCRIPT. OF GOODS　FOB SHANGHAI
WOODEN DESKS　AS PER S/C NO. LLD1232
WD001　600PCS　USD10. 00/PC
WD002　1000PCS　USD15. 00/PC
DOCUMENTS REQUIRED
+ SIGNED COMMERCIAL INVOICE IN THREE COPIES SHOWING INDENT NO. LL/5687/BU AND THE L/C NUMBER.
+ PACKING LIST IN THREE COPIES. SHOWING QUANTITY, NET WEIGHT, GROSS WEIGHT AND MEASUREMENT OF EACH PACKAGE.

+ 3/3 OCEAN ON BOARD BILLS OF LADING, MADE OUT TO ORDER AND BLANK ENDOSED, MARKED FREIGHT COLLECT AND NOTIFY APPLICANT.

+ CERTIFICATE OF ORIGIN IN 1 ORIGINAL AND 1 COPY CERTIFY ALL GOODS ARE CONFORM TO S/C NO. OM298.

+ BENEFICIARY'S CERTIFICATE THAT ONE SET OF NON - NEGOTIABLE DOCUMENTS HAS BEEN SENT TO APPLICANT BY UPS.

+ CERTIFICATE FROM SHIPPING COMPANY OR ITS AGENT THAT GOODS ARE SHIPPED IN FCL CONDITIONS

PRESENTATION PERIOD WITHIN 15DAYS AFTER THE DATE OF SHIPMENT BUT WITHIN THE VALIDITY OF THE CREDIT

CONFIRMATION WITHOUT

……

其他材料:

货物净重

尺码:WD001　20KGS

WD002　30KGS

唛头:WD/SALAM

包装箱重量、尺码:

WD001　2千克/个　80×60×40 cm

WD002　3千克/个 100×80×50 cm

包装:1只/箱

附　录

《跟单信用证统一惯例》(UCP600)

Article 1 Application of UCP

The Uniform Customs and Practice for Documentary Credits, 2007 Revision, ICC Publication no. 600 ("UCP") are rules that apply to any documentary credit ("credit") (including, to the extent to which they may be applicable, any standby letter of credit) when the text of the credit expressly indicates that it is subject to these rules. They are binding on all parties thereto unless expressly modified or excluded by the credit.

Article 2 Definitions

For the purpose of these rules:

Advising bank means the bank that advises the credit at the request of the issuing bank.

Applicant means the party on whose request the credit is issued.

Banking day means a day on which a bank is regularly open at the place at which an act subject to these rules is to be performed.

Beneficiary means the party in whose favour a credit is issued.

Complying presentation means a presentation that is in accordance with the terms and conditions of the credit, the applicable provisions of these rules and international standard banking practice.

Confirmation means a definite undertaking of the confirming bank, in addition to that of the issuing bank, to honour or negotiate a complying presentation.

Confirming bank means the bank that adds its confirmation to a credit upon the issuing bank's authorization or request.

Credit means any arrangement, however named or described, that is irrevocable and thereby constitutes a definite undertaking of the issuing bank to honour a complying presentation.

Honour means:

a. to pay at sight if the credit is available by sight payment.

b. to incur a deferred payment undertaking and pay at maturity if the credit is available by deferred payment.

c. to accept a bill of exchange ("draft") drawn by the beneficiary and pay at maturity if the credit is available by acceptance.

Issuing bank means the bank that issues a credit at the request of an applicant or on its own behalf.

Negotiation means the purchase by the nominated bank of drafts (drawn on a bank other than the nominated bank) and/or documents under a complying presentation, by advancing or agreeing to advance funds to the beneficiary on or before the banking day on which reimbursement is due to the nominated bank.

Nominated bank means the bank with which the credit is available or any bank in the case of a credit available with any bank.

Presentation means either the delivery of documents under a credit to the issuing bank or nominated bank or the documents so delivered.

Presenter means a beneficiary, bank or other party that makes a presentation

Article 3 Interpretations

For the purpose of these rules:

Where applicable, words in the singular include the plural and in the plural include the singular.

A credit is irrevocable even if there is no indication to that effect.

A document may be signed by handwriting, facsimile signature, perforated signature, stamp, symbol or any other mechanical or electronic method of authentication.

A requirement for a document to be legalized, visaed, certified or similar will be satisfied by any signature, mark, stamp or label on the document which appears to satisfy that requirement.

Branches of a bank in different countries are considered to be separate banks.

Terms such as "first class", "well known", "qualified", "independent", "official", "competent" or "local" used to describe the issuer of a document allow any issuer except the beneficiary to issue that document.

Unless required to be used in a document, words such as "prompt", "immediately" or "as soon as possible" will be disregarded.

The expression "on or about" or similar will be interpreted as a stipulation that an event is to occur during a period of five calendar days before until five calendar days after the specified date, both start and end dates included.

The words "to", "until", "till", "from" and "between" when used to determine a period of shipment include the date or dates mentioned, and the words "before" and "after" exclude the date mentioned.

The words "from" and "after" when used to determine a maturity date exclude the date mentioned.

The terms "first half" and "second half" of a month shall be construed respectively as the 1st to the 15th and the 16th to the last day of the month, all dates inclusive.

The terms "beginning", "middle" and "end" of a month shall be construed respectively as the 1st to the 10th, the 11th to the 20th and the 21st to the last day of the month, all dates inclusive.

Article 4 Credits v. Contracts

a. A credit by its nature is a separate transaction from the sale or other contract on which it may be based. Banks are in no way concerned with or bound by such contract, even if any reference whatsoever to it is included in the credit. Consequently, the undertaking of a bank to honour, to negotiate or to fulfil any other obligation under the credit is not subject to claims or defences by the applicant resulting from its relationships with the issuing bank or the beneficiary. A beneficiary can in no case avail itself of the contractual relationships existing between banks or between the applicant and the issuing bank.

b. An issuing bank should discourage any attempt by the applicant to include, as an integral part of the credit, copies of the underlying contract, proforma invoice and the like.

Article 5 Documents v. Goods, Services or Performance

Banks deal with documents and not with goods, services or performance to which the documents may relate.

Article 6 Availability, Expiry Date and Place for Presentation

a. A credit must state the bank with which it is available or whether it is available with any bank. A credit available with a nominated bank is also available with the issuing bank.

b. A credit must state whether it is available by sight payment, deferred payment, acceptance or negotiation.

c. A credit must not be issued available by a draft drawn on the applicant.

d. i. A credit must state an expiry date for presentation. An expiry date stated for honour or negotiation will be deemed to be an expiry date for presentation.

ii. The place of the bank with which the credit is available is the place for presentation. The place for presentation under a credit available with any bank is that of any bank. A place for presentation other than that of the issuing bank is in addition to the place of the issuing bank.

e. Except as provided in sub-article 29 (a), a presentation by or on behalf of the beneficiary must be made on or before the expiry date.

Article 7 Issuing Bank Undertaking

a. Provided that the stipulated documents are presented to the nominated bank or to the issuing bank and that they constitute a complying presentation, the issuing bank must honour if the credit is available by:

i. sight payment, deferred payment or acceptance with the issuing bank;

ii. sight payment with a nominated bank and that nominated bank does not pay;

iii. deferred payment with a nominated bank and that nominated bank does not incur its deferred payment undertaking or, having incurred its deferred payment undertaking, does not pay at maturity;

iv. acceptance with a nominated bank and that nominated bank does not accept a draft drawn on it or, having accepted a draft drawn on it, does not pay at maturity;

v. negotiation with a nominated bank and that nominated bank does not negotiate.

b. An issuing bank is irrevocably bound to honour as of the time it issues the credit.

c. An issuing bank undertakes to reimburse a nominated bank that has honoured or negotiated a complying presentation and forwarded the documents to the issuing bank. Reimbursement for the amount of a complying presentation under a credit available by acceptance or deferred payment is due at maturity, wheth-er or not the nominated bank prepaid or purchased before maturity. An issuing bank's undertaking to reimburse a nominated bank is independent of the issuin-g bank's undertaking to the beneficiary.

Article 8 Confirming Bank Undertaking

a. Provided that the stipulated documents are presented to the confirming bank or to any other nominated bank and that they constitute a complying presentation, the confirming bank must:

i. honour, if the credit is available by

a) sight payment, deferred payment or acceptance with the confirming bank;

b) sight payment with another nominated bank and that nominated bank doe-s not pay;

c) deferred payment with another nominated bank and that nominated bank does not incur its deferred payment undertaking or, having incurred its deferred payment undertaking, does not pay at maturity;

d) acceptance with another nominated bank and that nominated bank does not accept a draft drawn on it or, having accepted a draft drawn on it, does not pay at maturity;

e) negotiation with another nominated bank and that nominated bank does not negotiate.

ii. negotiate, without recourse, if the credit is available by negotiation with the confirming bank.

b. A confirming bank is irrevocably bound to honour or negotiate as of the time it adds its confirmation to the credit.

c. A confirming bank undertakes to reimburse another nominated bank that has honoured or negotiated a complying presentation and forwarded the documents to the confirming bank. Reimbursement for the amount of a complying presentation under a creditavailable by acceptance or deferred payment is due at maturity, whether or not another nominated bank prepaid or purchased before maturity. A confirming bank's undertaking to reimburse another nominated bank is independent of the confirming bank's undertaking to the beneficiary.

d. If a bank is authorized or requested by the issuing bank to confirm a credit but is not prepared to do so, it must inform the issuing bank without delay and may advise the credit without confirmation.

Article 9 Advising of Credits and Amendments

a. A credit and any amendment may be advised to a beneficiary through an advising bank. An advising bank that is not a confirming bank advises the credit and any amendment without any undertaking to honour or negotiate.

b. By advising the credit or amendment, the advising bank signifies that it has satisfied itself as to the apparent authenticity of the credit or amendment and that the advice accurately reflects the terms and conditions of the credit or amendment received.

c. An advising bank may utilize the services of another bank ("second advising bank") to advise the credit and any amendment to the beneficiary. By advising the credit or amendment, the second advising bank signifies that it has satisfied itself as to the apparent authenticity of the advice it has received and that the advice accurately reflects the terms and conditions of the credit or amendment received.

d. A bank utilizing the services of an advising bank or second advising bank to advise a credit must use the same bank to advise any amendment thereto.

e. If a bank is requested to advise a credit or amendment but elects not to do so, it must so inform, without delay, the bank from which the credit, amendment or advice has been received.

f. If a bank is requested to advise a credit or amendment but cannot satisfy itself as to the apparent authenticity of the credit, the amendment or the advice, it must so inform, without delay, the bank from which the instructions appear to have been received. If the advising bank or second advising bank elects nonetheless to advise the credit or amendment, it must inform the beneficiary or second advising bank that it has not been able to satisfy itself as to the apparent authenticity of the credit, the amendment or the advice.

Article 10 Amendments

a. Except as otherwise provided by article 38, a credit can neither be amended nor cancelled without the agreement of the issuing bank, the confirming bank, if any, and the beneficiary.

b. An issuing bank is irrevocably bound by an amendment as of the time it issues the amendment. A confirming bank may extend its confirmation to an amendment and will be irrevocably bound as of the time it advises the amendment. A confirming bank may, however, choose to advise an amendment without extending its confirmation and, if so, it must inform the issuing bank without delay and inform the beneficiary in its advice.

c. The terms and conditions of the original credit (or a credit incorporating previously accepted amendments) will remain in force for the beneficiary until the beneficiary communicates its acceptance of the amendment to the bank that advised such amendment. The beneficiary should give notification of acceptance or rejection of an amendment. If the beneficiary fails to give such notification, a presentation that complies with the credit and to any not yet accepted amendment will be deemed to be notification of acceptance by the beneficiary of such amendment. As of that moment the credit will be amended.

d. A bank that advises an amendment should inform the bank from which it received the amendment of any notification of acceptance or rejection.

e. Partial acceptance of an amendment is not allowed and will be deemed to be notification of rejection of the amendment.

f. A provision in an amendment to the effect that the amendment shall enter into force unless rejected by the beneficiary within a certain time shall be disregarded.

Article 11 Teletransmitted and Pre-Advised Credits and Amendments

a. An authenticated teletransmission of a credit or amendment will be deemed to be the operative credit or amendment, and any subsequent mail confirmation shall be disregarded. If a teletransmission states "full details to follow" (or words of similar effect), or states that the mail confirmation is to be the operative credit or amendment, then the teletransmission will not be deemed to be the operative credit or amendment. The issuing bank must then issue the operative credit or amendment without delay in terms not inconsistent with the teletransmission.

b. A preliminary advice of the issuance of a credit or amendment ("pre-advice") shall only be sent if the issuing bank is prepared to issue the operative credit or amendment. An issuing bank that sends a pre-advice is irrevocably committed to issue the operative credit or amendment, without delay, in terms not inconsistent with the pre-advice.

Article 12 Nomination

a. Unless a nominated bank is the confirming bank, an authorization to honour or negotiate does not impose any obligation on that nominated bank to honour or negotiate, except when expressly agreed to by that nominated bank and so communicated to the beneficiary.

b. By nominating a bank to accept a draft or incur a deferred payment undertaking, an issuing bank authorizes that nominated bank to prepay or purchase a draft accepted or a deferred payment undertaking incurred by that nominated bank.

c. Receipt or examination and forwarding of documents by a nominated bank that is not a confirming bank does not make that nominated bank liable to honour or negotiate, nor does it constitute honour or negotiation.

Article 13 Bank-to-Bank Reimbursement Arrangements

a. If a credit states that reimbursement is to be obtained by a nominated bank ("claiming bank") claiming on another party ("reimbursing bank"), the credit must state if the reimbursement is subject to the ICC rules for bank-to-bank reimbursements in effect on the date of issuance of the credit.

b. If a credit does not state that reimbursement is subject to the ICC rules for bank-to-bank reimbursements, the following apply:

  i. An issuing bank must provide a reimbursing bank with a reimbursement authorization that conforms with the availability stated in the credit. The reimbursement authorization should not be subject to an expiry date.

  ii. A claiming bank shall not be required to supply a reimbursing bank with a certificate of compliance with the terms and conditions of the credit.

  iii. An issuing bank will be responsible for any loss of interest, together with any expenses incurred, if reimbursement is not provided on first demand by a reimbursing bank in accordance with the terms and conditions of the credit.

  iv. A reimbursing bank's charges are for the account of the issuing bank. However, if the charges are for the account of the beneficiary, it is the responsibility of an issuing bank to so indicate in the credit and in the reimbursement authorization. If a reimbursing bank's charges are for the account of the beneficiary, they shall be deducted from the amount due to a claiming bank when reimbursement is made. If no reimbursement is made, the reimbursing bank's charges remain the obligation of the issuing bank.

c. An issuing bank is not relieved of any of its obligations to provide reimbursement if reimbursement is not made by a reimbursing bank on first demand.

Article 14 Standard for Examination of Documents

a. A nominated bank acting on its nomination, a confirming bank, if any, and the issuing bank must examine a presentation to determine, on the basis of the documents alone, whether or not the documents appear on their face to constitute a complying presentation.

b. A nominated bank acting on its nomination, a confirming bank, if any, and the issuing bank shall each have a maximum of five banking days following the day of presentation to determine if a presentation is complying. This period is not curtailed or otherwise affected by the occurrence on or after the date of presentation of any expiry date or last day for presentation.

c. A presentation including one or more original transport documents subject to articles 19, 20, 21, 22, 23, 24 or 25 must be made by or on behalf of the beneficiary not later than 21 calendar days after the date of shipment as described in these rules, but in any event not later than the expiry date of the credit.

d. Data in a document, when read in context with the credit, the document itself and international standard banking practice, need not be identical to, but must not conflict with, data in that document, any other stipulated document or the credit.

e. In documents other than the commercial invoice, the description of the goods, services or performance, if stated, may be in general terms not conflicting with their description in the credit.

f. If a credit requires presentation of a document other than a transport document, insurance document or commercial invoice, without stipulating by whom the document is to be issued or its data content, banks will accept the document as presented if its content appears to fulfil the function of the required document and otherwise complies with sub-article 14 (d).

g. A document presented but not required by the credit will be disregarded and may be returned to the presenter.

h. If a credit contains a condition without stipulating the document to indicate compliance with the condition, banks will deem such condition as not stated and will disregard it.

i. A document may be dated prior to the issuance date of the credit, but must not be dated later than its date of presentation.

j. When the addresses of the beneficiary and the applicant appear in any stipulated document, they need not be the same as those stated in the credit or in any other stipulated document, but must be within the same country as the respective addresses mentioned in the credit. Contact details (telefax, telephone, email and the like) stated as part of the beneficiary's and the applicant's address will be disregarded. However, when the address and contact details of the applicant appear as part of the consignee or notify party details on a transport document subject to articles 19, 20, 21, 22, 23, 24 or 25, they must be as stated in the credit.

k. The shipper or consignor of the goods indicated on any document need not be the beneficiary of the credit.

l. A transport document may be issued by any party other than a carrier, owner, master or charterer provided that the transport document meets the requirements of articles 19, 20, 21, 22, 23 or 24 of these rules.

Article 15 Complying Presentation

a. When an issuing bank determines that a presentation is complying, it must honour.

b. When a confirming bank determines that a presentation is complying, it must honour or negotiate and forward the documents to the issuing bank.

c. When a nominated bank determines that a presentation is complying and honours or negotiates, it must forward the documents to the confirming bank or issuing bank.

Article 16 Discrepant Documents, Waiver and Notice

a. When a nominated bank acting on its nomination, a confirming bank, if any, or the issuing bank determines that a presentation does not comply, it may refuse to honour or negotiate.

b. When an issuing bank determines that a presentation does not comply, it may in its sole judgement approach the applicant for a waiver of the discrepancies. This does not, however, extend the period mentioned in sub-article 14 (b).

c. When a nominated bank acting on its nomination, a confirming bank, if any, or the issuing bank decides to refuse to honour or negotiate, it must give a single notice to that effect to the presenter. The notice must state:

i. that the bank is refusing to honour or negotiate; and

ii. each discrepancy in respect of which the bank refuses to honour or negotiate; and

iii. a) that the bank is holding the documents pending further instructions from the presenter; or

b) that the issuing bank is holding the documents until it receives a waiver from the applicant and agrees to accept it, or receives further instructions from the presenter prior to agreeing to accept a waiver; or

c) that the bank is returning the documents; or

d) that the bank is acting in accordance with instructions previously received from the presenter.

d. The notice required in sub-article 16 (c) must be given by telecommunication or, if that is not possible, by other expeditious means no later than the close of the fifth banking day following the day of presentation.

e. A nominated bank acting on its nomination, a confirming bank, if any, or the issuing bank may, after providing notice required by sub-article 16 (c) (iii) (a) or (b), return the documents to the presenter at any time.

f. If an issuing bank or a confirming bank fails to act in accordance with the provisions of this article, it shall be precluded from claiming that the documents do not constitute a complying presentation.

g. When an issuing bank refuses to honour or a confirming bank refuses to honour or negotiate and has given notice to that effect in accordance with this article, it shall then be entitled to claim a refund, with interest, of any reimbursement made.

Article 17 Original Documents and Copies

a. At least one original of each document stipulated in the credit must be presented.

b. A bank shall treat as an original any document bearing an apparently original signature, mark, stamp, or label of the issuer of the document, unless the document itself indicates that it is not an original.

c. Unless a document indicates otherwise, a bank will also accept a document as original if it:

i. appears to be written, typed, perforated or stamped by the document issuer's hand; or

ii. appears to be on the document issuer's original stationery; or

iii. states that it is original, unless the statement appears not to apply to the document presented.

d. If a credit requires presentation of copies of documents, presentation of either originals or copies is permitted.

e. If a credit requires presentation of multiple documents by using terms such as "in duplicate", "in two fold" or "in two copies", this will be satisfied by the presentation of at least one original and the remaining number in copies, except when the document itself indicates otherwise.

Article 18 Commercial Invoice

a. A commercial invoice:

i. must appear to have been issued by the beneficiary (except as provided in article 38);

ii. must be made out in the name of the applicant (except as provided in sub-article 38 (g));

iii. must be made out in the same currency as the credit; and

iv. need not be signed.

b. A nominated bank acting on its nomination, a confirming bank, if any, or the issuing bank may accept a commercial invoice issued for an amount in excess of the amount permitted by the credit, and its decision will be binding upon all parties, provided the bank in question has not honoured or negotiated for an amount in excess of that permitted by the credit.

c. The description of the goods, services or performance in a commercial invoice must correspond with that appearing in the credit.

Article 19 Transport Document Covering at Least Two Different Modes of Transport

a. A transport document covering at least two different modes of transport (multimodal or combined transport document), however named, must appear to:

i. indicate the name of the carrier and be signed by:
the carrier or a named agent for or on behalf of the carrier, or the master or a named agent for or on behalf of the master. Any signature by the carrier, master or agent must be identified as that of the carrier, master or agent. Any signature by an agent must indicate whether the agent has signed for or on behalf of the carrier or for or on behalf of the master.

ii. indicate that the goods have been dispatched, taken in charge or shipped on board at the place stated in the credit, by: pre-printed wording, or a stamp or notation indicating the date on which the goods have been dispatched, taken in charge or shipped on board. The date of issuance of the transport document will be deemed to be the date of dispatch, taking in charge or shipped on board, and the date of shipment. However, if the transport document indicates, by stamp or notation, a date of dispatch, taking in charge or shipped on board, this date will be deemed to be the date of shipment.

iii. indicate the place of dispatch, taking in charge or shipment and the place of final destination stated in the credit, even if:

a) the transport document states, in addition, a different place of dispatch, taking in charge or shipment or place of final destination, or

b) the transport document contains the indication "intended" or similar qualification in relation to the vessel, port of loading or port of discharge.

iv. be the sole original transport document or, if issued in more than one original, be the full set as indicated on the transport document.

v. contain terms and conditions of carriage or make reference to another source containing the terms and conditions of carriage (short form or blank back transport document). Contents of terms and conditions of carriage will not be examined.

vi. contain no indication that it is subject to a charter party.

b. For the purpose of this article, transhipment means unloading from one means of conveyance and reloading to another means of conveyance (whether or not in different modes of transport) during the carriage from the place of dispatch, taking in charge or shipment to the place of final destination stated in the credit.

c. i. A transport document may indicate that the goods will or may be transhipped provided that the entire carriage is covered by one and the same transport document.

ii. A transport document indicating that transhipment will or may take place is acceptable, even if the credit prohibits transhipment.

Article 20 Bill of Lading

a. A bill of lading, however named, must appear to:

i. indicate the name of the carrier and be signed by:

● the carrier or a named agent for or on behalf of the carrier, or

● the master or a named agent for or on behalf of the master.

Any signature by the carrier, master or agent must be identified as that of the carrier, master or agent. Any signature by an agent must indicate whether the agent has signed for or on behalf of the carrier or for or on behalf of the master.

ii. indicate that the goods have been shipped on board a named vessel at the port of loading stated in the credit by: pre-printed wording, or an on board notation indicating the date on which the goods have been shipped on oard.

The date of issuance of the bill of lading will be deemed to be the date of shipment unless the bill of lading contains an on board notation indicating the date of shipment, in which case the date stated in the on board notation will be deemed to be the date of shipment. If the bill of lading contains the indication "intended vessel" or similar qualification in relation to the name of the vessel, an on board notation indicating the date of shipment and the name of the actual vessel is required.

iii. indicate shipment from the port of loading to the port of discharge stated in the credit. If the bill of lading does not indicate the port of loading stated in the credit as the port of loading, or if it contains the indication "intended" or similar qualification in relation to the port of loading, an on board notation indicating the port of loading as stated in the credit, the date of shipment and the name of the vessel is required. This provision applies even when loading on board or shipment on a named vessel is indicated by preprinted wording on the bill of lading.

iv. be the sole original bill of lading or, if issued in more than one original, be the full set as indicated on the bill of lading.

v. contain terms and conditions of carriage or make reference to another source containing the terms and conditions of carriage (short form or blank back bill of lading). Contents of terms and conditions of carriage will not be examined.

vi. contain no indication that it is subject to a charter party.

b. For the purpose of this article, transhipment means unloading from one vessel and reloading to another vessel during the carriage from the port of loading to the port of discharge stated in the credit.

c. i. A bill of lading may indicate that the goods will or may be transshipped provided that the entire carriage is covered by one and the same bill of lading.

ii. A bill of lading indicating that transhipment will or may take place is acceptable, even if the credit prohibits transhipment, if the goods have been shipped in a container, trailer or LASH barge as evidenced by the bill of lading.

d. Clauses in a bill of lading stating that the carrier reserves the right to tranship will be disregarded.

Article 21 Non-Negotiable Sea Waybill

a. A non-negotiable sea waybill, however named, must appear to:

i. indicate the name of the carrier and be signed by:

- the carrier or a named agent for or on behalf of the carrier, or
- the master or a named agent for or on behalf of the master.

Any signature by the carrier, master or agent must be identified as that of the carrier, master or agent. Any signature by an agent must indicate whether the agent has signed for or on behalf of the carrier or for or on behalf of the master.

ii. indicate that the goods have been shipped on board a named vessel at the port of loading stated in the credit by: pre-printed wording, or an on board notation indicating the date on which the goods have been shipped on board. The date of issuance of the non-negotiable sea waybill will be deemed to be the date of shipment unless the non-negotiable sea waybill contains an on board notation indicating the date of shipment, in which case the date stated in the on board notation will be deemed to be the date of shipment. If the non-negotiable sea waybill contains the indication "intended vessel" or similar qualification in relation to the name of the vessel, an on board notation indicating the date of shipment and the name of the actual vessel is required.

iii. indicate shipment from the port of loading to the port of discharge stated in the credit. If the non-negotiable sea waybill does not indicate the port of loading stated in the credit as the port of loading, or if it contains the indication "intended" or similar qualification in relation to the port of loading, an on board notation indicating the port of loading as stated in the credit, the date of shipment and the name of the vessel is required. This provision applies even when loading on board or shipment on a named vessel is indicated by pre-printed wording on the non-negotiable sea waybill.

iv. be the sole original non-negotiable sea waybill or, if issued in more than one original, be the full set as indicated on the non-negotiable sea waybill.

v. contain terms and conditions of carriage or make reference to another source containing the terms and conditions of carriage (short form or blank back non-negotiable sea waybill). Contents of terms and conditions of carriage will not be examined.

vi. contain no indication that it is subject to a charter party.

b. For the purpose of this article, transhipment means unloading from one vessel and reloading to another vessel during the carriage from the port of loading to the port of discharge stated in the credit.

c. i. A non-negotiable sea waybill may indicate that the goods will or may be transhipped provided that the entire carriage is covered by one and the same non-negotiable sea waybill.

ii. A non-negotiable sea waybill indicating that transhipment will or may take place is acceptable, even if the credit prohibits transhipment, if the goods have been shipped in a container, trailer or LASH barge as evidenced by the non-negotiable sea waybill.

d. Clauses in a non-negotiable sea waybill stating that the carrier reserves the right to tranship will be disregarded.

Article 22 Charter Party Bill of Lading

a. A bill of lading, however named, containing an indication that it is subject to a charter party (charter party bill of lading), must appear to:

i. be signed by:

the master or a named agent for or on behalf of the master, or the owner or a named agent for or on behalf of the owner, or the charterer or a named agent for or on behalf of the charterer. Any signature by the master, owner, charterer or agent must be identified as that of the master, owner, charterer or agent. Any signature by an agent must indicate whether the agent has signed for or on behalf of the master, owner or charterer. An agent signing for or on behalf of the owner or charterer must indicate the name of the owner or charterer.

ii. indicate that the goods have been shipped on board a named vessel at the port of loading stated in the credit by: pre-printed wording, or an on board notation indicating the date on which the goods have been shipped on board. The date of issuance of the charter party bill of lading will be deemed to be the date of shipment unless the charter party bill of lading contains an on board notation indicating the date of shipment, in which case the date stated in the on board notation will be deemed to be the date of shipment.

iii. indicate shipment from the port of loading to the port of discharge stated in the credit. The port of discharge may also be shown as a range of ports or a geographical area, as stated in the credit.

iv. be the sole original charter party bill of lading or, if issued in more than one original, be the full set as indicated on the charter party bill of lading.

b. A bank will not examine charter party contracts, even if they are required to be presented by the terms of the credit.

Article 23 Air Transport Document

a. An air transport document, however named, must appear to:

i. indicate the name of the carrier and be signed by: the carrier, or a named agent for or on behalf of the carrier. Any signature by the carrier or agent must be identified as that of the carrier or agent. Any signature by an agent must indicate that the agent has signed for or on behalf of the carrier.

ii. indicate that the goods have been accepted for carriage.

iii. indicate the date of issuance. This date will be deemed to be the date of shipment unless the air transport document contains a specific notation of the actual date of shipment, in which case the date stated in the notation will be deemed to be the date of shipment. Any other information appearing on the air transport document relative to the flight number and date will not be considered in determining the date of shipment.

iv. indicate the airport of departure and the airport of destination stated in the credit.

v. be the original for consignor or shipper, even if the credit stipulates a full set of originals.

vi. contain terms and conditions of carriage or make reference to another source containing the terms and conditions of carriage. Contents of terms and conditions of carriage will not be examined.

b. For the purpose of this article, transhipment means unloading from one aircraft and reloading to another aircraft during the carriage from the airport of departure to the airport of destination stated in the credit.

c. i. An air transport document may indicate that the goods will or may be transhipped, provided that the entire carriage is covered by one and the same air transport document.

ii. An air transport document indicating that transhipment will or may take place is acceptable, even if the credit prohibits transhipment.

Article 24 Road, Rail or Inland Waterway Transport Documents

a. A road, rail or inland waterway transport document, however named, must appear to:

i. indicate the name of the carrier and: be signed by the carrier or a named agent for or on behalf of the carrier, or indicate receipt of the goods by signature, stamp or notation by the carrier or a named agent for or on behalf of the carrier. Any signature, stamp or notation of receipt of the goods by the carrier or agent must be identified as that of the carrier or agent. Any signature, stamp or notation of receipt of the goods by the agent must indicate that the agent has signed or acted for or on behalf of the carrier. If a rail transport document does not identify the carrier, any signature or stamp of the railway company will be accepted as evidence of the document being signed by the carrier.

ii. indicate the date of shipment or the date the goods have been received for shipment, dispatch or carriage at the place stated in the credit. Unless the transport document contains a dated reception stamp, an indication of the date of receipt or a date of shipment, the date of issuance of the transport document will be deemed to be the date of shipment.

iii. indicate the place of shipment and the place of destination stated in the credit.

b. i. A road transport document must appear to be the original for consignor or shipper or bear no marking indicating for whom the document has been prepared.

ii. A rail transport document marked "duplicate" will be accepted as an original.

iii. A rail or inland waterway transport document will be accepted as an original whether marked as an original or not.

c. In the absence of an indication on the transport document as to the number of originals issued, the number presented will be deemed to constitute a full set.

d. For the purpose of this article, transhipment means unloading from one means of conveyance and reloading to another means of conveyance, within the same mode of transport, during the carriage from the place of shipment, dispatch or carriage to the place of destination stated in the credit.

e. i. A road, rail or inland waterway transport document may indicate that the goods will or may be transhipped provided that the entire carriage is covered by one and the same transport document.

ii. A road, rail or inland waterway transport document indicating that transhipment will or may take place is acceptable, even if the credit prohibits transhipment.

Article 25 Courier Receipt, Post Receipt or Certificate of Posting

a. A courier receipt, however named, evidencing receipt of goods for transport, must appear to:

i. indicate the name of the courier service and be stamped or signed by the named courier service at the place from which the credit states the goods are to be shipped; and

ii. indicate a date of pick-up or of receipt or wording to this effect. This date will be deemed to be the date of shipment.

b. A requirement that courier charges are to be paid or prepaid may be satisfied by a transport document issued by a courier service evidencing that courier charges are for the account of a party other than the consignee.

c. A post receipt or certificate of posting, however named, evidencing receipt of goods for transport, must appear to be stamped or signed and dated at the place from which the credit states the goods are to be shipped. This date will be deemed to be the date of shipment.

Article 26 "On Deck", "Shipper's Load and Count", "Said by Shipper to Contain" and Charges Additional to Freight

a. A transport document must not indicate that the goods are or will be loaded on deck. A clause on a transport document stating that the goods may be loaded on deck is acceptable.

b. A transport document bearing a clause such as "shipper's load and count" and "said by shipper to contain" is acceptable.

c. A transport document may bear a reference, by stamp or otherwise, to charges additional to the freight.

Article 27 Clean Transport Document

A bank will only accept a clean transport document. A clean transport document is one bearing no clause or notation expressly declaring a defective condition of the goods or their packaging. The word "clean" need not appear on a transport document, even if a credit has a requirement for that transport document to be "clean on board".

Article 28 Insurance Document and Coverage

a. An insurance document, such as an insurance policy, an insurance certificate or a declaration under an open cover, must appear to be issued and signed by an insurance company, an underwriter or their agents or their proxies. Any signature by an agent or proxy must indicate whether the agent or proxy has signed for or on behalf of the insurance company or underwriter.

b. When the insurance document indicates that it has been issued in more than one original, all originals must be presented.

c. Cover notes will not be accepted.

d. An insurance policy is acceptable in lieu of an insurance certificate or a declaration under an open cover.

e. The date of the insurance document must be no later than the date of shipment, unless it appears from the insurance document that the cover is effective from a date not later than the date of shipment.

f. i. The insurance document must indicate the amount of insurance coverage and be in the same currency as the credit.

ii. A requirement in the credit for insurance coverage to be for a percentage of the value of the goods, of the invoice value or similar is deemed to be the minimum amount of coverage required. If there is no indication in the credit of the insurance coverage required, the amount of insurance coverage must be at least 110% of the CIF or CIP value of the goods. When the CIF or CIP value cannot be determined from the documents, the amount of insurance coverage must be calculated on the basis of the amount for which honour or negotiation is requested or the gross value of the goods as shown on the invoice, whichever is greater.

iii. The insurance document must indicate that risks are covered at least between the place of taking in charge or shipment and the place of discharge or final destination as stated in the credit.

g. A credit should state the type of insurance required and, if any, the additional risks to be covered. An insurance document will be accepted without regard to any risks that are not covered if the credit uses imprecise terms such as "usual risks" or "customary risks".

h. When a credit requires insurance against "all risks" and an insurance document is presented containing any "all risks" notation or clause, whether or not bearing the heading "all risks", the insurance document will be accepted without regard to any risks stated to be excluded.

i. An insurance document may contain reference to any exclusion clause.

j. An insurance document may indicate that the cover is subject to a franchise or excess (deductible).

Article 29 Extension of Expiry Date or Last Day for Presentation

a. If the expiry date of a credit or the last day for presentation falls on a day when the bank to which presentation is to be made is closed for reasons other than those referred to in article 36, the expiry date or the last day for presentation, as the case may be, will be extended to the first following banking day.

b. If presentation is made on the first following banking day, a nominated bank must provide the issuing bank or confirming bank with a statement on its covering schedule that the presentation was made within the time limits extended in accordance with sub-article 29 (a).

c. The latest date for shipment will not be extended as a result of sub-article 29 (a).

Article 30 Tolerance in Credit Amount, Quantity and Unit Prices

a. The words "about" or "approximately" used in connection with the amount of the credit or the quantity or the unit price stated in the credit are to be construed as allowing a tolerance not to exceed 10% more or 10% less than the amount, the quantity or the unit price to which they refer.

b. A tolerance not to exceed 5% more or 5% less than the quantity of the goods is allowed, provided the credit does not state the quantity in terms of a stipulated number of packing units or individual items and the total amount of the drawings does not exceed the amount of the credit.

c. Even when partial shipments are not allowed, a tolerance not to exceed 5% less than the amount of the credit is allowed, provided that the quantity of the goods, if stated in the credit, is shipped in full and a unit price, if stated in the credit, is not reduced or that sub-article 30 (b) is not applicable. This tolerance does not apply when the credit stipulates a specific tolerance or uses the expressions referred to in sub-article 30 (a).

Article 31 Partial Drawings or Shipments

a. Partial drawings or shipments are allowed.

b. A presentation consisting of more than one set of transport documents evidencing shipment commencing on the same means of conveyance and for the same journey, provided they indicate the same destination, will not be regarded as covering a partial shipment, even if they indicate different dates of shipment or different ports of loading, places of taking in charge or dispatch. If the presentation consists of more than one set of transport documents, the latest date of shipment as evidenced on any of the sets of transport documents will be regarded as the date of shipment. A presentation consisting of one or more sets of transport documents evidencing shipment on more than one means of conveyance within the same mode of transport will be regarded as covering a partial shipment, even if the means of conveyance leave on the same day for the same destination.

c. A presentation consisting of more than one courier receipt, post receipt or certificate of posting will not be regarded as a partial shipment if the courier receipts, post receipts or certificates of posting appear to have been stamped or signed by the same courier or postal service at the same place and date and for the same destination.

Article 32 Instalment Drawings or Shipments

If a drawing or shipment by instalments within given periods is stipulated in the credit and any instalment is not drawn or shipped within the period allowed for that instalment, the credit ceases to be available for that and any subsequent instalment.

Article 33 Hours of Presentation

A bank has no obligation to accept a presentation outside of its banking hours.

Article 34 Disclaimer on Effectiveness of Documents

A bank assumes no liability or responsibility for the form, sufficiency, accuracy, genuineness, falsification or legal effect of any document, or for the general or particular conditions stipulated in a document or superimposed thereon; nor does it assume any liability or responsibility for the description, quantity, weight, quality, condition, packing, delivery, value or existence of the goods, services or other performance represented by any document, or for the good faith or acts or omissions, solvency, performance or standing of the consignor, the carrier, the forwarder, the consignee or the insurer of the goods or any other person.

Article 35 Disclaimer on Transmission and Translation

A bank assumes no liability or responsibility for the consequences arising out of delay, loss in transit, mutilation or other errors arising in the transmission of any messages or delivery of letters or documents, when such messages, letters or documents are transmitted or sent according to the requirements stated in the credit, or when the bank may have taken the initiative in the choice of the delivery service in the absence of such instructions in the credit.

If a nominated bank determines that a presentation is complying and forwards the documents to the issuing bank or confirming bank, whether or not the nominated bank has honoured or negotiated, an issuing bank or confirming bank must honour or negotiate, or reimburse that nominated bank, even when the documents have been lost in transit between the nominated bank and the issuing bank or confirming bank, or between the confirming bank and the issuing bank. A bank assumes no liability or responsibility for errors in translation or interpretation of technical terms and may transmit credit terms without translating them.

Article 36 Force Majeure

A bank assumes no liability or responsibility for the consequences arising out of the interruption of its business by Acts of God, riots, civil commotions, insurrections, wars, acts of terrorism, or by any strikes or lockouts or any other causes beyond its control. A bank will not, upon resumption of its business, honour or negotiate under a credit that expired during such interruption of its business.

Article 37 Disclaimer for Acts of an Instructed Party

a. A bank utilizing the services of another bank for the purpose of giving effect to the instructions of the applicant does so for the account and at the risk of the applicant.

b. An issuing bank or advising bank assumes no liability or responsibility should the instructions it transmits to another bank not be carried out, even if it has taken the initiative in the choice of that other bank.

c. A bank instructing another bank to perform services is liable for any commissions, fees, costs or expenses ("charges") incurred by that bank in connection with its instructions. If a credit states that charges are for the account of the beneficiary and charges cannot be collected or deducted from proceeds, the issuing bank remains liable for payment of charges. A credit or amendment should not stipulate that the advising to a beneficiary is conditional upon the receipt by the advising bank or second advising bank of its charges.

d. The applicant shall be bound by and liable to indemnify a bank against all obligations and responsibilities imposed by foreign laws and usages.

Article 38 Transferable Credits

a. A bank is under no obligation to transfer a credit except to the extent and in the manner expressly consented to by that bank.

b. For the purpose of this article: Transferable credit means a credit that specifically states it is "transferable". A transferable credit may be made available in whole or in part to another beneficiary ("second beneficiary") at the request of the beneficiary ("first beneficiary"). Transferring bank means a nominated bank that transfers the credit or, in a credit available with any bank, a bank that is specifically authorized by the issuing bank to transfer and that transfers the credit. An issuing bank may be a transferring bank. Transferred credit means a credit that has been made available by the transferring bank to a second beneficiary.

c. Unless otherwise agreed at the time of transfer, all charges (such as commissions, fees, costs or expenses) incurred in respect of a transfer must be paid by the first beneficiary.

d. A credit may be transferred in part to more than one second beneficiary provided partial drawings or shipments are allowed. A transferred credit cannot be transferred at the request of a second beneficiary to any subsequent beneficiary. The first beneficiary is not considered to be a subsequent beneficiary.

e. Any request for transfer must indicate if and under what conditions amendments may be advised to the second beneficiary. The transferred credit must clearly indicate those conditions.

f. If a credit is transferred to more than one second beneficiary, rejection of an amendment by one or more second beneficiary does not invalidate the acceptance by any other second beneficiary, with respect to which the transferred credit will be amended accordingly. For any second beneficiary that rejected the amendment, the transferred credit will remain unamended.

g. The transferred credit must accurately reflect the terms and conditions of the credit, including confirmation, if any, with the exception of:

—the amount of the credit,

—any unit price stated therein,

—the expiry date,

—the period for presentation, or

—the latest shipment date or given period for shipment, any or all of which may be reduced or curtailed.

The percentage for which insurance cover must be effected may be increased to provide the amount of cover stipulated in the credit or these articles. The name of the first beneficiary may be substituted for that of the applicant in the credit. If the name of the applicant is specifically required by the credit to appear in any document other than the invoice, such requirement must be reflected in the transferred credit.

h. The first beneficiary has the right to substitute its own invoice and draft, if any, for those of a second beneficiary for an amount not in excess of that stipulated in the credit, and upon such substitution the first beneficiary can draw under the credit for the difference, if any, between its invoice and the invoice of a second beneficiary.

i. If the first beneficiary is to present its own invoice and draft, if any, but fails to do so on first demand, or if the invoices presented by the first beneficiary create discrepancies that did not exist in the presentation made by the second beneficiary and the first beneficiary fails to correct them on first demand, the transferring bank has the right to present the documents as received from the second beneficiary to the issuing bank, without further responsibility to the first beneficiary.

j. The first beneficiary may, in its request for transfer, indicate that honour or negotiation is to be effected to a second beneficiary at the place to which the credit has been ransferred, up to and including the expiry date of the credit. This is without prejudice to the right of the first beneficiary in accordance with sub-article 38 (h).

k. Presentation of documents by or on behalf of a second beneficiary must be made to the transferring bank.

Article 39 Assignment of Proceeds

The fact that a credit is not stated to be transferable shall not affect the right of the beneficiary to assign any proceeds to which it may be or may become entitled under the credit, in accordance with the provisions of applicable law. This article relates only to the assignment of proceeds and not to the assignment of the right to perform under the credit.

参考文献

[1] 苏定东,王群飞. 国际贸易单证实务[M]. 北京:北京大学出版社,2015.

[2] 黎孝先,王健. 国际贸易实务[M]. 北京:对外经济贸易大学出版社,2017.

[3] 李贺,姚雷. 报检实务[M]. 上海:上海财经大学出版社,2016.

[4] 戴宾,陈有真. 外贸单证实务[M]. 成都:西南交通大学出版社,2002.

[5] 顾民. 外贸制单与结汇(第 3 版)[M]. 北京:对外经济贸易大学出版社,2001.

[6] 李一平. 跟单信用证项下出口审单实务[M]. 北京:中国商务出版社,2004.

[7] 李元旭,吴国新. 国际贸易单证实务[M]. 北京:清华大学出版社,2005.

[8] 刘启萍. 外贸英文制单[M]. 北京:对外经贸大学出版社,2005.

[9] 屈韬. 外贸单证处理技巧[M]. 广州:广东经济出版社,2000.

[10] 童宏祥. 外贸单证实务操作练习与解答[M]. 上海:华东理工大学出版社,2004.

[11] 王雪. 新编国际贸易单证实务[M]. 北京:化学工业出版社,2003.

[12] 许罗丹. 出口单据业务[M]. 广州:中山大学出版社,1996.

[13] 姚大伟. 新编对外贸易单证实务[M]. 上海:复旦大学出版社,1996.

[14] 尹哲. 国际贸易单证流转实务[M]. 北京:中国轻工业出版社,1999.

[15] 余世明,丛凤英. 国际商务单证[M]. 广州:暨南大学出版社,2004.

[16] 余心之. 新编外贸单证实务[M]. 北京:对外经济贸易大学出版社,2005.

[17] 俞涔,朱春兰. 外贸单证[M]. 杭州:浙江大学出版社,2004.

[18] 容静文. 外贸单证实务[M]. 北京:中国财政经济出版社,2015.

[19] 孟祥年. 外贸单证实务[M]. 北京:中国财政经济出版社,2014.

[20] 广银芳. 外贸单证实务[M]. 北京:中国轻工业出版社,2017.

[21] 王海鸥. 外贸单证实务[M]. 北京:北京交通大学出版社,2011.